'In her latest book, renowned historian Sheila Fitzpatrick recounts the remarkable wartime odyssey of Michael Danos (1922–1999), known also at various times as Mikelis/Mischa/Mischka, the theoretical physicist to whom she was married until his death. Drawing on diaries and letters, she retraces Mischka's journey from occupied Riga via a displaced persons camp to Heidelberg, where his career began to take off. Fitzpatrick does not claim that Mischka's story was representative, indeed she thinks of it as "singular". It's an honest and sometimes unflinching account: we learn of his devotion to his mother, his fledgling scientific career (he regularly carried in his suitcase twenty volumes of the *Zeitschrift für Physik*), his love of sport and music, and his multiple liaisons. When he and his first wife reached the USA in 1951, he proclaimed "We made it". In this labour of love, Fitzpatrick shows how they did, and why it matters.'

Peter Gatrell, Professor of Economic History, Manchester University and author of *The Making of the Modern Refugee*

'At once tender and forensic: a beguiling combination of scholarship and love.'

Anna Goldsworthy, author of *Piano Lessons*

'Two dramas are played out in Sheila Fitzpatrick's *Mischka's War*: that of Misha, navigating the European catastrophe with an equanimity that often threatens to confound our understanding of it; and the author's own drama, as she tries to preserve the historian's objectivity and "distance" from even the most terrible events, while uncovering the story of one man among the millions caught up in them—the man she met and fell in love with long after the war was over. The result is an absorbing, unsettling, rare and memorable book.'

Don Watson, author of *The Bush*

— Sheila Fitzpatrick —

MISCHKA'S WAR

A Story of Survival
from War-Torn Europe
to New York

I.B. TAURIS
LONDON · NEW YORK

Published in 2017 by
I.B.Tauris & Co. Ltd
London • New York
www.ibtauris.com

Copyright © 2017 Sheila Fitzpatrick

ISBN: 978 1 78831 022 2
eISBN: 978 1 78672 254 6
ePDF: 978 1 78673 254 5

A full CIP record for this book is available from the British Library
A full CIP record is available from the Library of Congress

Library of Congress Catalog Card Number: available

Printed and bound in Sweden by ScandBook AB

Contents

Introduction

Misha in Paris cafe, 1990.

EVERYBODY always asks me about my accent, and Misha was no exception; he thought I was Danish. It was unlike him to behave like anybody else, as I soon found out, but there are only so many pick-up lines to use on strange women on planes. At least it was better than his gently melancholy remark the next day, 'I must be twice your age,' to which I was able to give the once-in-a-lifetime riposte: 'You're 96, then?' In any case, I didn't waste time on the boring answer that I was an Australian with an unplaceable hybrid accent, and batted the Danish question back—where was *he* from? I thought I already knew the answer, having observed that he was writing a letter to *Chère Agnès* and decided he was French. 'The Baltics', was the reply.

'Which one?' I asked, slightly irritated.

'The middle one.'

That was vintage Misha, always avoiding a direct answer, and not just because he liked to tease; he liked not releasing information, too. In a schoolmarmish tone, I informed him that, as a Soviet historian by trade, I knew which of the Baltics was which. 'So you speak Russian?' That was great good luck, because Russian had escaped the deep freeze into which depression had put my English, though (*pace* Misha) English was my native language. The conversation took off at a Russian gallop before slowing abruptly as Misha switched back into English. Later he explained that he had run headlong into the second-person pronoun, which in Russian comes in either a familiar or an impersonal form: as a European born in 1922, he could not use the intimate Russian form with a woman he had just met, but as a romantic he couldn't *not* use it, because he was falling in love. That was vintage Misha, too, both the belief in instant intuitive knowledge and the willingness to act on it. I was temperamentally more cautious, but in this case, unlike him, I had nothing to lose. The year was 1989, *annus mirabilis* in the Eastern bloc.

We married and lived happily ever after, which turned out to be ten years—by coincidence or not, the number I had bargained with God about at the beginning, for the first and only time in my life ('Five years if you must, but please, if you possibly can, ten years, and I'll pay you back with ten years of mine'). I should have asked for more, of course. Misha had his first stroke on 23 September 1999 and his second, the one that destroyed his brain, on the 24th. As the incumbent wife, I summoned his three children and his second wife, Vicky (who lived nearby), to the deathbed. Helga, his first wife, was in town too, looking after the grandchildren, but I didn't invite her to the hospital because she and Misha were not on good terms. None of us had dealt with a death in the family before, and Misha, a resolute denier of death in the spirit of Kingsley Amis's anti-death league, had left no instructions. We held a wake in our little cottage in Washington, DC, not far from the Potomac River and the C&O Canal that runs beside it; the guests were mainly work colleagues, physicists, like Misha. 'Which is the wife?' I heard someone ask. In fact, all three were present.

After the wake, we had a family meeting to discuss what to do with his ashes. We thought of scattering them in the Potomac, but decided against it because of legal doubts (did one need a permit?) and some unwillingness on my part to acknowledge an American claim on him. Riga seemed the obvious alternative, consoling for his surviving brothers who still lived there, though a bit out of sync with his conspicuous lack of desire to embrace Latvia as his lost homeland. Finally, Vicky, Misha's second wife, came up with the solution: take his ashes to Riga and scatter them in the Baltic, thus giving him access to all the oceans of the world, as befitted a world citizen. That's what we did.

After Misha's death, I got in the habit of going to his eldest child Johanna's house each year for the anniversary. Johanna had the box that Misha had told me contained his mother's papers, and on the sixth year we decided to open it and look for photographs. It turned out that the papers there were not just his mother's but also Misha's, dating from the late 1930s, when Misha was an adolescent in Riga, through the 1940s and early '50s, when he and his mother were both 'displaced persons' (DPs) in Germany before resettling in the United States. Misha's diaries were there, along with his mother Olga's diaries; correspondence between the two of them about all manner of things (news, business, music and, on Misha's part, physics, philosophy and sport); letters from Misha's brothers and old friends; official documents relating to their DP status; Misha's notebooks with physics jottings; address books; letters between Misha and Helga Heimers, the young German woman he met at the sports club in Hanover and married in 1949; as well as lots of photographs, including a whole bunch of Misha flying through the air as a pole vaulter.

Does the opening of the box explain why I am writing this book? In a way it does, as it is a historian's natural instinct on finding a collection of previously undiscovered papers to use them for something. For a few years this was the justification I gave for doing what I was doing, namely cataloguing the papers, translating them (they are mainly in German, with excursions into Latvian and Russian, odd sentences in English and, in Olga's case, even some diary entries in Italian) and seeking out family and friends who knew him in the 1940s to interview.

But of course that explanation isn't good enough. You don't write a book about a time in your husband's life when you didn't even know him, when he wasn't your husband but someone else's, just because you discover a nice set of documents. So I must have had other reasons, and I recognised one of them when, around the same time, I started writing a memoir of my own Australian childhood and discovered at first hand the power to bring the dead back to life by writing about them. If I could do this for my parents and great-aunt in the Australian memoir, why not for Misha, the person I most wanted back from the dead?

That still left the question of why I should choose to write about Misha not in the time I knew him but half a century before I met him. It took me a while to work this one out, but finally I got there. It was because this was the part of his life I didn't understand, the part that had worried me a little from the beginning. I remember our first conversation about the war, when he said he had gone to Germany in the spring of 1944. In 1944? With the war still on and the Nazis in power? I was shocked, even frightened. Why would one do such a thing? Misha explained that in his family's judgement, the Germans were going to lose the war, and then the Soviets would come back into Latvia, which in everyday-life terms was worse than the Nazis, unless one happened to be a Jew, which he was not. He wanted to get out so as to study physics in Germany (before the war, the best place in the world for it, or so he thought), escape the coming second Soviet occupation of the Baltics and have a chance of getting to the West when the war was over. That was a shock too; up to then, without really thinking about it, I had assumed that living under the Nazis was worse than under the Soviets because they had the nastier ideology. But when I thought about it, I saw that it made sense. Misha told me all this in a matter-of-fact way, without embarrassment, but I remember wondering (though silently) if it had caused any problems for him when he was a DP in Europe applying for a US visa.

That was how things stood until a few years after Misha died, when his daughter Johanna visited the Danos family in Riga and came back with the news that Misha's Hungarian father was Jewish. This was even more of a shock, both because of the danger Misha had put himself in by going to Nazi Germany and because, in this important early conversation with me, he had so clearly indicated that he was *not* Jewish. How could he, the son of a Jew, even if passing as Aryan, have taken the incredible risk of going willingly to Germany in the spring of 1944? Was it possible that he didn't know about the Jewish forebears in Hungary? And a more visceral reaction: how could he have misled me?

Whether he knew or didn't know is a complicated story. Helga and her two daughters didn't know anything about any Jewish connections of the Danos family. Misha's brother Jan said he (Jan) had found out only in the 1980s, from the last surviving Hungarian relative, that the family was at least half Jewish and had changed their name from Deutsch to Danos around 1900, and that he had passed the news on to Misha. Vicky, Misha's wife at that time, confirms this; she remembers Misha reporting it humorously as a rather pleasing discovery—'Now I can say I am [Massachusetts Institute of Technology physicist Martin] Deutsch's cousin.' But he had evidently forgotten again by the time I asked him or, to put it another way, did not consider it a significant datum: the point he was making to me was that persons identified/identifying as Jews were at risk in Nazi Germany, but he was not such a person. No doubt if I had said to him, 'But wasn't your father half-Jewish?' he would have said yes, but so what?—the father was secular, Catholic by official religion, an atheist by conviction, not known as a Jew in Riga and not interested in the whole question, and neither were we. But I didn't know to ask that question.

So there are some mysteries and hidden things in Misha's 1940s story. That raises the question about whether, in that case, I should write about it. Misha was honest but secretive by temperament, or at least not a gratuitous discloser; he would tell you what he saw as the deep truth and ignore what he considered to be trivial aspects. Thus, in our second conversation, he told me with considerable emotion that he had been found to have a kidney problem that was likely to be fatal within a short time. I remember the awful sinking feeling with which I heard it—finally I meet the right man and it turns out he's dying!—and the jarring though happy reversal when it turned out, in response to my cross-examination, that the kidney crisis had occurred twenty years ago, at the end of his first marriage, and that he had been functioning perfectly well on whatever proportion was left to him ever since.

Is it a betrayal, then, to try to find out and understand more about Misha in the 1940s?

Misha had a natural sense of loyalty to those he loved, which to some extent inhibited his critical judgement of them: this was so when he spoke of his mother or his elder brother Arpad, for example, and it was evident in his unquestioningly high evaluation of me as a historian and of Vicky as an artist (not that I'm saying he was wrong, but the judgement was axiomatic rather than derived from observation). Whenever I told him about a disagreement I had had with a colleague, he was always unreservedly on my side. It was how his own mother had been with him, and the opposite of how my mother had been with me, and I found it extraordinarily lovable.

But I could never be like that. I am a committed ferreter out of detail, personally as well as professionally; no matter how much I love someone, I have never been able to take their self-evaluation on trust, as Misha could sometimes do, but always wanted to find out all about them, including things they might not have intended to tell me. Having fallen in love, Misha was eager in principle to tell me everything about himself, as well as to learn everything about me; that's how we come to have the occasional reflections on his life and thoughts, which he called 'musings', on which I draw in this book. (For more on the musings, mainly originating as emails to me in the 1990s, see the Sources section.) It has even occurred to me that in writing the musings, he might in a way have anticipated a book like this one, although at that stage of my life I had never written anything like it. I am a historian, after all, and the source base he left me was at least partly consciously created. A close reading of his diaries suggests that even earlier in his life, when he wrote things down, it was not just to record but also to communicate.

As is evident from the Jewish story, however, not everything struck Misha as 'non-trivial' enough (a favourite word) to pass on. He would answer questions, but there were times when the impossibility of communicating a deep truth frustrated him to the point of anger (he had the same problem as a physicist talking to other physicists), and other times when he would resent an attempt to put him in a category (for example, as a Latvian; as a native speaker of German; or in more or less any way other than as a theoretical physicist) and burst out that it was irrelevant, he was not one of those people in normal categories, he was himself, uncategorisable.

When, in our first year together, Misha conducted what was in effect an informal psychoanalysis of me, he was puzzled by the way in which I recounted my life, as if it were something from which I was detached. Initially he thought of this as neurotic, but after a while he changed his mind and redefined this detachment of mine as a virtue, even an object of his admiration. He didn't do detachment: as he explained, he had had to give up experimental physics because his intense engagement influenced outcomes, whereas my extreme form of it was, he concluded, the secret of my success as an 'experimentalist' (this was his term, borrowed from the natural sciences, for all empirical historians not driven by Grand Theory, which in history—though not in physics—he despised).

This is a historian's book, not a memoir, but it's also a wife's book about her husband. There are tensions between those two purposes, sometimes commented on. I hope they turn out to be the kind of tensions that make things more interesting rather than the spoiling kind. Appropriately for a wife's book, I draw on my own memories, along with things Misha told me about his life, but I behave like a historian in dealing with documents and the memories of those who knew him in the 1940s. (Sometimes I even quietly throw in a few archival nuggets, by-products of my current academic work on DPs, which in turn owes its origin indirectly to Misha.)

In describing the German years, I'm not going to call him Misha, the Russian diminutive that was my name for him, and also his family's back in Riga. Instead, I will use the name by which he was known in Germany in the 1940s, and throughout his life to Helga and his children: Mischka. For his early years, and throughout the text when I interpolate something based on my own direct knowledge from the 1990s, I'll call him Misha. Misha/Mischka would answer to both names, as well as to Michael, Mikhail, Michel, Mikelis, Michika and Mike, but he would never say which of the formal versions was his 'real' name (his documents give both Michael and the Latvian Mikelis) or admit that any of the three languages he spoke in childhood (German, Latvian and Russian) was his native language. When his daughter Johanna and I talk about him, she calls him Mischka and I call him Misha, not in a spirit of disagreement but rather of recognition of separate claims. My use of Mischka in the book is perhaps the same kind of recognition. It's a reminder to myself and the reader that the man I am writing about is, and is not, my husband.

I can't tell for sure how Misha/Mischka would have felt about being the posthumous subject of my detached (or, to be honest, relatively detached) enquiry. He thought himself wiser than me with respect to philosophy and morals, but not necessarily with respect to people and everyday life: after a while he conceded that people were my realm, just as nature and anything mechanical were his, and that my gaze, although detached, was, in another of his favourite words, 'benign'. It was important for him that I understood him as a Person (his word, his capitalisation); that's why he wrote the musings.

More broadly, it was important to him to be understood (and presumably remembered, too, though his anti-death stance did not allow discussion of this) in all his unique individuality; his sense of his own stature required it. Aware that he had repressed some aspects of the 1940s, he tried in the 1990s to recover memories from this time—the musings on the Dresden bombing and the Jewish graves in the forest outside Riga are examples—which he would email to me as presents when I was away at my job in Chicago. Although I am by no means certain of this, he may even have thought that I had a better chance of sorting out the residual mess inside him from the 1940s than he did. In any case, he didn't have time to finish the sorting out, and this book is my attempt to do so—an offering of love that is also, I hope not contradictorily, a search for knowledge and, finally, a completely selfish effort of mine to join his anti-death league and have him back.

Mischka and Olga

Michael and Olga Danos, 1940s.

THIS mother-and-son photo from the Danos family collection is undated, but Misha, born in Riga, Latvia, in 1922, looks to be in his early twenties, which puts Olga in her mid forties. The photo could have been taken any time during the war or even after it, but not later than 1949. That was the year that Misha, having become Mischka in his new German context, married the young German Helga Heimers. Unlike the slapdash Olga, or Mischka-the-budding-physicist with his mind on higher things, Helga was an orderly person who labelled and dated family photographs.

If the photo was taken in 1940, that was the year Misha had just finished school and started his first job at Riga's State Electrotechnical Factory, (VEF). Olga at that point was separated from his father and living in the workshop of her fashion atelier, but the sons remained in close contact and often dropped round for tea (the object bottom right in the photo seems to be a teapot; the things or person obscuring Misha's right shoulder are unidentified). Or it could have been taken in the autumn of 1941, when Misha entered the University of Riga as an engineering student. In this short period, Latvia had changed its status more than once, successively falling under Soviet occupation, ceasing to be an independent state and becoming a constituent part of the Soviet Union, and then being occupied by the Germans. Misha, of call-up age under all three regimes, had managed to avoid conscription into any of these armies, which was a good thing as the Danoses—despite their competence in all three languages—had no enthusiasm for any of the regimes.

There were lots of leave-takings and reunions in 1944–45, any one of which could have been the occasion for the photo. In the spring of 1944, to escape the conscription into the German forces that now seemed inevitable, Misha went off to study in Germany, a scheme probably hatched by Olga. In the following months, as Soviet forces advanced and it became clear that they were about to reoccupy Latvia, Olga started planning her own departure and that of the other two sons. The photo could have been taken in Riga in the summer, when Mischka made a brief farewell visit from Germany, or a few months later in Dresden or the Sudetenland, where he and Olga met up again after she moved her tailoring business to the region. By this time, it was clear that they were the only two family members who had got out: an attempt by the other two sons to leave Latvia by sea, organised by Olga, had failed, and as Latvia had been incorporated into the Soviet Union, they were now willy-nilly Soviet citizens living behind a closed border.

Or it could conceivably have been taken in Flensburg, in the north of Germany, close to the Danish border, where Mischka and Olga met up in the spring of 1945 after making their separate ways across Germany in the months before its final capitulation and, in Mischka's case, surviving both the Allied bombing of Dresden and a bout of diphtheria en route. I doubt this, however: Olga looks too spruce for a refugee and Mischka too healthy for someone still recovering from a serious illness. It was in Flensburg that the two of them officially became DPs, under the care of UNRRA (the United National Relief and Rehabilitation Administration) and the British occupation forces.

What the picture captures beautifully, whenever it was taken, is the relationship between the two. Olga leans towards him, straightforwardly warm and affectionate and engaged, and Mischka accepts her affection, even returns it, but preserves his independence by looking slightly away. This is exactly how they were in the letters they exchanged regularly over the years of their residence in Germany, 1944–51. Fortunately for us, they were generally not living in the same city. For much of 1944, the correspondence was between Mischka in Dresden and Olga in Riga and then various towns in the Sudetenland. Then, after some months together in Flensburg, Mischka moved to Hanover to study at the technical university there. Olga, by now developing a career as a sculptor as well as running a tailoring business, moved to Fulda in the American zone in 1947. She was still there two years later when Mischka went to Heidelberg, also in the American zone, to do his PhD in physics, marrying Helga, whom he had met in the Hanover sports club shortly before the move. The correspondence turns international at the end of 1950, when Olga emigrated to the United States, sponsored by one of the Jews she had protected back in Riga during the German occupation. It ends when

Mischka and Helga arrived in New York as immigrants a year later and were reunited with Olga.

All this time, Olga was writing warm, chatty, practical, informative letters about what she was doing, in her rather untidy handwriting and with quite a few mistakes in the German, while Mischka responded in better German and more legible handwriting, giving Olga his thoughts on physics, philosophy and (when he was having girlfriend trouble) relations between the sexes, but rarely condescending, despite her repeated requests, to give her the mundane details about his everyday and student life that she, sometimes with a certain asperity, requested. That parsimoniousness with information, along with a teasing tendency to obfuscation ('Which Baltic state?' 'The middle one') was as recognisable to me as his handwriting, which hadn't changed in forty years.

When the correspondence starts, Olga writes as a parent—caring but also authoritative, generous with advice and sometimes admonition. As it develops, she yields some authority to Mischka and even starts to defer to him on business and organisational questions. This undoubtedly reflects the fact that he was growing up, but also suggests that the canny Olga was encouraging him to do so, even tutoring him in the new role. The depth of Olga's affection is evident in her letters; the depth of Mischka's perhaps only from his diary. But as Olga once wrote to him, it didn't matter whether he expressed his affection openly or not because she could always decode him. For the six or seven years they were in Germany, each was for the other the closest and most important person in the world. That's why a book that was meant to be just about Mischka ended up as a book about Mischka and Olga.

1
Family

Olga and Arpad Danos around
the time of their marriage, 1920.

NOSTALGIA for the home we once slammed the door on often creeps up on expatriates. But not on Misha. Uniquely, in my experience, he held firm to his original conviction that the place he had grown up in was a provincial backwater that he had been right to leave at the earliest possible moment. His two brothers had stayed in Riga, though not exactly by choice. In the 1990s, when Latvia emerged from the Soviet Union and opened up again, Misha resisted, for as long as he could, his brother Jan's urgent invitations to visit Riga, then yielded unwillingly, and squirmed all the time he was there. He and I had both, as teenagers, longed to leave the parochial, narrow-minded, intolerant place that we had, by some cosmic mistake, been born in and get out into the real world. But my feelings about Australia had mellowed over the years, while rational Misha had seen no reason to change his attitude. Or perhaps it wasn't the rational Misha who held so strongly to this position: the Riga past was a bit of an emotional minefield for him. He cherished the memory of Olga and his elder brother Arpad, a sometime prisoner of Gulag of whom Misha spoke almost with reverence. But Olga had ended up, like him, in America; and it was the remembered Arpad that he felt close to, not the still-living one, long back in Riga but permanently damaged by his Soviet experiences. The only thing in Riga to which Misha had a straightforward 'this is my own, my native land' response was Rigās Jūrmala, the beloved beach resort of his childhood. I found it on the bleak side.

Misha had a strong sense of himself as a European. But he was skittish about nationality, refusing even to commit himself to a native language (he said German, Latvian and Russian were all spoken in his milieu, and resisted my suggestion that German *seemed* to be his native language, since his German was much better than his Russian or, as far as I could tell, his Latvian). This was one of the few contexts in which his father, the multilingual cosmopolitan, was cited with unreserved approval, particularly for his dismissive attitude to things Latvian. Misha never expressed any particular feeling of kinship with Latvians, whose interwar (and, in the displaced persons camps, postwar) nationalism had left unpleasant memories. He displayed marginally more interest in Hungarians, of whom there were many in his chosen community of physics, though I couldn't say it went as far as a feeling of kinship (skill at entering revolving doors behind you and exiting in front was emphasised, and Misha did not have that skill). Still, I thought he might be interested in going to Hungary, since we travelled a lot in Europe, and given the Hungarian father, but he wasn't at all. Quite the contrary. We never went there, which given my professional ties with Eastern Europe, almost amounted to a statement.

Of the stories Misha told me about his childhood, the one I remember most vividly was about his expulsion from the Riga German classical gymnasium (academic high school), for rudeness to a teacher, which he considered outrageous since all he had been doing was non-disruptively pointing out that the man didn't know what he was talking about. Even sixty years later, he didn't really see why the teacher had been so annoyed; unlike the rest of us as we get older, he had not become persuaded that seniority deserves respect. When he started to write his musings for me, not much about his childhood or family background struck him as significant enough to be remembered. There was a memory, from the family's prosperous days in the early 1920s, of going upstairs to the kitchen to the warm, comfortable presence of the servants, who though welcoming, conveyed some sense that he wasn't supposed to be there. After a while, he worked out that this must be his mother's edict, based on the principle of non-fraternisation between classes, which opened up a small crack in his previously wholesale acceptance of his mother's wisdom. But that, from Misha, was not a story about the beginning of class consciousness. His dislike of separation into hierarchical categories in which some were held to be inferior extended in practice not only to age (he had no special way of treating either five- or 95-year-olds) but even to species (he treated dogs as not clearly distinct from humans, and in return they seemed to treat him as not clearly distinct from a dog).

Another memory was of his strong internal protest against the indignity of having to get rotten apples from the market because they were cheap—a consequence of the family's financial crisis in the early 1930s. It was a memory of humiliation stemming from a sense of pride, and thus potentially contradictory to the anti-distinction position I have just outlined. But Misha would have said that the pride that was damaged by the rotten apples was his pride as an individual, unique and unrepeatable, not his pride as the member of a family that had formerly been prosperous but was now poor. In any case, it was a story implicitly critical of his father (who argued that rotten apples were only rotten in parts and remained basically eatable) and supportive of his mother, who evidently thought that the family's plight did not justify quite such extreme measures. That, as he was growing up and the parents were quarrelling, was Misha's usual choice of allegiance.

The one musing he wrote on family history, entitled 'Stories from the Grandfather's Times', concerned his mother's Latvian father, not the essentially unknown Hungarian (or Jewish) grandfather on the paternal side. There was a reason for Misha's interest in the Latvian grandfather that we will come to later. But the substance of the musing is notable for its scrupulous attention to detail, especially geographic, economic and technological. As I read it, I am irresistibly reminded of going for walks with Misha along the C&O Canal near our house in Washington. The canal runs beside the Potomac River. As we walked, Misha would be registering water levels, landscape contours, vegetation, and wildlife in and out of the water, and at the same time carefully examining any machine or construction along the way to determine its purpose and operational principles. I saw virtually none of these things, not only because I am short-sighted but also because I don't pay attention. The only things that would strike me on the towpath were the people we passed, from whose dress, facial expression, demeanour and behaviour to each other I would make some quick, automatic deductions about character, social status, relationship to each other and so on. But Misha didn't even notice them.

'The grandmother, Julia, was born 1870' is how 'Stories from the Grandfather's Times' starts. But we hear no more of Julia, though she lived in the Danos household for most of Misha's childhood, something of a kill-joy presence as far as I could gather from Misha's rare remarks about her. As the musing continues,

> the grandfather, Janis Viksne, was a little, not much, older; probably born 1865, i.e., after, even though not much after, the removal of serfdom. Thus, a few, very few, serfdom stories survived, but only from Julia's side … My mother was born in 1897, into a household, an economic enterprise, based on a water mill, with a dam across the Jugla river, a tributary to the Jugla lake (Stintsee in German), not far from Riga. In German it would be called 'ein Bach', not 'ein Fluss'. I have not seen that place; my mother visited it: nothing had survived WWI, not even the dam. At any rate, the power generated by that water wheel was sufficient to power not only a wood-working shop, but even an electric generator, supplying electric lights to the Viksne population. That aspect was a thorn in the side of the local German baron—the ex-serfholder of that region: 'This Viksne, he has electricity and I do not!' Actually, that was the first electricity in the district, if not the Baltics; I think his electricity certainly predates the electrification of Riga; probably not that of some of Riga's industries.

The electricity motif had some personal significance for Misha because of his work as a young man at the VEF, Riga's great electrotechnical factory. But it had significance in the history of Latvia as well, because Riga in the decades before the First World War was one of the Russian Empire's economic showpieces. Large, modern industrial plants, many of them foreign-owned, had sprung up in the latter part of the nineteenth century, metalworking, mechanical engineering and chemicals being the biggest industries. In the decade before the First World War, Latvia's annual growth rate was a spectacular 6.4 per cent, while Riga's population doubled. Misha's grandfather was a beneficiary, since he had set up a woodworking shop at his mill that made stopcocks (external valves regulating the flow of liquid) for beer kegs, and Riga's breweries constituted a flourishing market.

Latvia is a small country wedged between two big ones, Germany and Russia, whose periodic incursions provided many of the great events of its history. Up to the First World War, it was a part of the Russian Empire, having been won from the Swedes by Peter the Great at the beginning of the eighteenth century. For a century before, it had been a site of contestation between the Teutonic Knights, the Polish– Lithuanian Commonwealth, Sweden and Russia. Before that, from the twelfth to the sixteenth century, Riga had been an important town in the Hanseatic League, connecting it with the German language, culture and trading network.

Since the Reformation, the majority of the population of present-day Latvia identified as Lutheran by confession, although the eastern region of Latgale remained Roman Catholic, and Orthodoxy made inroads in the Russian period. The German presence remained large, with German nobles— the so-called 'Baltic barons'—the main landowners. Their serfs, mainly ethnic Latvians, were for the most part emancipated in the early nineteenth century, but resentment against the Baltic barons remained. Russification policies of the 1880–90s aimed to reduce the German dominance, including linguistically, but in the short term their effect was mainly to sharpen Latvian resentment against Russians as well as Germans.

Latvia's population grew rapidly in the course of the nineteenth century, from a base of 720,000 to two million, with large-scale and varied immigration, which reduced the ethnic Latvian proportion of the population from 90 per cent at the beginning of the century to 68 per cent at the end. The biggest minorities at the turn of the century were Russians (8 per cent), Germans (7 per cent) and Jews (6 per cent)—the figures, from Latvian sources, may err on the low side—and in Riga both German and Russian were officially recognised languages. In culture, German remained the dominant influence: it wasn't only ethnic Germans who spoke German at home and sent their children to German schools, but also many others.

Rapid social and economic change brought a variety of discontents, including, as a by-product of industrialisation, the appearance of a large and radical working class, from which came a whole cohort of Latvian revolutionaries. In the 1905 Revolution, which plunged the whole of the Russian Empire into chaos for more than a year, Riga was in the forefront. Misha's grandfather was not a revolutionary, but— appropriately for an ancestor of Misha's—he was interested in technology, including photography. He had got too rich, according to Misha's analysis (perhaps based on his mother's report) and was 'bored to death':

> So he dabbled with this and that, and tended to disappear for months at a time, reappearing dead drunk in the middle of the night, to disappear again some months later. His last entry in the book of history was in 1905, when he assembled photographic equipment and left to photograph and document the [Russian] revolution. He never returned.

That was the part of the grandfather's story Misha particularly liked, the reason the grandfather deserved a musing. Provincial

Latvia had bored Grandfather Janis, so he left. Misha as an adolescent approved of that. He had similar plans for himself, though in his case the idea was to go west rather than east.

Olga was one of Janis and Julia's three children, including an older sister, Mary, and a son who played the violin, fought in the First World War and either died there or, in one version, went off to fight for the Reds in the Russian Civil War (around 1918) and never came back. The departure of Olga's father when she was eight must have made for a difficult childhood, all the more since her mother was away for months in hospital and sanatorium. As the family—Olga does not specify its members, but it included an uncle and a piano-playing cousin—gathered to celebrate Julia's long-awaited return, her fourteen-year-old cousin played a Chopin étude that was forever marked in Olga's memory.

I never knew Olga, who died long before I met Misha, and his unfailingly admiring comments about his mother inspired a certain unspoken scepticism on my part: someone so wise, benevolent and generally saintly seemed not only implausible but almost dull (how wrong I was about that). It didn't help that Misha expressed to me in the 1990s the same feelings about the sanctity of motherhood and the special qualities of maternal love that, as I now know, he had written in almost identical words in his diary in his twenties. This was alien territory for me, and for a long time it turned me off Olga. When I first started doing research on the family, I started with his father.

The bare outlines of the story that I got from Misha were as follows. Arpad Danos, born in 1882, was a Hungarian who, as a singer with the Hamburg Opera, was touring in Riga when the First World War broke out. Since Hungary was on the Axis side in the war and Russia on the Allied, Arpad became overnight an enemy alien. He solved this problem by going undercover as a soloist with the Riga opera, using his stage name of Arimondi (this overt way of going underground greatly appealed to Misha). There he met and married a young Latvian singer in the opera chorus, Olga Viksne, daughter of the absconding miller and his wife Julia. A gymnasium graduate and cosmopolitan Anglophile, he subscribed to the London newspaper the *Morning Post*, probably more for its excellent international and cultural coverage than for its conservative politics. Arpad was not only an opera singer but also a sportsman: he had competed in the Paris Olympic Games in 1900 in the triple jump, Misha said, but gave up competitive sport on the insistence of his singing teacher. Twenty years later, and pushing forty, he had acquired a girth suitable for an opera singer of the day but definitely not for a triple jumper—as we see from the photograph at the head of this chapter.

Now *there's* an interesting parent, I thought. Indeed, I think so to this day, although much about Arpad remains frustratingly elusive. The puzzles start with his family back in Hungary. Misha, although photographed at the age of six in Hungarian costume, had little interest either as child or adult in Hungary or the ramifications of the Danos family. His brothers Arpad Jr and Jan were more attentive, and much of what I found out about the family after Misha's death came from them. They both remembered visits from the Danos aunts who brought the Hungarian costumes at the end of the 1920s, and Arpad Jr knew the Hungarian side of the family quite well, having as a fifteen-year-old spent a year with them in Hungary because of ill health. According to their accounts, the paternal grandfather, Josef Deutsch, was a Catholic schoolteacher of German colonist stock who, as a civil servant at the turn of the century, had to take a Hungarian name because of the government's Magyarisation policies, and chose the name of Danos. He was married to a Spaniard, the impressively named

Johanna da Quilla, and they had nine children (though Arpad remembered the names of only eight of them), of whom Arpad was the third. Jan amended the original version, after postwar contact with surviving members of the Hungarian family in which he discovered that the family was at least partly Jewish, to make grandmother Johanna da Quilla a Spanish Jew and a baroness.

Given my curiosity about the Jewish part of the family tree, I was fascinated but also puzzled by this information. Did Spanish Jew mean Sephardic? Were Spanish Jews likely to be baronesses, and if so, according to whose titles of nobility? I pestered all my friends with expertise in Jewish history about these questions and essentially came up with a blank. Nobody knew anything about aristocratic, possibly Sephardic, Jews called da Quilla, in Hungary or anywhere else. So I found a young Hungarian researcher, Kata Bohus, and set her on a search in the birth and marriage and other contemporary records. She came up with a marriage record for Joszef (sic) Deutsch, but alas the wife had the more prosaic name of Janka Weiner. The parents' name change was not recorded, but in 1898, four of their sons registered a change of last name to Danos.

The parents' marriage certificate contained no information on the nationality, race or religion of the couple, but all the other documents Kata found, as well as some in Jan's private archive, indicated that the children of the marriage were consistently identified as 'Israelite', both in their school records and in the registration of name changes. It may be, as Jan suggests, that for Hungarian bureaucratic purposes in cases of mixed marriages, the mother's nationality was passed to the children, and that the Danos children were baptised and brought up as Catholic and identified as such. Certainly Arpad Sr called himself a Catholic when marrying Olga in Riga. Of the family remaining in Hungary under the Nazis in the Second World War, most came through alive, but one sister was denounced as a Jew and perished in a concentration camp. Deutsch, however, was often a Jewish name in Eastern Europe, and other Hungarian families who changed their name from Deutsch to Danos in the same period appear to have been Jewish, though not necessarily identifying as such. My sense, and Kata's, is that the Josef Danos family was very likely Jewish on both sides, albeit assimilated, German-speaking and secular.

Everybody gets their family stories a bit wrong and it's a shame to spoil a good one. But as regards other elements of the family, I must sadly report that according to Kata's researches, Arpad Sr did *not* compete in the Paris Olympic Games, despite Arpad Jr and Jan confirming Misha's recollection on this point. Still, you can see why the Olympics lodged in family memory as a shorthand. Arpad Sr actually was a promising athlete, first mentioned in the Budapest sporting press around 1899, whose best events initially were the long jump and the triple jump, and who then became Hungarian national champion in the high jump in 1903. He did indeed qualify for the Olympics in 1900, but lack of funds evidently prevented him from going to Paris to compete.

Arpad landed in Riga accidentally and never seems to have thought much of Latvia, although by a quirk of fate he would be the only member of the family who did not try to leave it in 1944. Yet when he arrived there in 1914, Riga was in the midst of an artistic flowering; not at all a bad place to be as far as culture was concerned. A spectacular local Art Nouveau movement in architecture in the prewar decade, led by the Russian-educated Latvian German Mikhail Eisenstein (father of the famous Soviet filmmaker Sergei), had given Riga the highest concentration of this style in the world. In the 1920s, Arpad Danos and his family would live in one of the Art Nouveau apartment blocks, with the family of Isaiah Berlin (the British philosopher) round the corner in another. Arpad's affinity with the modern in music, particularly the art songs of the French composer Claude Debussy, would have been congenial to the international- and modern-minded Riga public. Opera was also flourishing. Up to 1913, it was mainly performed in the German Theatre by touring companies like Arpad's, but in that year, a Latvian opera company was formed, whose soloists included Paul Sakss, Arpad's future brother-in-law, and later Arpad himself.

It was the First World War that essentially destroyed Riga as a lively, modern, cosmopolitan city, turning it into the depressed backwater that Misha grew up in and his parents in varying degrees disdained. The war inflicted tremendous damage on Latvia, particularly on Riga. There was fighting on Latvian territory from the first months of the war, and by 1915 several major Latvian cities had fallen to the Germans, although Riga held out amid fierce fighting until the summer of 1917. The Russians carried out a wholesale evacuation of industry from Latvia in 1915, which according to Latvian nationalist sources, amounted to a 'wholesale plunder', and about a quarter of a million Riga workers and their families left for the Russian heartland in a departure that often proved to be permanent. This, incidentally, seems to have affected the Viksne family fortunes, since Olga's mother owned houses occupied by workers in the Riga suburbs, and after the workers' evacuation eastward, these houses had been arbitrarily demolished. Over a hundred thousand Jews—three-quarters of Latvia's Jewish population—also went east, either in flight or through forcible relocation by the Russian military (who regarded them as sympathetic to the Germans). The result was that by 1920, Latvia's population had lost a million people (down from 2.6 to 1.6 million), and Riga's population had halved, down to under 200,000. As one historian writes, 'from a noisy, bustling industrial and cultural metropolis, Riga was transformed into a quiet provincial centre'.

Schools and public institutions were evacuated to Russia during the war too, which was evidently how the teenage Olga Viksne found herself in Petrograd (the wartime name of the capital, formerly St Petersburg) around the time that the country was sliding once again into revolution. Her sons came up with various versions of how she got there, but Olga herself settled the question in an autobiographical fragment found in her papers: 'My school was transferred from Riga to Petrograd. My sister was married to an opera singer and was herself studying singing in the State conservatory in Petrograd, so I went to live with them.' Her school was quartered in one of the elite Russian girls' schools in the very centre of the capital, taking the afternoon shift. Since Olga had the mornings free, she used to wander around the fashionable centre of the city, where the atmosphere was 'exceedingly gay and lighthearted', and officers could be seen walking with 'beautiful fur-clad women' as if they were on holiday, not in the midst of a war. She must have travelled, too: one of her diary entries in the 1920s recalls two visits to the provincial town of Iaroslavl, north-east of Moscow, the first time during the war to some event in the officers' school, when the mood was still upbeat and extravagant, and a few years later, in 1918 or 1919, when 'fear was already blowing openly through the streets'.

This mysterious second visit to Iaroslavl, when, alone for the first time in her life, she lived 'unforgettable days of hunger and self-elected loneliness', suggests that Olga's life at this point was in chaos, along with Russia's and Latvia's. At the time of Russia's October 1917 Revolution, which brought the Bolsheviks to power, Riga and the rest of Latvia were in German hands, and the Treaty of Brest (signed under duress in March 1918 by the new Soviet government) gave Latvia to the Germans. With German defeat in November 1918, however, this became null, and the region sank into near anarchy, with various groups seizing power in quick succession. Latvian politicians immediately declared the country's independence, but after the Bolsheviks' Red Army came in, a Latvian Socialist Soviet Republic government (allied with Soviet Russia) was established. This lasted only a year or so before Riga was seized by the German Freikorps (freebooters from the defeated German imperial army), who launched a 'White terror' against the Reds. An independent Latvian state with the constitution of a parliamentary republic emerged tentatively at the beginning of the 1920s.

Sometime in this chaotic period, young Olga married a postal official, probably Russian, and began a brief career as a coloratura soprano with the Riga opera (the sequence of these events, and the place of her first marriage, is not clear). In any event, after seven and a half months, she left her husband (this could perhaps explain the period of self-elected loneliness in Iaroslavl) and ran off with the operatic tenor Arpad Danos. The version Misha had from his mother, somewhat bowdlerised, had her boarding a train to Petrograd to marry her fiancé when Arpad appeared dramatically at the station and snatched her off. In fact, she was with a husband, not a fiancé, when Arpad, who had also been married, came on the scene.

Arpad may not look like a romantic hero in the photos we have of him from this time, but Olga certainly saw their relationship in high romantic terms. As she later recalled their first meeting, he saw her at a concert and said to his friend and fellow-musician Hans Schmidt, 'That is my bride, I will sing her the *Dichterliebe* (Schumann's song cycle, *A Poet's Love*).' He duly launched into the cycle's first song, 'Im wunderschönen Monat Mai' ('In the Wonderful Month of May'), which to Olga became 'their' song. Afterwards, 'Hans Schmidt led me to the window, took both my hands, and said "Let me look at you. You want to marry this man. Are you brave enough?" "Does one need to be *so* brave?" "To live with a man of genius, yes."'

No marriage certificate survives in Olga's papers, nor any indication of how (or if) she and Arpad managed to disengage themselves legally from previous spouses. According to Olga's diary, the date of the wedding was 19 May 1919, a month after the Bolsheviks had taken power in Riga, and they were married in a Catholic church in Riga. This was not because they were religious but because a church marriage was important to Olga's mother Julia (although her own confession seems to have been Protestant) and because Arpad, whose official identification in Latvia was Catholic, often sang there. It was the groom's thirty-seventh birthday; the bride was twenty-two. Olga put up her long hair in what she described wryly as an 'enemy-of-the-people' style (meaning that the puritanical Bolsheviks would have regarded it as 'bourgeois') and wore a white dress she made herself from odd bits of material from a second-hand shop. For the reception, so her mama informed her, they had nothing to offer but potatoes.

The young couple were evidently not Bolshevik supporters, but Olga seemed inclined, at least in retrospect, to treat this first Soviet occupation with humour, as one of those upheavals in the external world you just have to cope with as best you can. As it turned out, Arpad and Olga did rather well out of the Bolsheviks, albeit indirectly. Their first marital apartment had six rooms, fully furnished and with a little garden, and on top of that it came for free. That was because the owner—a friend of Arpad's with the title of baron, whose pastor brother had fled—was in bad odour with the Bolsheviks and wanted to protect it from nationalisation by putting friendly and politically inconspicuous tenants in.

It was a marriage of passion that, according to Olga's later reflections, she saw as shaky from the start. '*A wedding?*' she wrote a few weeks before the event, in a diary entry simmering with jealousy sparked by the discovery of a photograph of his former wife in his drawer. (The entry is in Russian rather than the usual German, the language she and Arpad mainly used at home.)

> Will I manage not to torment him, weak as I am? Jealousy of his past tortures me unbearably ... A wedding awaits me, I'm going to marry him ... When I married [illegible], I was sure that I would live my whole life with him. And then I left him after 7 and a half months. Now I already know in advance, that we can't stand this mutual tormenting for long, yet all the same, there's going to be a wedding ... My God, how I hate him, how jealous I am of him. How ridiculous and pitiful he seems to me, and how I respect him. How I despise him and how I loved him—love him now!

She must have been already pregnant with Arpad Jr, who was born in January 1920, seven months after the marriage. Michael (Mikelis) followed in 1922, and Jan (Janis, Jochen) in 1924. Years later, in a subsequent journal kept in America, Olga remembered that at the time of Misha's birth, the marriage was already in trouble: 'I loved my husband and was unhappy. Actually, when Mischi was born, the watershed was already behind me. I had already begun to get used to being inwardly alone.' Perhaps so, but the operatic passions of love and jealousy continue to dominate her original diary (written in a notebook entitled 'the book of my marriage') throughout the 1920s.

2
Childhood

Three Danos boys—from left Arpad, Jan
and Misha—in Hungarian costume, 1928.

MISHA'S parents were riding high in his childhood. Servants were part of the household, the family slept between 'top-quality sheets', and their multilingual cosmopolitanism was, if anything, a social advantage in the cultural elite in which they moved. All that changed in his adolescence, when Arpad Sr lost his money and his singing voice, the parents separated and a new spirit of assertive Latvian nationalism made foreigners like Arpad feel unwanted.

The family's prosperity in the 1920s was not based on Arpad's singing career, although that seems to have been going well enough, but on a windfall made possible by the Bolsheviks and their brief reign in Riga. Aristocrats, capitalists, high officials and anyone who had been privileged under the old regime feared the Bolsheviks sufficiently to flee, leaving most of their property behind them. Arpad became a millionaire in the early 1920s, according to his son Jan, by selling antique furniture and paintings left behind in Riga by the refugees or confiscated from them. The deals were struck through contacts in the British and American embassies, notably a certain Major Bell. Jan says he was Misha's godfather and describes him as a friend and fellow-explorer of Jack London, the American adventure-story writer, whose fame in Eastern Europe in the first half of the twentieth century was tremendous. Misha never mentioned a godfather to me, or revealed any special interest in London, although as a child of his time he had surely read him; and I can find no record of a Major Bell (admittedly a common name) in the US Embassy. Perhaps we should banish him to the anteroom of colourful but fictional characters like Johanna da Quilla. Still, Jan's story makes sense: there would have been money to be made that way, and Arpad was probably sufficiently well connected and enough of a connoisseur to have done it. It would explain how, around 1926, Arpad and Olga had the funds to pay for an extravagant year for the whole family in Italy.

Misha remembered that year in Palermo fondly, his vividest memory being a spectacular win in a pissing contest with local boys. He learnt Italian, though he forgot it again later. For the parents, it became a second household language (Latvian and Russian were only spoken outside, in the street, or to the grandmother), used for *'pas devant les enfants'* purposes. The parents hired an Italian nanny for the children and spent a lot of time off concertising, according to Jan. Olga later gave a slightly different version: she had given up singing after her marriage, she told the *Miami Herald* in 1954, thinking that she and her husband should not be in the same business, and switched to sculpture, studying in the studio of Richard Maur (probably in Riga) and 'later spen[ding] over two years doing direct carving in Rome'. The marriage seems to have looked up in this period, although this is partly a deduction based on the lack of diary entries: Olga used 'the book of my marriage' mainly for theatrical expression of moods of melancholy and anguish, so a lack of entries seems prima facie evidence of an upswing. They probably hoped to remain permanently in Italy, but the money ran out (Misha's version), and in addition (Jan's version) they may have had problems in Sicily with the Mafia.

The family seems to have been back in Riga by Easter 1927, when Olga's diary resumes. Arpad Sr was having trouble with his voice, and she wasn't sure if he would be able to keep singing professionally. She described him as being at a loose end, frequenting cafes and not sure what to do with himself; perhaps a more sympathetic version would cast him as a flâneur. As his combination of musical and sporting skills suggests, he was a man of parts, interested in and well informed on a wide range of subjects, from international affairs to physics. Apparently he was trying to establish himself in the import/export business, trading particularly with Russia. According to Latvian sources, he was one of the founders of the 'Rosemary' canning and sausage company, whose investors included his sister-in-law Mary and her husband Paul Sakss. His son Arpad remembered toothpaste (Olga's diaries contain references to the dubious fortunes of 'Chlorodon') and oil as the mainstays of the export business. Jan said he was a fool as a businessman. His son Arpad was kinder, saying he was too trusting and was often cheated.

In any case, he lost all his money at the beginning of the 1930s, with the onset of the Great Depression, which hit Latvia with force. Misha linked this with the establishment of a state monopoly on certain types of import/export by the Ulmanis government, making his father a victim of growing Latvian nationalism, but the other brothers—perhaps more tolerant of Latvian nationalism than Misha—weren't sure about this. As Misha's friend Andrejs Bičevskis, who knew the family slightly in Riga, remembered the story, when Arpad Sr's oil-import business was bought out or nationalised, he was offered the choice of a lump sum or employment, took the latter and was fired after a month.

The children's upbringing was Olga's domain, and she seems to have let them run reasonably wild and follow their own interests. Olga's mother lived with them, providing a corrective to the otherwise somewhat bohemian mores of the household, and they saw a lot of their two slightly older cousins, Mary's daughters Ariadna and Jogita. Olga may have homeschooled her children in their early years, since Misha (and probably Arpad too) didn't go to school until he was about twelve. The two elder boys, Arpad and Misha, were very close, with Jan the younger odd man out. There was a lot of music in the household. Misha sang in a boys' choir until his voice broke (he told me he was allowed to continue too long, thus damaging his voice as an adult, a fate he claimed to share with the composer Joseph Haydn) and also played the piano. As they grew up, the two older boys became passionate and talented sportsmen.

Olga's child-raising approach, as she later described it, was to maintain a certain detachment, avoid overemotionalism, including physical manifestations of love, and encourage independent thinking. Misha thought she brought them up in exactly the right way, but Jan, at least as a young adult, was more critical: he considered that she should have set clearer boundaries and perhaps have been a bit more conventional all along the line. More Latvian as well, or at least this was Olga's interpretation of his criticism. Addressing Jan in her diary on his name-day in 1947, she wrote sadly that 'we never celebrated your name-day properly. When you were little, we wove garlands and sung folksongs, but it wasn't genuine. I was then alienated from Latvian society, and partly also from Latvian customs.' Indeed, three-year-old Jan is virtually swamped in his garland of leaves in the photographs at the head of this chapter, but the costumes he and his brothers are wearing are not Latvian but the gift of a Hungarian aunt.

When I tried to read up on Riga's history, I was taken aback to find that the city's historians tend to write about just one national history—German Riga, Russian Riga, Jewish Riga, Latvian Riga—as if the others didn't exist. But families like the Danoses straddled the boundaries, whether they wanted to or not. The Danos parents normally spoke German to each other and the children at home. Olga was equally at ease in Russian (in fact, her Russian was probably better than her German in her youth), and apparently Arpad Sr was too. The children spoke Latvian to their grandmother and Russian and Latvian on the street. This was nothing remarkable in multiethnic Riga. The Danos family, or at least its head, had Hungarian passports, according to Jan, until growing nationalist pressure led them to take Latvian citizenship in 1934. Misha's memory was that his father had had a Nansen (stateless) passport after the war.

In Riga, everyone agrees, the Germans constituted the social elite. What is not so clear is the social standing of German speakers like the Danoses who were not actually German. Jan holds strongly to the view that the Danoses were part of 'German society' in Riga, although conceding that within

German society, they counted as Hungarians. But Misha himself never claimed such membership for the family, and friends of Misha's whom I interviewed later in life denied that the Danoses could be so described. For one thing, I gathered, they were not elite enough, especially after Arpad lost his money. While the two eldest children were sent to the German classical gymnasium, Jan went first to a French school and then to the Latvian gymnasium, perhaps because by the time he was of high-school age, Latvian identity looked the more likely to improve your life chances. But Jan, like the others, spoke a more or less native German as well as Latvian and a Russian that, by the time I knew him (after decades of Soviet rule), was more or less native too, and much more fluent than Misha's.

At the end of his school years, Misha kept a diary—in German, of course—which was less a day-to-day chronicle than a series of meditations on the meaning of his life so far. One of the main topics was his sense of himself as culturally German. 'I was actually from earliest childhood brought up absolutely German,' he wrote, 'speaking German at home, then and now, and being given mainly German children's literature to read.' (Wilhelm Busch's classic German story in verse of boyish pranks, *Max und Moritz*, remained a prime favourite of Misha's until the end of his life.) He loved the German gymnasium when he finally got there after a preliminary year in Grade 6 of the German elementary school.

In the gymnasium, it was at first not his fellow pupils who made an impact ('I had no close friend, and also didn't feel any particular need of one') but the teachers, especially the maths teacher, Herr Kupfer. They were, he said, 'not teachers for me so much as friendly acquaintances, to some extent even more than acquaintances; they all without exception liked me'; they also treated him as an equal, encouraged his already evident talents in maths and physics and left him to spend his time at school more or less as he pleased. That's the way he put it in his diary, but from what I gathered from his later recollections, it didn't mean he slacked off, but rather that if he felt like going to a class, even an advanced class in physics when he was still a junior, they let him. It can't, at any rate, have been too undisciplined, as he retained a remarkable amount of Latin and Greek, which were merely peripheral interests to him, for the rest of his life.

'I didn't behave as a schoolboy but in a much freer way', he wrote, looking back from the heights of seventeen, and I can believe it: behaving as a schoolboy/subordinate/member of a subaltern collective was never in his repertoire when I knew him. It wasn't that he lacked the bump of reverence: he had enormous respect (much greater than I could generally muster) for various mentors in physics and for individuals whose understanding or simply humanity impressed him. But he had an absolute aversion to acknowledging claims to superior status or position and could be outright rude—though generally a mild-mannered man—when he saw it was expected of him. The converse was that he made no such claims himself, and consequently established the easiest of rapports with the young in later life because he really did talk to them as equals. It's odd, given the Germans' alleged love of hierarchy and discipline, that a German gymnasium should have been the first external environment that validated Misha's 'free' approach to adults, presumably learnt in his somewhat bohemian home.

The discovery of friends of his own age came a bit later, outside school and through the sports club. This being Riga, there was of course not just a general sports club for adolescents but a German one, a Latvian one and no doubt Russian and Jewish ones as well. Misha and Arpad Jr were both sports-minded, good at a variety of forms of athletics (Misha was a middle-distance runner and also a pole vaulter,

Arpad a sprinter), and both competed at national level, but for different sports clubs—Misha the German club and Arpad the Latvian. Joining the sports club was 'a decisive moment in my life', Mischa wrote in his diary at seventeen: 'I acquired comrades and was set off in another direction, namely as a young man (*Junge*). I learnt to understand comradeship and became more and more German.'

Another discovery was no less important: radio. Misha became a passionate radio amateur, though whether this means ham radio (experimenting with wireless communication) or simply building radios and taking them apart I don't know. As he told the story,

> In the autumn of 1937 I chanced to notice in a newspaper, with which I was otherwise never in contact, an announcement for a course for radio amateurs; I enrolled in it immediately. There I was by far the youngest participant [at fifteen], but technically one of the best, if not the best.

One of the lecturers to the group was the head of Riga's commercial radio station, and acquaintance with him seems to have been a factor in Misha's obtaining a job at the VEF, one of the world's leading radio manufacturers, after leaving school. But Misha's sense of the importance of amateur radio in his life went way beyond the contingent. In a letter to his prospective in-laws twelve years later, he included it as one of the decisive moments in his life's trajectory, whose meaning was the pursuit of *Wissenschaft* ('science' in the broad German sense of 'knowledge').

Neither Misha's diary nor Olga's sheds much light on what was happening at home in his high-school years. Undoubtedly it was depressing. Misha's rotten apples story indicates his dislike of the family's declining fortunes. When he spoke about the period to me, it was in terms of quarrels between his parents about money, with Arpad Sr continuing his old habits of generous hospitality, including putting up impecunious friends for months at a time, and Olga objecting that they couldn't afford it. This must have stopped when they moved out of their good apartment in the centre of the city and went to live in a little house outside the city (perhaps, indeed, that was part of Olga's intention). But nobody liked that set-up, and after a few years the family moved back to the centre, now in Elizabetes Street in the Art Nouveau section, living in the same apartment block as Olga's sister Mary (probably now divorced) and her two daughters. Arpad Sr tried to make a living as a singing teacher, but not very successfully. The Danoses sold off some of their expensive furniture and art objects. In the end, it was Olga who recouped the family fortunes, establishing an *atelier des modes* in the mid 1930s that by the end of the decade was providing most of the family's income.

Information on Olga's enterprise was comparatively sparse until one day, out of the blue, an email arrived in my inbox from a Latvian scholar, Līvija Baumane, who had discovered Olga and was giving a chapter to her in a study of entrepreneurial Latvian women in prewar Riga. From Līvija, I found out that Olga's arrival on the commercial scene was hailed in nationalist terms in 1938 as a sign that the centre of Riga was being 'conquered by Latvian-owned businesses—up until then, members of other nationalities had dominated in the local business and trade sectors'. This sounds like shorthand for the extrusion of Jews and Germans. Among the successful Jewish businessmen in Riga's apparel trade was David Mirkin, a maker of men's and women's gloves with a haberdashery business in the same quarter as Olga's shop, whom she almost certainly knew (I drop his name here because the Mirkin family is going to reappear in the story). Olga was aiming at the upscale market. The Danoses seem to have had a wide circle of friends and acquaintances in Riga's elites, which Olga both used and expanded with her atelier. According to a contemporary newspaper report, her salon provided an entrée into 'a world of elegance', receiving patterns 'directly from the fashion capital of Paris as well as New York City', and also featuring designs by Olga herself. The reporter was 'able to view the original gold-coloured garment with blue panne flowers belonging to "the well known socialite Mrs. N. N." And an assistant was just wrapping a parcel containing a beautiful evening dress for the wife of an ambassador—black lace and white tulle, a very current combination ...' Olga was able to open a subsidiary in a resort on Rigās Jūrmala, the favourite seaside haunt of Misha's childhood, and then in 1939 joined forces with a milliner, Mrs Vera Dagilis, to establish a salon now billed in French as *'Haute couture et chapeaux. On parle toutes les langues principales'* ('High fashion and hats. All main languages spoken').

At some point in this period, the Danoses separated, with Olga moving out to a small apartment in the Old City, leaving the boys with their father in the city apartment, perhaps because it was closer to their school. The sources of Olga's dissatisfaction, or some of them, can be found in a conversation Misha reported in his diary, without comment, on 24 October 1939. Papa was 'extraordinarily capable in all areas', Olga had told Misha. He understood a great deal about economics and politics, was 'extraordinarily gifted' in the arts, writing good poetry and short stories and singing Debussy like no other. He had even 'done something creative' in the area of theoretical physics. The trouble was, he had made nothing of his gifts, ending up as 'a miserable little [import/export] agent'. 'In his youth, he set out to conquer the world,' but he was 'egocentric' without being ambitious: evidently, in the end, he didn't care enough about success and just did what he felt like. This was clearly a disappointment for Olga, with her early sense that she was marrying a genius; but her analysis, for Misha's ears alone, could also be read as a message that geniuses should not fritter away their gifts but go out and 'conquer the world'. (Olga had already decided that Misha was the cleverest of her children, and thus the bearer of hopes.) Misha's diary entry records Olga's words with such a complete absence of commentary that one becomes all the more curious to know how he interpreted them.

Misha disliked the new living arrangements, and his relations with his father deteriorated. No doubt he also shared something of his mother's disappointment with his father, as adolescents are prone to do. He must have spent a fair amount of time over at his mother's shop, because years later, when I was playing Russian popular songs from the 1920s, he recognised them as songs that Olga's Russian seamstresses used to sing as they worked. He also learnt to judge the fit of a jacket like a professional tailor, an unexpected skill in one who, at least when I knew him, never owned a suit and liked his sports coats shabby—though, like Olga, he wore his clothes with an air. Whether this meant that he sometimes actually worked in the shop, or simply learnt the skill through his automatic habit of closely observing any technical process, I don't know.

Recalling this period in the 1990s and 2000s, all three brothers agreed that the parents had separated but were uncertain whether they had divorced. This in itself tells us something about the family's relatively bohemian mores. None of them mentioned affairs on the part of either parent as a reason for separation, but Olga was the spouse who moved out, and it's clear from her diary that the direction of marital jealousy had switched: while in the 1920s it was Olga who was constantly jealous of Arpad and his connections with other women, in the 1930s it was Arpad who, as she remembered later, 'pestered me with jealousy'. The diary notes the existence of 'one I loved apart from you [her husband], whose name in this book will not be named', but we know no more of him other than the fact that, as of 1948, he was dead.

The political atmosphere in Riga, and indeed all over Europe, was souring in the late 1930s. In Latvia, an increasingly assertive and parochial Latvian nationalism had brought Kārlis Ulmanis to power. Ulmanis, an agricultural expert by profession, had been a nationalist activist in the 1905 Revolution and after independence had headed the conservative Farmers' Party. 'Our micro Mussolini', as Misha always called him, took dictatorial powers by a coup in 1934, abolishing the parliament and all political parties, including his own, giving privileges to a paramilitary home guard, Aizsargi, and pursuing economic and cultural policies of Latvianisation. Arpad Sr, an anglophile liberal, strongly disliked the Ulmanis regime, but Arpad Jr evidently had some sympathy with it, which may have been the cause of the tensions between them that Misha remembered.

Misha, sharing the political views of the older Arpad, was nevertheless annoyed by his (dismissive? contemptuous?) treatment of the younger one. Although he was Misha's elder by two years, Misha, who had always been the stronger and the cleverer, developed a protective attitude towards his older brother. In the 1990s, he remembered that 'when OB [the older brother, i.e. Arpad] was ill: it was disturbing, seemed unfair (why should he be [ill]?); also I felt that I could have an easier time coping with it—being stronger'. Arpad's unspecified illness, and whether or not he should be kept in school, was one of the bones of contention between the parents as well. Olga later felt guilty because, obedient to my husband, I let it happen that you [Arpad] overtaxed your strength in school … I was until then an obedient wife. Then I freed myself from him … but for you it was too late. You had to live with the damage to your health for many years.

The autonomy of the German school system in Latvia was under threat under the Ulmanis regime, along with the extensive German cultural and sporting network that had been set up. But there was worse to come. The Nazi–Soviet Pact of August 1939 put Latvia and the other Baltic states in the Soviet zone of influence. In 1940, this would result in Soviet occupation of the Baltic states and their incorporation into the Soviet Union, but the writing was already on the wall in October 1939 when Ulmanis was forced to accept the stationing of Soviet troops in Latvia. Most of the Riga Germans didn't want to stay under those circumstances, and indeed Hitler's regime officially called them 'home to the Reich', offering them assistance in resettling (mainly in the western part of Poland, which had gone to Germany under the Nazi–Soviet Pact). Almost sixty thousand Baltic Germans left Latvia in 1939–40. These were tumultuous times for Riga's German classical gymnasium, many of whose pupils were preparing to depart at the beginning of the 1939–40 school year. The gymnasium seems to have kept functioning, but Misha's German sports club, the place where he had just learnt comradeship, was closed down in 1939.

To top off a miserable year, Misha managed to get himself expelled from the gymnasium for rudeness to a teacher. Exactly how this happened is not entirely clear. Misha's favourite teacher, Herr Kupfer, had retired by this time, and no doubt his successors lacked Kupfer's special appreciation of Misha and gave him less latitude. The problem arose with a new teacher in physics, where Misha had always felt himself supreme, knowing more than what was taught in class and therefore not always bothering to attend. According to his brother Arpad's version, the incident that led to Misha's expulsion was that the physics teacher gave the wrong explanation for something, Misha corrected him, the teacher stuck to his version, and Misha made the gesture of screwing a hole in the side of his head, meaning 'He's crazy'. Misha's version omitted the gesture and emphasised the teacher's unreasonableness in being unable to accept correction. In his diary at the time, his sense of being hard done by was slightly tempered by the recognition that he didn't handle such things well:

It was because of my straightforwardness, because of my absolute inability to think up something untrue to say. It wasn't that I was such an angel that I wouldn't lie for ethical reasons. But I was so untalented at it, that it just didn't occur to me to make a 'scene'. In this case the possible scene was so obvious, and would have been completely convincing, so everyone called me the biggest idiot in world history … Obviously this teacher held, perhaps unconsciously, to the principle that it's how things look that matters most, not wisdom. That the clever man can be in a bar and not get beaten up while the stupid one gets clobbered even in church. Back then for the first time it was darkly borne in on me that one doesn't get far with honesty. With my brain I seem to understand this, but I still haven't really grasped it and probably never will …

He was basically right in that gloomy prophesy. Even though he was going to have to pick up some basic skills of tactical evasion and selective truth-telling in the next few years, he never learnt to apologise, particularly when he was sure he was in the right, and he didn't internalise automatic respect for authority either. The outcome of this bit of tactless disrespect was that Misha had to leave the German gymnasium and spend his last school year in the Latvian city gymnasium, a place so 'bleak' and 'spiritually dead' that he had to force himself to get up and go to school in the morning. After a while, he evidently stopped forcing himself and dropped out as a full-time student, graduating from high school as an external student in the autumn of 1940.

It was just at this time that Misha's German friends from school and the sports club started leaving with their families for Germany. '*Aus!*' ('Out!') is the one-word entry in Misha's diary for 11 November 1939. That 'Out!' is explained a few pages later in an undated entry:

> When the news came that we, that is the local Germans, will be going to the Reich, it was quite clear to me: I'm going too! I just have to get this through at home. I hope I can manage to convince them both. Actually I have had the plan for a long time to go to Germany after finishing secondary school and make my life there.

The political aspect of such a move seems not to have occurred to him. Sometime in the late 1930s, when he was still singing, he had gone with a choir to Germany and later remembered watching crowds streaming to one of the Nazi rallies and thinking how stupid they were. It was not the (no doubt ephemeral) Nazi regime in Germany that appealed to him but the centuries of German culture to which, like many German speakers in Eastern Europe, he felt himself heir. The Ulmanis regime had been bad enough, but with the prospect of Soviet occupation imminent, Latvia was about to be drawn downwards, from Misha's point of view, into eastern backwardness and chaos, which made it more than ever a place to leave. Jan remembers feeling the same way, and thinks the third brother, Arpad, may have too. But, unusually in a family where the mother generally ruled the roost, their father put his foot down. Nobody was going to go to Germany, he ruled. He 'wasn't going to give up his sons for cannon-fodder for Adolf', and that was that. The family stayed in Riga.

3

Riga under the Soviets

State Electrotechnical Factory (VEF), Riga, Wikimedia
Commons photo.

A S Misha was finishing school, the Soviets were moving towards occupying Latvia and overthrowing the Ulmanis government. They had the green light to do this on the basis of the secret treaties attached to the non-aggression pact signed by Soviet foreign minister Vyacheslav Molotov and German foreign minister Joachim von Ribbentrop in August 1939. Soviet troops marched into Riga in the middle of June 1940 and remained for a little over a year. In this period, Latvia and the other Baltic states were formally incorporated into the Soviet Union, but since the Germans threw the Soviets out in

July 1941 and occupied the Baltic states themselves, Misha didn't have long to enjoy his new Soviet citizenship. It was a dangerous time for a young man to approach his eighteenth birthday (which Misha celebrated on 10 January 1940), but Latvian military call-up age was twenty-one, so he avoided that; and his stint working on a farm in the summer of 1940—probably the result of a labour draft of schoolchildren by the Ulmanis government to help with the harvest—provoked only the diary comment that agricultural work might build up stamina but was really dull. The Soviets didn't get round to conscripting him in the six months that he was, in theory, eligible for military service.

Misha was scarcely a committed follower of politics at this point, but he had started reading newspapers, 'not religiously, but with a certain interest: there was turmoil in the world'. Evidently his newspaper reading was international, which suggests that his father was still able to subscribe to foreign newspapers in the last Ulmanis years, though the Soviets surely soon put a stop to this bourgeois habit. Misha found the Latvian press to be 'laudatory towards our micro-Mussolini but rather objective on world events', somewhere on the comparative scale between the ideologically charged German press and the English, with its scrupulous separation of news and opinion.

He also observed Latvia's war preparations, as displayed in military parades, with his usual eye for technological detail, and found them slightly comic:

> The air force had about 20 planes, bombers and fighters; all of them bi-planes, of frame plus canvas construction. Top speed of bombers about 100 miles per hour; of the fighters about 110 miles per hour. The motors of the tanks tended to stall; so as to be prepared for the case that the motor refused

to re-start, every tank had a heavy hook front and back, and carried a heavy chain. It so happened that this refusal to re-start happened during one of these parades; so the chain was hooked between that stalled and a non-stalled tank, and the functioning tank started to move, but the stalled did not; the pull evidently was too strong for the armor plate; hook plus a chunk of tank armor moved; tank with hole in armor stayed put. Cannon was horse-drawn.

The entry of Soviet military forces into Riga was a low-key affair:

> After a few days of confusing newspaper articles the Russian tanks rolled in, a thousand or more of them; Russian two-motor bombers, made of metal, flew low over Riga. Ulmanis said over the radio: You stay in your place, I will stay in my place (meaning of 'place': post); that was the last heard from and of him. The planes continued over-flights, not only on that rolling-in day, but now and then for some further days.

The Finns, receiving a similar ultimatum to those delivered to the Baltic states requiring the resignation of their governments and the entry of Soviet forces, resisted and managed to embarrass the Soviets significantly by their stubbornness in the Winter War of 1940–41. But the small Baltic states were more easily intimidated. Kārlis Ulmanis accepted the Soviet ultimatum without offering even symbolic resistance, let alone military, and resigned on 16 June. Perhaps as a reward, he was subsequently allowed to work for a year in Southern Russia at his original profession of agricultural specialist before being arrested a month after the German invasion. But the political and diplomatic manoeuvring took place out of sight of Latvia's inhabitants. As Misha later wrote, after reading a scholarly study of the diplomacy,

> all the activities taking place there had no impact, and were essentially unknown. What was known was that the Soviet military bases were generated, later that the [Soviet] army was on its way to Riga, and that [Soviet] planes were flying overhead. That diplomatic life seems so disconnected, self-contained, void of content, arbitrary, unreal. Then, suddenly, there are the tanks.

In Riga, the first impact of Soviet occupation as Misha observed it was comparatively mild: 'some arrests took place, but not in such numbers as to be perceived as really alarming'. What astonished him was the new kind of public discourse in the newspapers. The moment the Soviets took charge,

> the papers flipped over; objective reporting was gone; everything which had been white turned black, and vice versa ... Very soon every-day life set in. What remained: weird, extraordinary, against previous experience: the writing in the newspapers. It was known, clearly under-stood, that it was transparently disconnected from truth; it was irreal, surreal—but did not let up.

Misha concluded that the Soviets lived in a fantasy world.

The Soviet occupation turned out to be something like a working gap year between school and university for Misha. Whether the gap was a matter of choice, general chaos, late graduation on his part or a labour draft is unclear. His friend Andrejs Bičevskis, born in the same year and graduating from high school around the same time, remembered that the Soviets had some kind of work assignment system that would have landed him (Bičevskis) in a labouring job in a glass factory if he hadn't pulled strings to have himself reassigned to clerical work in a government ministry. In the end, he said, he never had to take up this assignment because in the autumn of 1941 (with Latvia under German rule) he went to university instead. Misha's job may have enabled him to fulfil a work requirement, but it was far too good to have been the result of random assignment (he probably got it through his connections as a radio amateur), and Misha found it fascinating. The job was at VEF, (Valsts Elektrotechniskā Fabrika), which was the high-tech pride of Latvian industry.

VEF, established in Riga as a state enterprise soon after the First World War and housed in a remarkable Art Deco building designed by German architect Peter Behrens, was at the cutting edge of independent Latvia's attempts to re-establish an industrial base after the wartime destruction and removal of the old one. It made radio receivers, audio amplifiers, telephone equipment and such, and had acquired a worldwide reputation by the 1930s. The Minox subminiature camera, then the smallest in the world, was invented here. After the Second World War, VEF, once again Soviet, would manufacture the extremely popular Spidola transistor radios for the Soviet market. Misha had long been fascinated by radio technology, and his adolescent diaries are dotted with entries (impenetrable to me) on the subject. He kept up the hands-on tinkering, even in later life, as a theoretical physicist, when he had a side occupation as an inventor and 'gadgeteer'. He loved working at VEF and retained an identification with it for the rest of his life. One of my fond memories from the 1990s is of Misha sitting opposite me in the reading room of the Riga state archives, transformed into a historian and totally immersed in the VEF files. He had come along to help me with any documents in Latvian, but as it turned out, postwar

Latvia had become enough of a colonial outpost for its political documents to be all in Russian. So Misha took the opportunity to do some independent research into VEF's technical history, bringing an expertise that no historian is ever going to match, and told me many things about it that I only half understood. I have forgotten the details, and this makes me angry with myself because now Misha is gone and with him all that knowledge.

Misha had already been working at VEF for a few months before the Soviets took over. They knew its value and immediately declared it to be an industrial enterprise of 'all-Union' significance—that is, subordinate to the central Soviet industrial ministry, not local authorities, and financed on the central Soviet budget. An abrupt transition to Soviet-style management and work practices followed, introduced by engineers who, though ethnically Latvian, had just been sent from Moscow. Misha was most unfavourably impressed. The first task, in Soviet eyes, was to speed up production ruthlessly to meet high output targets, just as was done in the Soviet Union. If that produced high reject rates—Misha used the Russian term for spoiled production, *brak*, since it was such a typical Soviet phenomenon—so be it. All Soviet factories had high reject rates.

> After the Russians had been there some time, it must have been around December 1940, or perhaps January 1941, the verdict of the Moscow engineers was: What a waste! With that beautiful production facility you could build twice as many radios per month! [It was already running two shifts.] You simply should run the conveyor belt in the assembly line faster; look at the leisurely pace [at which] these women do their soldering! OK, so you object; but

20% faster you simply will have to; that is an order (the number 20% may be inaccurate). So it was. I do not know how long the re-scheduling and reorganization took, but by March the walls of the assembly shop already were lined with non-functioning radios.

After a while, the plant ran out of space to store the rejects. The whole staff of the research and development labs, including Misha, were mobilised to investigate the faults and clear the shelves. It turned out that because of the speed-up of the conveyer belt, one particular solder joint tended to be defective. This wasn't hard to fix, but there were other more subtle problems that took more time. Despite the R&D people working two shifts, the number of rejects kept piling up. So the new Soviet management turned to another typically Soviet administrative practice: threats and intimidation.

About that time, March or April, a Meeting of the Whole VEF Collective was called, with the program: there will be some speeches by the (Latvian!) Moscow engineers, then there will be beer and dancing. So we went there, all the several thousand. Indeed, it started with the Moscow engineer, talking in Latvian. So, what did he have to say? 'We all know that the production has deteriorated. The high quality of the VEF radios is very well known, throughout the Union. Unfortunately, as we also know, recently *brak* production has arisen. (Full agreement by the audience.) We must stop that. We must find the culprits, the saboteurs, and we must get rid of them.' (Full disagreement by the audience; a faint chill.) The foreman of one of the sub-assembly shops, the one where the chassis and other hardware was produced, whom I had seen many a time, and whom I had considered to be highly competent, both technically and in interaction with the workers, asked to say a few words, which was granted: 'We know that there is *brak* production. In order to get rid of it, rather than to look for culprits, it might be more useful to look for the reasons for this faulty production. Once these reasons have been found and delineated it will be possible to address and rectify them.' (Enthusiastic applause by the audience.) Back comes the Moscow engineer: 'Perhaps this shop foreman is one of the saboteurs? Was he not a member of the Aizsargi [the nationalist and anti-Soviet home guard]? or perhaps he still is in a counterrevolutionary cell?' (Total, chilled silence by the audience.) End of meeting; no beer, no dancing.

Misha's musing on VEF is among the longest he wrote on any subject. Perhaps that was partly to make me—a Soviet historian, but ignorant of factory life—understand what Soviet management meant in practice, but it also reflected his attachment to the place. At VEF, Misha found that, as in the halcyon days of the German gymnasium under Herr Knupfer, people not only appreciated his talents but also let him do things his own way. In the newly Soviet factory, as in the German gymnasium, that meant wandering around to see what was happening in the various parts of the enterprise and staying to watch if there was something to learn:

After having been there a few months I began my investigations of that place. I went into one of the two Electrical Productions Buildings, entered some floor, and looked it over; depending on the subject I lingered more or less long times, watching what took place, how the workers acted, what the machines were doing, etc. These excursions, hence my absences from my official work place, lasted different amounts of time; I do not think less than one hour, but also not more than three. It never occurred to me to ask, it also never occurred to me to be surprised that nobody asked me about my absences—correction: I remember that once the immediate boss, Harjess, enquired, what I had seen, and I told him about it; with no further comment by Harjess. At any rate, when I was supposed to build a new design of an amplifier from scratch, I knew where to go.

His move to the design lab to work on the development of audio amplifiers came in December 1940. Only later on, when he wanted to enter university and the factory was unexpectedly uncooperative about letting him go, did it strike him that his bosses' tolerance of his wandering habits (under both Soviet and German occupations!) probably meant that they had marked him down as a bright lad and were grooming him for higher things.

Apart from VEF, what most preoccupied Misha during Riga's first Soviet year was his social and particularly his romantic life. I put a lot of effort into working out exactly who and what is being talked about in his diary entries on the topic, which are often elliptical, replete with some heavy crossings-out, pangs of conscience and a lot of abstract discussion of the nature of love. In the process I was guiltily reminded of my own distress as a child when the man next door discovered my diary hidden in the hedge and politely returned it to me (he could have read about my schoolgirl crushes!). So in the end I decided to skip the detail, since the people in question are mainly unknown anyway, and just offer Misha's retrospective summary from a diary entry for 5 May 1945, written in hospital in Germany just before the end of the war. It was a time when the Soviets had reoccupied and re-annexed Latvia, meaning that for those who, like the

Danoses, had left, there was no way back. In this entry, he was looking back on a lost past whose fragments war had scattered to the winds:

> It [his first relationship with a girl] began in spring of 1940; the parting came in spring 1941; however, it continued on for a while, and then in the spring of 1942 AK gradually entered the scene, which then in this way anyway gave the waning relationship a new twist. Then AK. It began in spring 1942 and went on with various struggles up to the summer of 1944, when the impact relatively quickly faded.

AK is Austra Krumins, the most important girlfriend of the Riga years according to Arpad Jr's later memory; she was a Latvian, met at university, who remained in Latvia. This last characteristic was not all that common among the friends of Misha's Riga years, or at least the ones whose contacts with him have left records. Take Valka, the Russian diminutive by which Waldtraut Hernberger, probably of mixed Russian and German origin, was known to Misha in Riga. She remembered pleasant winter evenings when the two of them strolled beside the river, having 'deep conversations about religion and such like', after which, 'frozen with rather mauve noses', they would retreat to her place to have tea with jam. Valka went to Germany sometime at the beginning of the 1940s and spent the war in Berlin; her sister had married a man who took her to England, while her mother was arrested and deported by the Soviets in 1941 and spent the war in the Soviet Union. After the war, Valka, along with her sister (now probably divorced) and her mother (finally released from Soviet exile), settled in Canada.

Or take the Klumbergs: Arvid (Didi) was Misha's best friend from the German school, and his sister Elena, known as 'Baby', was two years older than Misha and a classmate of Valka's at the German gymnasium. The father of the Klumberg family was a successful Baltic German lawyer who had married a Russian woman while working in Moscow; German and Russian were both spoken at home, and the boys were brought up as Lutheran and the girls Orthodox. Misha visited them several times at their summer place in Baldone, south of Riga, in 1940. Baby's family was so cosmopolitan and wealthy that they had sent her for a year at the end of the 1930s to a finishing school in Switzerland, where she learnt French and also picked up some English. They had a bad time under the Soviet occupation, when the Russians regarded her father as a 'big capitalist' and expropriated most of his assets, even nationalising their house and making the family pay rent. Baby, Didi and their mother moved to Germany in 1941 (the parents were divorced by this time), and Didi later fought in the German Army as an officer, on the Eastern Front. Baby herself shuttled back and forth between Riga and Berlin in the early war years, working in Riga for a German businessman, a Nazi who played Hitler's speeches on the radio to the girls in his office, but was congenial. Later in the war, she moved south in Germany, ending up at war's end in the US zone, where she married an American GI and moved to Chicago. Didi, who ended the war as a German prisoner, studied architecture in Germany as a postwar DP and then moved to Bolivia, following his remarried father, who had business interests there.

There is a lot about Baby in Misha's diary, including a worried discussion about why 'people' (evidently Baby) thought of him as 'a cold, dry, calculating machine'. I had Baby pegged as the leading candidate for the unnamed 1940–41 girlfriend, but this was strongly denied by Mrs Helen Machen, aka Baby Klumberg, when I interviewed her in Chicago in

2007. Misha was very nice, kind and polite, she said, but there was 'no funny business between us, no mushiness'. Well, who knows.

Olga Danos wasn't in Klumberg's league as a business-woman, but she was still, from the Soviet point of view, a capitalist, which was a source of possible danger during the Soviet occupation. The last prewar years had been difficult for a business aimed at the high-end market, since international tensions discouraged luxury consumption. Olga had to retool for a new 'era of frugality', as announced by President Ulmanis, but she did so with panache. The President himself attended a 'frugality' fashion show in the spring of 1940 in which Olga's light-coloured summer dress, made of a new and inexpensive 'amber fabric', earned his particular commendation. During the Soviet occupation, Olga was penalised, along with many other capitalist business owners, for 'speculative raising of prices and other violations', and threatened with closure, although it is not clear if her atelier was actually closed down.

Tensions were mounting in the spring of 1941, both inter-nally and on the international scene. Rumours that Germany was planning an attack on the Soviet Union flew around in diplomatic circles, and despite desperate Soviet efforts to conciliate the Germans, it appeared ever more likely that the Nazi–Soviet Non-Aggression Pact would break down. In that case, of course, Latvia and the other Baltic states were right in the firing line.

On the night of 14–15 June 1941, the Soviets unleashed an unprecedented wave of terror on the Baltic states, arrest-ing and deporting more than fifteen thousand people, or over 1 per cent of the total population, from Latvia. This operation was well prepared, according to the archival record, and not random, specifically targeting particular social and political categories regarded as dangerous (businessmen, army officers, landowners, police etc.). But the secret had been well kept, and it came as a total shock to the population. In Riga, there 'had been no signs, no rumors, no nothing, indicating the knowledge, suspicion, fear, on anybody's part of the impending "doom"', Misha recalled.

At that time I was working at VEF; starting time—generally obeyed!—was 7:30. I left the house around 7; overcast, grey, morning light, the street emptier than usual, deserted, except for now and then a group of people walking together, silent; impression surrealistic, weird, at the lab, collaborators [i.e. workmates] dazed, one missing, the others saying, quietly, this or that acquaintance or relative taken during the night, standing around, no work done.

Naturally, being Misha, he tried to work out what this was all about, attempting a quantitative method:

I began, without a conscious decision, to gather statistics, of who it was who had been taken. In a few days I started to tally it more consciously, after the first data, stories, did not reveal any logic, made no sense: no pattern had emerged. The distribution seemed fully random. I had expected that there would emerge a preponderance of 'the privileged classes' in the deportee population. Instead, the distribution seemed, and remained so, to really be random; there were more workers than doctors, etc.; sometimes the whole family was taken, sometimes only one or two members, and even being [a] party member seemed to make no difference: the representation in the deportees represented as cleanly as I could see the composition of the population at large: no preponderance of bosses, or members of former privileged classes, or party members, or anything. Democratic to the hilt.

This is not what the official record (now released from the archives) suggests, but Misha may well have been right. Historians should never be too trusting of bureaucratic documents, which in general tend to say that what happened was what was supposed to happen, but in this case there is an additional reason for scepticism, in that the key document setting out the arrests and deportations of target groups is either misdated or else claims as accomplished fact something that had not yet occurred. In any case, Misha was not alone in perceiving it as a bolt from the blue, hitting random victims. According to a recent Latvian history, the deportations 'created such fear and hatred in the populace that in a very short period the common view of Germans ("the black knights") as the Latvians' primary enemies—developed over the centuries— was suddenly replaced by the view that the primary enemy was Russia and the Communists'.

Nobody from the Danos family was taken on 14–15 June, although they very easily could have been, either on a random basis or, if we give the Soviets more credit for precision, because of Olga's 'capitalist' activities. According to Misha's musing, presumably based on contemporary rumour, 'the arrests of that memorable night was the first installment; our family, complete, was on the list for the second wave, which never took place, having been preempted by the outbreak of the war on the Eastern front'. But already, a month or so earlier than the mass arrests, the family had lost two of its members to Soviet terror.

Ariadna Sakss, daughter of Olga's sister Mary, the wild 'gypsy' one in Jan's recollection, had just married a Danish sailor in an attempt to get out of the country. Misha had given the bride away, which in the Latvian version of the marriage ceremony involves holding a gold crown—very heavy, as he remembered—over the bride's head as the priest performs the rite. The departure plan backfired: not only was Ariadna unable to leave for Scandinavia, but she, and for good measure her sister Jogita as well, was also arrested for treason and then deported into the interior of the Soviet Union. Misha never saw either of them again. Jogita was to die during the war as a deportee in Krasnoiarsk in Siberia. Ariadna, who was twenty-two when she was arrested, survived fifteen years' exile in either Ufa in Bashkiria (now Bashkortostan) or Vorkuta in the far north, returning to Riga with three young children and shattered health in 1956.

The cousins' arrest and disappearance were the first of a sequence of personal wartime disasters that Misha in later life would occasionally recall without commenting on his own reactions. The way he told the story, you could get hit from every side, Soviet, German or whatever. Getting hit was mainly a random outcome, but there were some strategies for self-protection (young Ariadna, with her tousled brown curls and challenging eyes, had not had the time or inclination to learn these). When there was danger around, you had to go on 'autopilot', a favourite word of his, and make yourself as still and unnoticeable as possible, all the while looking for a chance to melt away from the scene of danger. (I actually saw him do this twice in the 1990s, once in a threatened mugging by black teenagers in Washington and the other time in an actual mugging in Moscow, and was astonished to see how this worked. It was as if he had made himself invisible in plain sight, becoming an object that gave out no signals to the aggressors, until the moment came to make a dash for it.)

Still, while the dangers came from every side in Misha's narrative, the Soviet danger was particularly acute and unpleasant. He and Olga probably revised their view of the Soviet Union in 1940–41 along with the rest of the population. Before 1939, there is no sign of particular antipathy in the

Danos family to the Russians or even the Soviets. Admittedly the teenage Misha was a Germanophile with little apparent interest in Russia, though he knew the language for everyday purposes. But Olga's early orientation was more Russian than German, and she saw something of the Bolshevik Revolution at firsthand without demonising it. Arpad Sr, similarly, had good Russian and had tried to build a business on the basis of trade with the Soviet Union in the 1920s and early '30s, which suggests that he probably had contacts and spent time there. Somebody in the family, or close to it, even produced a whole novel in Russian about a foreign specialist working in the Soviet Union, written in the spirit of critical sympathy with 'the Soviet experiment' common on the moderate international Left in the mid 1930s (the typescript, without a title page, was in the box of Olga's papers; nobody in the family knows anything about its provenance).

Yet in 1941, when the Germans came in, it never crossed the mind of anybody in the Danos family to remove themselves *eastward* to escape them, though some Jewish neighbours did exactly that and survived the war as evacuees in the Soviet Union. The Danoses took it for granted that if they moved, it would be westward. In 1944, with the Soviets likely to reoccupy the Baltic states, Olga, Arpad Jr and Jan were agreed that they should try to leave at any cost to avoid living under Soviet rule again. Misha had already left, though for different reasons, but his attitude to the Soviets at this point was probably similar to theirs. Arpad Sr must have seen things a bit differently, since he did not try to leave: we have no full insight into his reasons, but Misha quoted him as saying that he had been a displaced person once in his life already, during the First World War, and did not choose to repeat the experience.

By the late 1940s, both Misha and Olga saw the Soviets as enemy No. 1, which they, but unfortunately not Arpad Jr and Jan, had managed to escape. This was a view common to most DPs in Europe, particularly those from the Baltic states; Misha and Olga were unusual only in not taking on the aggressive Latvian nationalism that often went with it. When they moved to the United States, it was at the height of the Cold War, with European DPs firmly categorised as victims of Communism. Neither of them left any comment on American political attitudes at this period; no doubt they were still trying to get a handle on them. In the 1950s, judging by her diary entries, Olga had fully internalised a Cold War attitude to Communism, lamenting the fate of her two sons left trapped inside the Soviet Union, 'suffering in Russia' and 'pursued by hunger and cold'.

From his firsthand encounters and later DP conditioning, Misha emerged with an Orwellian view of the Soviet Union as a totalitarian society, pathologically deformed by doubletalk, curdled idealism and violence, in which fear was the dominant emotion. To be sure, his professional contacts with Soviet physicists and visits to the country, starting in the late 1960s, slightly qualified that, but as he told me many times, up until perestroika he always felt a heavy 'pressure' on flying into Moscow's Sheremetyevo Airport. There was a certain irony, therefore, in the fact that, in marrying me, he had inadvertently allied himself with one of the main critics of the totalitarian interpretation among professional Sovietologists. Strangely enough, this never caused any problems between us, or even arguments. He was the eyewitness, an unusually accurate and observant one in my judgement; I was the historian, whom he considered to be fair-minded. Mind you, he more or less had to see me like that because it was not in him to be basically critical of a person he loved. I could live with knowing that we had somewhat different views on something, but that wasn't acceptable to Misha.

I see, re-reading his musings, that Misha didn't acknowledge that any differences of interpretation of the Soviet Union existed between us. This had the odd consequence that when he changed his mind on something, it couldn't be because of my influence. For example, Misha wrote a musing in 1994 entitled 'Everyday in the Soviet Union' in which he wrote that in the Soviet Union, material shortages of just about everything, from shoes to housing, were more on most people's minds than fear. In the musing, Misha notes that while his previous view had been that fear was dominant in all strata of society, he had now changed his mind, at least as far as the mass of non-privileged citizens was concerned. Since this is actually the main argument of the book I was then working on, the logical presumption would be that he got the idea from me—but in the musing, he explicitly gives his sources, and I'm not one of them. Yet it occurs to me as I write that there's also another way of looking at this story, which is that while Misha's revised conclusion undoubtedly reflected my general line of thought as of 1994, my book wasn't actually written for another four years, which means that there was also time for his rather clear and concise formulation to come back and influence *me*.

As I've said before, Misha was a man whose loyalty to those he loved was absolute. Thus, when my old Sovietological battles about totalitarianism briefly flared up again with the collapse of the Soviet Union in 1991, he was outraged on my behalf, much more than I was, writing a private musing in 1993 calling my most prominent critics 'assassinators' moved by prejudice, hatred, self-hatred and self-interest. I didn't see it in such stark black-and-white terms, and indeed would have been highly embarrassed had he ever met the 'assassinators' face to face and denounced them on my behalf, as he would very likely have done. But who wouldn't have such a loyal knight, ready to fight their battles, at their side? I marvelled at my good fortune. It was fortunate, too, that Misha happened never to have read any of the assassinators' books before he met me. He would almost certainly have liked them.

4

Riga under the Germans

Misha the pole vaulter.

OPERATION Barbarossa, launched against the Soviet Union on 22 June 1941, was a spectacular success. It took the German forces less than two weeks to advance into the Baltics and occupy Riga. Misha's VEF, being classified as of national (Soviet) significance, had to be evacuated to the east, in circumstances of high alarm and danger for all concerned as the Germans advanced; very likely some of the more valuable personnel were evacuated east as well. Misha was assigned to help with the loading of machinery and materials, but by good luck—everyone who survived the war living in war zones had to have had luck at many points, and Misha was no exception—he was temporarily absent from the scene at the crucial moment:

> In this loading [of machinery and materials for evacuation] I sustained an injury (by playing around), which I got taken care of in the medical office; since I could not continue with the loading operation I was given an official paper sending me home. As I found out much later, I was the last person to leave the compound: a troup of Russian soldiers arrived to oversee the operation, and they immediately sealed all exits. At some point a number of the employees were already lined up against a wall to be shot; that was prevented by a Russian officer who came upon the scene. I know of no details about this event. I was not too unhappy for not having been present.

Artillery shells fell on Riga as the Germans advanced, 'and then the war was over, for the time being: suddenly it was totally quiet':

> I ventured out, and on the square by the station I saw the first dead soldier: a young, perhaps 18-year-old Russian, sitting in a normal position at the wheel of a truck, seemingly alive, but actually dead. Lying around were rifles, other war materiel, abandoned vehicles. The population was in a jubilant mood, showing it; I had never thought that the Latvians, usually restrained, were capable of that. There already stood young men, 20–30, in columns of twos, 10 deep, with rifles picked up from the ground, ready to join in the fight against the Russians. They were disbanded: 'Thank you. We do not need your help.' (I saw the older brother, standing in one of these columns.)

This is a typically laconic account, especially of the unwelcome sight of his brother Arpad. Misha thought that the Latvian nationalist would-be collaborators were naive fools, as he told me in an only slightly elaborated verbal account of this sighting, but he was always unwilling to criticise Arpad, whom he once described to me as 'a kind of Solzhenitsyn', meaning by that a man of rare moral conscience, but unworldly. (In my observation, Arpad was indeed unworldly and almost pathologically ethical in his approach to life, but gentle and humanly disengaged as well, quite unlike the provocative and belligerent Solzhenitsyn; Dostoevsky's Prince Myshkin might have been a better analogy.)

As with the Soviet occupiers, Misha's first experience of the German occupiers was in his capacity as an employee of VEF. How much the Soviets succeeded in evacuating before they themselves were driven out is unclear, but in any case the factory kept going under the Germans:

> At the time the news of the German invasion arrived I was in the assembly line shop; as the news was announced over the factory speaker system, activities in the shop stopped; one of the soldering girls jumped up and flung herself onto the lap of the boss: now life will end, one way or another, so, until then, over the remaining days: sex. I saw that, with a mixture of feeling bad, compassion for the girl, surprise about that unexpected reaction of hers, and a vague, unspecified foreboding.

When, after a month or so, Misha recovered from his injury and went back to work at VEF, he found that

> things had changed, not too much in form, but the emphasis of the production was changing by responding to the needs

and demands of the German war machine. Most obvious, and also unexpected, was the loosening of the discipline, associated with the disappearance of the fear factor. Under the Russians, the work was scheduled to begin at 7.30 in the morning, and one was to remain on the premises until, if I remember correctly, 17.30. Everybody was there at 7.30. No question. Tardiness was punishable by almost death, so it seemed. Upon the arrival of the Germans, that threat—and, in the beginning, any other threat—was gone. We began arriving later and later, and leaving for lunch outside of the factory, going earlier and earlier; nothing happened.

With the factory back to normal, more or less, Misha resumed his prowlings around the shops, observing different aspects of production. Since he knew German, he was given the task of translating the operating manuals from Russian into German, which he did at his own pace, using the opportunity to teach himself to touch-type—something that, as was his wont, he invented from scratch with a fine imperviousness to any possible precedents ('I devised the optimal system of how to type with minimal hand motions, which then would allow typing without looking').

A couple of months later, in the autumn of 1941, Misha managed to enrol at the university as an electrical engineering student, so he went to the VEF bosses and told them he was quitting. They accepted his decision, though unwillingly. He was lucky again in his timing—or perhaps his practical mother was keeping an eye on things—as shortly afterwards work at VEF was declared essential for the German war effort, and quitting became impossible. But Misha got in under the wire.

At university, Misha 'wouldn't play the game', according to Andrejs Bičevskis, meaning he often failed to attend lectures, preferred to offer his own proofs in assignments rather than those taught in class and refused to memorise his notes for exams. As a result, his grades were not as good as they should have been, although, Bičevskis noted, there were some professors who thought he was exceptional. Misha himself always recognised that, not boastfully but as a given, and so had his early teachers at the gymnasium and—as a strongly supportive constant in his life—his mother. He tended to assume that teachers and colleagues who failed to do so were dullards, best avoided.

The University of Riga—founded in 1919 on the basis of the Riga Polytechnic—was probably quite strong in engineering, but it was not the top higher educational institution in the Baltics: that title was held by the University of Tartu (formerly Dorpat University) in Estonia. Misha told me little about his university experience in Riga, and his only musing on the subject is about the lack of German impact on university affairs: the old professors ('of course minus the ones exterminated during the Soviet occupation') stayed on, working as they had always done. My impression was that he didn't think he was learning anything new, had no particular respect for his professors and generally wasn't interested. Sports gained more of his attention. He joined the university sports club, Universitates Sports, after the closing of the German one, and ran the 800 metres, in which he was, according to Bičevskis, good but not at the very top of Riga's sportsmen. He then switched to pole vaulting, where he showed typical fearlessness (it was dangerous in those days, with bamboo poles and nothing much to fall on) and went right to the top in the local scene. He played ice hockey too, playing goalie first in the German Union team and then in the university's second team, generally distinguishing himself sufficiently to be included in a history of Latvian sport in this capacity. He was even elected to the board of directors of the university club, being, as he related with some pride, the youngest member.

When Misha later remembered the German occupation, implicitly comparing it with the Russian, it was its comparatively normal, laissez-faire quality that struck him. The Germans, in his account, just brought in the top people in every sector (civil service, university, police) and left the Latvians to run things the same way they had run them before the Russians came. He didn't notice any overt Germanising or de-Latvianising activities and observed that, in contrast to the Soviets, they didn't change the street names or even write them in German. It was, in fact, a decision made by Hitler that the Baltics were not to be put under military rule but allowed a certain amount of autonomy.

Apart from Arpad Jr, the Danos family does not seem to have welcomed the German invaders, even as a counterforce to the Soviets, but they didn't oppose them either; rather, the attitude seems to have been one of wary observation: what now? In later life, Misha thought it self-evident that the Soviets were more dangerous as occupiers than the Germans because of their propensity to casual violence, their lack of respect for law and property, and the randomness of their targets. That came as a shock to me at first: born into a left-wing family in Australia during the war, when the Soviet Union was our ally and Nazi Germany the enemy, I had grown up assuming the opposite, namely that however bad the Soviets may have been, the Nazis were worse. As an adult, I had, of course, heard versions of Misha's judgement before, since it is shared by virtually all who experienced both occupations in the Baltics, except Jews, but I had put it down to anti-Communist prejudice. I couldn't dismiss Misha's judgement like that. Perhaps, I decided, he was right. The Germans seem in fact to have killed more people (most of them Jews), but they also had a longer period of occupation to do it in. And there was no nightmarish equivalent of the sudden large-scale Soviet deportations of June 1941 to shock the population.

Not that Misha had a good opinion of the German occupiers. From 1941, there are no more diary reflections on his kinship with Germans or German culture. The Germans' racial theories repelled him:

> Concerning the long range plans, I heard that at a party where the Latvian top officials, of course subordinates to the Germans, were present, and who heard that the plan as far as the members of the German Ministry for the Occupied Eastern Region was concerned, the Jews of course will have been exterminated; the Poles were to be the unskilled workers, while the Baltics were higher race and were going to be foremen. This the Germans talked about without bothering to notice the presence of the Latvians.

This has the characteristic ring of Misha's automatic hostility to anyone's categorical claims to superiority, whether it be on grounds of race, status, descent or anything else. In addition, it sounds as if he was now identifying at least partially as a Latvian, a definite shift from his position a couple of years earlier. A sporting contemporary remembers a similar comment from him on the occasion of a competition with a German team, which, it appears, the Latvians won—'and they consider us a lesser race!'

The great exception to the Germans' relative tolerance was their response to Jews. Among their first order of business was to round up Jews—that is, those so identified in Riga's highly compartmentalised society—and put them in a ghetto. After a few months, they started shooting the Latvian Jews in the ghetto: about twenty-five thousand Jews from the Riga ghetto are estimated to have been shot in November–December 1941, partly to make room for the trainloads of Jews from Central Europe who were being brought in at the same time, many of them to be killed in their turn. Misha doesn't seem to have personally known anybody who suffered this fate; Olga, as we shall see, did. He knew about the ghetto, however, and he also knew that the Germans were bringing in Jews from Germany and Austria to the Riga ghetto, 'where after a while most of them were shot'.

Nobody in the Danos family ever mentioned any anxiety on their own part during the German occupation about the possibility of being taken for, and punished as, Jews. The sons may not have known of the Jewish Hungarian ancestry, but their father obviously did, and surely their mother also. When, in the 2000s, I quizzed two of Misha's Latvian friends from the 1940s about whether they had thought his father might be Jewish, they conceded after some prevarication that yes, the thought had fleetingly crossed their minds, not that they cared either way. If the thought might have crossed their minds, it might also have crossed those of malicious neighbours and business and professional rivals, but actually Arpad Sr was lucky: he never was denounced as a Jew, as far as we know, and lived through both occupations without any particular problems. Olga's sister Mary Sakss was not so fortunate.

Mary and Olga were pure ethnic Latvians without a stain on their racial character. But they didn't like the Nazi persecution of Jews, and acted accordingly. Mary hid Jews in her apartment to save them from the Gestapo and was denounced for it by a neighbour. The Germans promptly arrested her on 18 March 1943 and sent her first to Salaspils concentration camp outside Riga and then to Ravensbrück, north of Berlin. This was the second disaster to have struck her family, the

first being the Soviet authorities' arrest and deportation eastward of both her children. When Misha later spoke of this,
he as usual said nothing about his own emotional reactions
at the time. Coming across a discussion in the 1990s of the
motivations of non-Jews in hiding Jews during the war, he
seemed a bit bemused by the question: he had not thought to
wonder about Mary's reasons for doing something obviously
right, though risky. In retrospect, however, he regretted not
having asked her.

About a month after Mary's arrest, Misha had an experience that remained with him as one of the two most traumatic
events of the war (the other was the bombing of Dresden in
1945). The musing on this topic is called 'Mass Graves', and
the graves were those of Jews shot by the Nazis. I will quote it
almost in its entirety:

> It was on Easter Sunday, that year which had the extreme
> winter; I think it was 1943. No sign yet of spring. Deep snow,
> sunshine. I went skiing in the Shmerl woods, west of Riga,
> accessible by tram. As appropriate to the day and weather,
> the ski hut and the environs teemed with Sunday skiers.
> To evade the crowds I decided to go off in a direction I had
> not tried before. Indeed, the crowds thinned and soon there
> was nobody. Quite pleasing. Underbrush a little uncom-
> fortably dense; evidently a rather recently (10 years ago?)
> re-planted tree stand. It should not last too long, I hoped;
> underbrush was not standard in these woods, which were
> quite well-maintained. Indeed, the woods changed to the
> rather transparent 50-year stand. The topography was that
> of that area: irregular hills and depressions of 10 to 15 m
> height, a pleasant cross-country terrain, with practically
> non-used snow; it was far off the beaten track, with nobody
> in sight.

After not too long a chain of hills came into sight; unexpectedly through the gaps between the hills a line of people became visible; families with grandparents and children, all walking like in a procession towards about where I was on the other side of the hills. I proceeded through a gap to their side. A total change: the snow flattened by having been walked over; there were truck tracks; here and there coal and ashes remnants of little fires; here and there empty and half-empty wooden barrels with calcium chlorate. The people went up the hills, and stood around at the tops; I took off the skis and joined them. The size of the top was something like 20 by 20 meters; it had a 10 by 10 by more than 6 m deep square hole, filled to that level with corpses, which were partially covered with calcium chlorate. The holes in the previous hills had already had been covered with earth; on the next hill a new hole already had been started. So that was the Jews' graveyard.

I took off, in a state, through the people-free terrain: it must have been an unspecified fear, shock, mental-emotional short-circuit; immense relief emerged as the first person became visible.

Arriving at the ski hut I collected my stuff and left for home.

The thought which emerged irrepressibly at that time: what is in their mind, taking the children to drink in the horror? How is it that this is a Sunday afternoon enjoyment? The distance to the then closest housing is several kilometers, non-trivial, in particular for children.

'So that was the Jews' graveyard' suggests that Misha already knew something about the killing of Jews from the Riga ghetto. But to be confronted suddenly by the reality first-hand, and to see the crowds of spectators enjoying it, made that knowledge unendurable. He tried to explain to me, in a postscript to the 'Mass Graves' email, how it had affected him. It closed off access to some part of himself, like switching off a light or closing a door. He was most aware of this when he played the piano, particularly Beethoven's *Moonlight Sonata*, because he couldn't access the emotional depths anymore—'the playing of the piece remains incomplete, just skimming the surface'. As we shall see, about five years later he thought that this situation had improved, but even forty years later (in 1996), he found that the door was still almost fully closed, with just 'a crack, allowing a glimpse, but not an entry'. Writing the musing was part of his effort to get the door open again.

After his encounter with the graves, Misha went straight home and—contrary to his usual habit of keeping things to himself—told his parents about the horrors he had seen. To his surprise, they already knew.

Olga knew a lot of things, and she also knew a lot of people. The people included German officers, on the one hand, and Jews who had been put in the ghetto, on the other. During the German occupation, she used her contacts with the former to help the latter, making her simultaneously a righteous gentile (though she doesn't seem to have got on Yad Vashem's list) and, in a less generous interpretation, a collaborator. Unlike her sister, she didn't get caught, and it was thanks to one of the Jews she helped that she and Misha would ultimately get to the United States.

Her sons knew about both these activities, more or less, although for their own protection she didn't tell them any details about what she was doing for Jews. Basically she had turned her fashion atelier into a tailoring workshop, where, under contract with the German Army, she made suspenders and straw sandals, employing a dozen or so Jews from the ghetto, whom she was able, at a minimum version of the story (Arpad Jr's), to feed and, at a maximum (Olga's own), to extract and smuggle out of the country.

As Olga told a reporter on the *Miami Herald* in 1954, she

assisted in saving and hiding what she describes as 'an army of refugees,' during several years work, being arrested only once, and detained that time for a single day. Her scheme was to contract to supply 60,000 pairs of suspenders for the German army, and on the strength of that to get passes to fly to Prague over-frequently 'for materials.' Arrangements for hiding, feeding, and passing on the refugees were made during these Prague visits. Many of them she also employed surreptitiously in the 'factory.' She never actually supplied more than a few thousand of the article contracted for.

I don't know how close this story is to the literal truth. Her sons Misha and Jan knew about her employing, helping and supporting Jews, but not about smuggling them out; her son Arpad told me that her Jewish workers were escorted to and from the ghetto in convoy, but sometimes one managed to disappear without either Olga or her contact getting into trouble. He didn't know anything about any further arrangements to save them she may have made. On the face of it, landlocked Prague was a surprising way station for smuggling out Jews, but certainly Olga did go there on business during the war, as well as to a number of other cities in the greater Reich; according to Jan, she was importing Czech glass and medicine from Prague. The one Jewish protégé I have been able to trace—her later US immigration sponsor, Simon Mirkin— was *not* smuggled out but, after surviving 'selections' in the Riga ghetto thanks to Olga's help, served a short term in the Stutthof concentration camp in the waning days of the war and ended up liberated by the Americans in Germany. Simon was the son of a prosperous Jewish businessman—probably a prewar acquaintance of Olga's—who was also protected by her and survived Stutthof but died in Buchenwald in February 1945. The young Mirkin later suggested that the whole Mirkin family was at one point living in Olga's workshop.

As Misha remembered, Olga was able to help the Jews because of the collusion of two anti-Nazi German officers with whom she had become friendly:

> Herr Major v. Koelln was Kommandant of the Riga airport, Spilve. By now the airport has been moved twice. Spilve's runways were grass; that was fine with the WW2 planes; all of them could land there. The background of v. K. was German Nobility; he was born in St Petersburg, son of the then ambassador of the then Kaiser Wilhelm to the then Tzar. Herr Seeliger was of humble origins, blue collar worker family. His position in Riga was also of different kind; he was commandant of the Riga Ghetto; it contained besides the not insignificant number of Riga Jews, which still made up the minority, a significantly larger number of imports, principally from Austria. Each of them did whatever they could, to keep alive as many as possible of their charges, POWs by v. K; Jews by S. A deadly balancing act. In particular for S.

'Von Koelln' becomes 'Koellner' in Olga's letters after the war, when she encountered him as a hotel porter in Wiesbaden and commented that 'he is no more a true porter than he was a true airbase commander' in Riga. I can find no record of a man with either of these names serving as airbase commander, but not much information is easily available about airbase personnel, so he may have done. The Riga ghetto is another matter, as it has been extensively documented in memoirs and scholarly studies. They name the ghetto commandant, and he was not Seeliger. Since the name in this case is unambiguous, Seeliger was presumably working in the German ghetto administration but lower down in the administrative chain.

> For reasons which I never knew, never asked about, and was not told, my parents knew both of them, evidently quite well. They visited our apartment, separately, more than once; besides saying Good Evening, my presence was not desired.
>
> Nonetheless, my mother thought it prudent to tell me a little about these people. The main point was that they were deeply, violently, anti-Nazi. Evidently they did not hold back in venting their feelings during these visits. I am sure they used different language in these explanations. I do not know how come they felt this confidence, but they did. I also knew better than to ask; whatever I was told I listened to.

This image of himself listening and watching, without being really drawn in, often recurred in Misha's stories about the war. In lighter contexts, he would throw in a proverbial Russian expression of insouciance, *'Vas'ka slushaet, da est'* ('Vas'ka listens, but goes on eating'). Here Misha is not insouciant, but he is very emphatically only a listener, an observer and not a participant of action. Nevertheless, he knew both the Germans well enough to be sent greetings in a letter from Seeliger to Olga in 1951, and also to form his own impression of their ability to act for good from within an institutional setting with quite different purposes. Seeliger, he thought, was a fairly simple character who saved lives when he could and felt more satisfaction at his success in saving some individual lives than distress at the killing of many other Jews for which, by virtue of his official job, he was also responsible. Von Koelln, an intellectual, had more complex reactions: his 'limited success in saving a few lives' (by keeping POWs from being executed) afforded him less satisfaction because he was 'evidently more bothered by general inhumaneness'. Misha assumed that in staying within the system, both were affected by the general logic that 'if I don't do it then that, or that, or that guy will, and he is real bad news'.

Olga was not particularly inclined to introspection (except, in her diary, about her sentimental life), and her motives for helping Jews—and for using her contact with friendly Germans as a way of doing so—went essentially undiscussed. In the 1954 newspaper interview, she explained to the American reporter that, although not Jewish herself, she had helped the Jews 'because I found it so ugly a situation'. Evidently it seemed to her, as to Misha, an obvious thing to do, for reasons of simple humanity, as long as she could get away with it. It would also have been obvious to her, though perhaps not to Misha, that the best way to get away with it, as well as secure her and her family's position in general, was to have some protection within German officialdom.

Koelln's and Seeliger's visits were evidently made to the Danos family apartment, although it seems that as a result of the marital separation, Olga was no longer actually living there but in her workshop in the old city. Thus Arpad Sr was involved in these contacts (as Misha's comments confirm), but we know even less about his motives and reactions than about Olga's. Later, when Olga was trying to get her oldest and youngest son out of Latvia as the Soviet Army approached in 1944, Arpad Sr seems to have approved her plans but assumed that initiatives of this kind belonged to her sphere of action rather than his. Perhaps it was the same here. If we factor in his being at least half Jewish, and Olga possibly having an affair with (the anti-Nazi Nazi) Seeliger, the complexities are multiplied, no doubt a salutary reminder that all marriages are complicated, and this one more than most.

None of Olga's sons seem to have been surprised by her (or Mary's) actions in trying to save Jews or to have thought they needed special explanation. As Misha wrote later, 'At that time it seemed the most natural thing to do; it never even occurred to me to see any problem in that action, or to ask anybody about any motivations,' and his brothers, interviewed in the 2000s, seemed to feel the same. As far as the purpose of the action (saving Jews) is concerned, I'm sure this is an accurate report of his feelings at the time. About his reaction to the means Olga used, I'm not so sure. Olga's shrewd worldliness and optimistic interventionist instincts were not part of her son's make-up. He never hinted at any uneasiness about his mother's connections with the German officers, either to me or in his correspondence with her in Germany, when she ran across both of them again. But that goes almost without saying, since he virtually never questioned or criticised any of her actions. Yet all his life, Misha made a point of *not* cultivating people with power, often to his detriment. Whether he recognised it or not, his instincts here were very different from Olga's approach.

With regard to Olga's cultivation of German officials and Misha's reaction to it, Helen Machen, the former Baby Klumberg, provided an interesting vignette. Helen had gone with her family to Germany with the Baltic Germans in 1941, but came back on her own to Riga a year or so later. Shortly after her return (as she related in a conversation with me in 2008), she went round to look for Misha at the house his family were then living in and found a lively party in full swing. Misha's mother was there (she didn't see any sign of his father) and some German officers. There was an element of unspoken disapproval in Helen's account, though I couldn't be sure of what: not fraternisation, surely, since Helen herself had been working happily enough for a nice Nazi official since her return to Riga; perhaps the milieu was a bit bohemian for her? Anyway, she didn't see Misha at the party, asked for him, and was told that he was up in his room, not feeling well. Baby went up (nobody offered to take her) and found him in bed, depressed but not apparently sick. He was pleased to see her but did not tell her what was bothering him.

Of course there were a lot of things that could have prevented him being in a party mood that night. One perennial cause of anxiety and melancholy was his personal life, as we can see from his diary (a useful reminder that this is often what people are actually thinking about when, as historians, we expect them to be contemplating the big historic events like war and displacement). Another one was military conscription.

All three Danos brothers were of call-up age, and none of them wanted to serve in the German Army (Waffen-SS). Jan was the first one in real trouble. Called up for military service in the autumn of 1943, he failed to appear before the mobilisation commission and went into hiding for a month but was caught and imprisoned for six months. He became ill with pleurisy in prison and in February 1944 was released from prison to hospital. After his recovery, he was again liable for the draft and again went into hiding. Arpad, meanwhile, was safe, at least for the time being, as a worker in an aviation factory, a protected occupation.

Misha came before the mobilisation commission a couple of months later, on 9 December 1943. He was told that he was temporarily excused but would be drafted at the next call-up. His temporary protection was probably that he was back working as a radio technician at VEF on a labour draft, but this was not going to be enough to keep him out of the army for long. In the spring of 1944, he (or Olga) discovered a way of beating the draft: to go to Germany as an exchange student.

Misha's laconic description of these events is contained in an undated statement, written in English in 1946 in Hanover, probably for some kind of political screening process by the British military authorities. I have left his English uncorrected; the German phrase in parenthesis is his:

> I remained in Riga til the end of May, 1944. Then I had passed a mobilization commission which took place December, 9th 1943, and where I had been excused from mobilization up til the next order (bis zum nächsten Befehl).
>
> Beginning with 1942 it was possible each semester for ca 10 students of the University of Riga to continue their studies at an University in Germany. In April, 1944 I asked the german authorities the permission to go to an University in Germany. I did so for the following reasons:
>
> a) I had been excused once from mobilization in December, 1943, and it was clear that at the next commission I would be mobilized,
>
> b) The german eastern front was collapsing and nobody could tell how long a time it would take the russians to conquer Riga.
>
> Both reasons a) and b) were urgent enough to try to get away from Riga. At that time the only other possibility to do so was to volunteer to work in Germany. By asking the permission to go as a student I tried to escape both from mobilization and the Russians without helping the germans in a single way to make war.
>
> I got the permission to go to Dresden in the middle of May without any political screening. Would the Germans

have done so they would not have let me go my aunt being in concentration camp and with the precendent of my yunger brother ...

Finally, I would like to remark that none of us three brothers has been a single day in the german army.

This part of Misha's story of his life, when told to me for the first time, took my breath away. How could he have dared to go to Germany, throwing himself into the lion's den? The explanation given in the 1945 statement is pretty well how he explained it to me in 1989: if he stayed, he would be called up; if he went to Germany, he wouldn't be. It makes perfect sense, assuming he didn't know about the Jewish grandparent(s). The residual astonishment I have focusses on Olga, who surely must have known that Misha had a Jewish grandmother. But when I think about it, that makes sense too. The Danoses' files were in Riga, and if Arpad Sr were ever denounced as a Jew, that was where it was going to happen. Anywhere *not* Riga was arguably safer.

After Misha's death, I tried to find out more about this student exchange between Latvia and Germany and became increasingly sceptical that such a thing ever existed. Neither Misha's friend Andrej Bičevskis nor his wife Anna, both members of the Latvian DP community in Germany after the war, had ever heard of anyone besides Misha who had gone from Riga to a German university on an exchange during the war. Andrej thought it had to have been a special deal that Olga, with her contacts, had organised, and another Riga friend, Dailonis Stauvers, thought the same.

DPs lied to the authorities all the time about their origins, movements and relations with the Germans, as I knew from my own archival research for a separate project; it was part of their survival strategy. I started to think that even Misha, in general a very truthful man, was gilding the lily a bit. But I shouldn't have doubted him. The story he told the British occupation authorities turned out to be true.

I discovered the existence of a formal exchange in an obscure German scholarly monograph. Latvians were relatively high up on the Germans' racial scale, and it seems that the Germans were interested in such an exchange in order to promote Germanisation via the dispatch of German professors of literature and the like to the Baltics, as well as the sending of Latvian students to Germany to further their exposure to German culture and language. Misha even gave the correct year for its establishment. The exchange covered engineering, medicine and law as well as the humanities. Apparently the initial response of Baltic students was tepid: only about a hundred Latvians and Estonians, including Misha, went to study in Germany during the war. Why it wasn't more widely noticed as a way of dodging the draft is not clear. Very likely, noticing it was Olga's achievement, and she may also have pulled some strings to get Misha on the list.

One thing that surprised me in Misha's story, although as a historian I probably should have known it, was how early the Danos family concluded that Germany was going to lose the war and the Baltic states would be reoccupied by the Soviet Union. This may have been part of Olga's strategy, even in the first months of 1944, when Misha's participation in the exchange must have been organised. At that point, the Soviet Army had already won back most of their own territory (excluding the Baltic states) that the Germans had occupied and were preparing for a summer offensive to clear the Germans out of Eastern Europe. The Allies landed in Normandy in the summer and started pressing eastward. By the autumn, the Baltic states had been reoccupied by the Soviets, moving steadily westward. Olga wanted her sons and herself out of Latvia, to avoid falling under Soviet rule, and Germany was not the destination but a way station in her plans. The idea was to go west, which of course meant going into and through Germany, with the aim of ending up as close as possible to a western border in the hope of crossing into Allied territory when the final defeat came. Misha was the first to go, in the spring of 1944. The rest of the family (except Misha's father) would try to follow him westwards, with varying success.

5

Wartime Germany

Arpad Danos, 'der Alte',
1944. Photograph enclosed
in his last letter to Olga.

IT must have been towards the end of April 1944 that Misha
set off to study in Germany (and, in my story, now becomes
Mischka), for Olga was fretting about not having received a
letter from him on 2 May. When a letter finally came ten
days later, reporting that various last-minute problems had
been solved, its mood was buoyant and confident. This wasn't
the passive 'Vas'ka who listens' while his mother makes the
important decisions, but a new take-charge, now-I-am-an-
adult Mischka. Of course, he might well have been in a good
mood: five years earlier, he had wanted to go to Germany and
had been prevented, and now he had made it, albeit with a
less sanguine view of Germans as a result of the occupation.
The way it comes across from his letters, it wasn't so much

going to Germany that now excited him but rather setting off on his first adventure on his own. When he later told me the story of his wanderings in Europe, it had a fairytale cadence and I immediately pictured him as Dick Whittington in the children's rhyme, off to London with his bundle on his back to make his fortune. Olga saw his departure in similar terms, and gave him appropriate sage advice. Speaking of her great hopes of him, she wrote on 20 May:

> Listen, don't disappoint us with the high spirits of the all-too-gifted man [shades of her critique of his father, with his wasted talents!]. Protect your gifts; that means, work hard, because they are not only your property. Nature gives out gifts sparingly, and he who has many of them has to use them to help his fellow men …

Going to study in Germany certainly let Mischka see a lot of the Central European world. A diary entry in the spring of 1945 summarises his travels over the previous year: 'Vienna–Prague–Berlin–Vienna–Berlin–Dresden–Vienna–Dresden–Vienna–Dresden–Riga–Vienna–Dresden'. Vienna, evidently, was the base; he stayed there with Frau Loefer and her husband, probably acquaintances of his parents, and gave that as his permanent address. Mischka was very taken with Vienna—'it is already high spring, the plum and peach and apple trees are in bloom'—and he liked the Loefers. By 4 May, he had joined the Foreign Student Club in Vienna—identifying himself as Michael (not Latvian Mikelis) Danos, citizen of Latvia, nationality Hungarian, native language German—and made some sporting connections.

But his university placement had yet to be confirmed, and the first problem was that this had to be done in Berlin. Off he went to Berlin, and there made contact with Dr Hans Boening, one of Olga's German patrons, who informed him that the relevant official—an important 'Herr Professor', too busy to see Mischka—wanted to send him to one of the technical universities at Stuttgart or Dresden, though Mischka was evidently hoping for Vienna. Now, as he informed his family, he was unfortunately out of money but had several 'support points' in the Reich: a very good one in Vienna, a good one in Berlin (a widowed landlady with a daughter—her son had died at Stalingrad), and even, in case of need, one in Prague, where he had had to make a stopover en route to Berlin. 'For the rest,' he concluded grandly, 'I have as little respect as ever for difficulties. Moreover I have a new motto for myself: KL [*kompromisslosigkeit*, 'uncompromisingness'].

Mischka's Berlin trips had put him back in touch with friends from Riga days: first Valka (who now becomes a German Walka or even Waldtraut) Herrnberger and then, through her, both Baby Klumberg, recently arrived and rooming in the same house, and Baby's brother Didi. Baby was working as a secretary, perhaps in the home office of the German firm she had worked for in Riga. Didi, who had just graduated from the Dresden Technical University, at which Mischka was about to enrol, was serving as a radio operator in the Wehrmacht, stationed not far from Berlin.

Walka, working in an office in Berlin, seems to have been in an unhappy frame of mind. She fastened on Mischka as soon as he arrived in Berlin, sending him in the next couple of months a dozen letters about her depression and loneliness and the 'beautiful and carefree hours' they spent together when she visited him in Dresden in the summer. Even though Mischka evidently kept his distance (Walka complained about this), I rather took against Walka, with her dreams of lying in a white bed in a hospital being looked after and her tendency to whine, but perhaps this was just because she was so clearly on the hunt for Mischka.

And there was another reason: a document that looks to be in Walka's handwriting on a half sheet of paper, headed *Verpflichtung* ('Undertaking'), dated Berlin 13 May 1944 (the same date on which Mischka wrote his first letter home, giving his address as 'temporarily Berlin'). The document reads, 'I, Waldtraut Herrnberger, born 22 October 1919 in Riga, undertake in the course of two weeks after my divorce from Mr Michael Danos to leave him without claims to alimony from your (sic) divorce.' Naturally, as a subsequent wife of Mischka's, this got my attention. It was hard to imagine Mischka up and marrying Walka within days of his arrival in Berlin, having had no apparent contact with her for the past four years, and at the same time writing so cheerfully to his family about his progress (he mentioned her in a letter home as 'Frau W. Herrnberger [whom] you will remember', who had helped him find his Berlin lodgings). Yet there it was, one of the few apparently unambiguous and completely legible papers in my Danos files; surely it must mean something.

But it's one of the infuriating things about personal documentation that really valuable stuff disappears and meaningless things—jokes, party games or whatever—get accidentally kept. I had to conclude that Walka's *Verpflichtung* was in that category, even if Walka was not being altogether frank about her relations with Mischka when I asked her about it. When I showed it to Helen Machen (the former Baby Klumberg), she was astonished: Walka had her own boyfriend, she said, an older German gentleman with two PhDs, and she never knew of any romantic attachment, let alone a marriage and divorce, between her and Mischka. Helen was sufficiently intrigued to pick up the telephone and call Mrs Wally Ayers, formerly Walka, in Canada and ask her about it. But Walka denied all knowledge of the document, suggesting that someone else might have written it pretending to be her, and also disclaimed any romantic connection with Mischka: he was a nice man, quiet and almost shy, respectful of women, but she didn't know him well. Anyway, she didn't want to talk about those miserable times; it was better to forget the past.

By the time Walka's letters started coming, Mischka was already in Dresden. That was where he was assigned as a student by the Reich Education Ministry, initially for one semester only, with a new application to be made before the beginning of the winter semester of 1944–45.

Mischka struck it lucky in Dresden. Four of his courses that first summer semester were with Professor Heinrich Barkhausen, a physicist who held the first chair in electrical engineering at Dresden Technische Hochschule (TH) and founded the Institute of High-Frequency Electron-Tube Technology there. Barkhausen was in his sixties when he encountered Mischka, no doubt with his major work behind him, but still active and engaged. All his life, Misha spoke with the greatest respect of Barkhausen. He was the first of his physics mentors as an adult, and although it was Misha's habit to deny that he ever learnt anything from anyone, he did admit that Barkhausen had made a contribution. (What he attributed to Barkhausen was the reassurance that it was OK in physics to see things in pictures, thus 'legalising' a habit Mischka had kept quiet about.)

It didn't take Barkhausen long to see that he, too, had struck it lucky with Mischka. Mischka's letters home in those first months are full of the excitement of having his talents recognised and seeing vistas of science opening up before him. He wrote on 21 July 1944:

> I have already made a good impression on one of my professors. It happened like this. Barkhausen always comes to the Low Voltage practicum and talks to the people working

there. I as a so-called beginner got the simplest task to do at the beginning. I was working with a young man from Riga, and the work was going very quickly. Officially, one had 4 hours to complete it, but we only needed 1 hour. In that time the Herr Professor was walking round and talking to people, and he came to us as well. Since that occasion he comes to us every time. We are gradually getting ever more difficult assignments, and he has separated me from my partner and put me with someone else. As it happens, this new partner is in his last semester and is doing the most advanced experiments. Thus, to sum up, after 6 weeks he [Barkhausen] has given me the same assignments that you get after two and a half semesters.

A week later, he was able to report that he had been appointed as a junior assistant to Barkhausen—not a teaching position, he explained, but a technical one, with the task of upgrading the Low Voltage practicum. 'As a job it's not worth anything much,' he wrote to Olga, 'but rather as a principal step in the direction of the future and reputation.' Olga was as usual warmly appreciative: 'Dear Mischulein,' she replied, 'you can imagine what joy the news of your success has brought us. Arpad has told some friends about it. Some were pleased but some were also envious. As always.' This is the first indication in Mischka's papers of him thinking in terms of making a career (something to which he would generally be disinclined all his life). Before, he had simply been fascinated by physical processes as such, both in a practical and theoretical way. Barkhausen quickly took on the role of patron. In a letter recommending extension of his stipend, dated 17 August 1944, he wrote that 'Mr Danos is well known to me from the Low Voltage practicum. He is particularly gifted theoretically and also possesses excellent practical knowledge, so that I have appointed him Junior Assistant during the vacation.' A To-Whom-It-May-Concern letter a few months later stated that 'Mr Michael Danos is occupied in important, necessary work in the Institute for Low Power Technology. It is requested that he be supported in carrying out his work.'

In the semester break in September, Mischka wrote to his mother: 'We have vacation at the moment, and must do war work (Kriegseinsatz) for a while. "We" means foreigners who are citizens of various small nations. I personally don't feel any difference, as my work for Barkhausen counts as war work.'

He was thinking a lot about physics—he had had 'ideas of both a general and technical nature', as he wrote to his mother, 'and am working out some of them, and have come to the astonishing realisation that despite everything I am still making progress'. On 16 June, a large part of his letter to Olga was devoted to thoughts on mathematical relativity, by analogy with relativity in modern physics, and a critique of mathematical absolutism. He admitted that such thoughts might 'lead to the madhouse', a sentiment that Olga seemed to share, though acknowledging that she hadn't understood half of what he wrote. Then, in a letter that also asked Olga to send darning wool, he explored, at length, the concept of logic, which he regarded as not innate but based on activated memory—something that, if the philosophers realised it, would send *them* to the madhouse, 'seeing the unfruitfulness of their lives'. Logic, he now understood, was just one of the 'humanly generated systems for the consistent ordering of observed phenomena', but people hated to admit this. 'I don't know if anyone has had the courage to say this, because it would destroy the nimbus of absolute truth.' And there was more of the critique of logic in a letter of 3 September, with Mischka rising effortlessly above the mundane issues of Latvia's Soviet reoccupation, Olga's departure and the failed efforts of his two brothers to get out.

'Your egocentric son Michael' was how he signed one of these philosophical letters, and Olga, proud though she was of him, must surely have agreed. Of course, up until Olga's departure at the beginning of October, these were letters that were bound to be passed on to the rest of the family, with the two Arpads, father and son, more philosophically and scientifically inclined than Olga. Perhaps it was even, in part, Mischka's way of keeping up the connection with his father, which, thanks to external as well as domestic developments, was becoming ever more tenuous. In December (with the Soviets firmly in control in Latvia, and the two Arpads and Jan trapped inside), Mischka ended a paragraph on how solving scientific problems is easier than finding the right problems to solve with a sudden, almost wistful reference to his father: 'By the way, I heard this thesis once from Papa in Elisabetes Street, but naturally rejected it out of contrariness. But this thing gave me no peace, and soon I had to recognise its correctness, but of course I haven't spoken of it again.' He was thinking about his father again in a diary entry a few months later, noting that there was something he had to think about more deeply: 'the appreciation and more correct understanding of life's tragedy and the problem and achievements of my father'.

Sport was another prominent topic of Mischka's letters to Olga, sometimes with explicit requests to pass something on to his brother and fellow athlete Arpad. Even in his brief stay in Vienna, Mischka had established sporting contacts, as he noted in a letter of 13 May, although 'unfortunately they will probably remain unused'. A long letter of 16 June combined information about his efforts to get into the sporting scene in Dresden with a critical assessment of Germans. My assumption is that this curious mix, which makes the letter uncharacteristically unfocussed and wandering, was partly an intentional camouflage for the politically dangerous suggestion that politics and propaganda were playing too large a role in German universities and that Germans seemed 'apathetic and passive', without enthusiasm or initiative. At the same time, it comes through clearly that Mischka was very annoyed by the local sports bureaucracy, which tried first to prevent him, as a foreigner, from participating in Dresden's regional sports meet, and then to disqualify him from officially winning or placing in the events. They hadn't bothered to get the formalities taken care of, despite the fact that Mischka had carefully explained to them what they needed to do. On top of that, they had only managed to produce an inadequate pole for his pole vaulting, although he was sure they had a better one. By the end of the letter, he moves out of the realm of political commentary and into straightforward reporting of sporting prowess:

> Could you tell Arpad that I have begun my season with 12.0? [It's not clear what competition this is—perhaps triple jump?] And something else. The day before yesterday for the first time this year I did some pole vaulting ... And despite the lack of technical training and the inferior pole, I got the training height up to 3.35. [So despite everything] it's working! Even with primitive means! And not at all badly.

There is no more political comment in the letters or diary of this period, but that is not to say that Mischka was completely oblivious to the darker side of German life. This is evident in his reaction to a casual meeting with a German nurse, which he wrote about in a musing fifty years later:

> Late summer or early fall 1944, downtown Dresden. The weather was pleasant, relaxed, the sidewalks were full; it must have been Sunday afternoon. I do not remember how, but I struck up a conversation with a perhaps 25 year old, non-uniformed girl, pleasant looking, but evidently alone,

not having anything particularly in mind. Looked as if not from Dresden; even somewhat lost. That may have been the reason I took up the conversation. Very quickly I ascertained that she indeed is non-local; on vacation from somewhere in the South of Germany; possibly from [somewhere] not far from Munich ... I found her a very pleasant, warm personality; but evidently troubled. I, of course, began to ask questions. She is a hospital nurse; under heavy stress. Hence was sent away to relax, recuperate, away from her place of residence, away from colleagues, environment. She did not answer any more detailed questions; she intimated that her job was secret. It did not take much of contemplation to reach the conclusion that she was involved in medical experimentation in a concentration camp.

It turned out to be the last day of her vacation, and she had to leave early the next morning. At his suggestion, they had a pleasant dinner together ('having lots of ration cards, she felt free to accept'). As they left the restaurant, she suddenly became ill, and then almost immediately left: '*Auf Wiedersehen* (the meaningless breaking off; can mean see you tomorrow, or, see you never). I was not happy to see her go.' He struggled afterwards with the contradiction of a nice, seemingly kind girl who had apparently been drawn into something horrible and inhuman:

> I had no difficulty in reconstructing her path: having the caring personality, she chose the most helpful profession: hospital nurse. Having graduated, she was recruited into a job which, being secret, she did not know anything about. But, it being war, there were all kind of secret places, activities, around: 'Vorsicht, Feind höhrt mit!'['Careful, the enemy is listening!'] She must have been told that it is a

very important job, that it is so important that one can not talk about it. Once in it, there was no way out. The aspect which impressed me so strongly, then, and still now, was the discrepancy between her caring person, her aims, dreams of helpfulness, and the reality she found herself in.

'No wonder she had the breakdown,' he concluded sadly. 'I do not think she made it through denazification.'

This was a rare direct contact with what Misha later called the totalitarian side of German life. Normal life, as he encountered it lodging with ordinary working-class families in Dresden and elsewhere, seems to have been remarkably free of police-state or even wartime pressures. He observed 'no fear of the Gestapo' or any kind of surveillance:

There existed a neighborhood Party member (Blockwart if my memory is correct) who was invisible, whose existence was totally ignored. Was Blockwart an informer? Perhaps, but who cares. The local people talked freely to me, a foreigner. Having had no bombings, Dresden was at peace; in contrast Riga was at war. Even though being an eminently draftable specimen I was never asked to produce personal documents, except when travelling on the fast non-stop long-distance trains (D-Zug or Fern-D-Zug), not even on long-distance 'local' trains (Bummelzug), which stop at all intermediate stations ... The police state, the totalitarianism, did not concern the population. It only concerned the 'other', who were essentially invisible (forced labourers from the East; POWs) ... In interpersonal relations, both concerning civil and criminal cases, the state functioned as always; there was no need to use subterfuge, and perhaps even very little chance of success. No lawlessness in the society. Law and order prevailed.

This last assertion was not just a general observation but based on actual research—one of Mischka's landladies, the widow of a lawyer, put transcripts of Third Reich court cases in the lavatory as toilet paper, and evidently it was Mischka's habit to read them before use. (This detail of everyday life reminded me how in Moscow in the 1960s, *Pravda* was often used for the same purpose, and I used to read it that way too.)

Mischka's student status was extended for two more semesters by the education minister in December. That was a weight off his mind, as it guaranteed his stipend. In addition to his school studies, he had started to read the German physics journal *Zeitschrift für Physik*, which was to acquire almost talismanic significance for him as he lugged his copies—twenty volumes!—around in the coming years of displacement. Nevertheless, he was back to his old tricks of missing lectures, informing Olga that he hadn't been to a single one this semester (it's to be hoped that the two courses he was doing with Barkhausen listed on his transcript were not lecture courses).

One rather dubious achievement of this period is not overtly discussed in Mischka's and Olga's correspondence— namely, an invention of his that was praised by the Reich Ministry for Armaments and War Production. We know about it only because a letter dated 15 December 1944 survives from a Colonel Geist in the ministry to Dr H. Boening, President of the District Work Office, Reichenburg, the patron of Olga's who had helped Mischka set up his German studies in Berlin:

Subject: The invention proposal of Mischka Danos
In reference to: Communication of 16 October 1944

Very respected Mr President!
    The communication from Herr Dr Schmelter along with the exposition of the discovery of student Mischka Danos was forwarded to me for consideration.

It concerns an acoustic pathfinding apparatus [*Zielsuchgerät*] ... Since Danos correctly sees the electro-acoustic problem with his assessment of the applicability limits, I have sent his model for testing to the special commission 'Munition Accessories' to Herr Dr Runge in the development high commission 'Elektrotechnik', with the request that they make direct contact with the inventor.

I beg to thank your protégé for his trouble and the great interest he shows for the defence of the German Reich.

Heil Hitler!

I know nothing of the outcome (no evidence of 'direct contact' is to be found in the files), but clearly if Mischka had anything to do with the submission of his invention, it contradicts his later claim to have systematically sought *not* to help the German war effort. My hypothesis—of course, the reader might suspect I *would* say this—is that Mischka himself did not submit his invention to the ministry, but that it was done on the initiative of Barkhausen or whoever Dr Schmelter was, to whom he had showed it. Mischka now called himself Michael Danos in all official interactions, though German friends called him Mischka. The inventor in this document is identified, rather patronisingly, as 'the student Mischka Danos', a self-description Mischka would never have used in such a context. But all this is speculation. The only further light to be shed on the topic—and it may not in fact be about Mischka Danos's commendation by the Reich—is in a carefully worded sentence in one of Olga's letters a month later to the effect that she would rather not comment on some recent excitement or perturbation he had written about because they would soon be able to discuss it face to face.

Certainly there is no other indication that Mischka was interested in contributing to the defence of the Reich. His reaction to the suggestion that his younger brother Jan wanted to join the Latvian Legion—that is, the Latvian units of the Waffen-SS—was sharply negative. Olga had written to tell Mischka that 'Janschi was set on joining the Legion. He explained to me at great length that the eternal hiding is suffocating him and he will end up weak and without will. In the Legion he would find a broad and specialised development field.' Jan had actually gone to the induction commission to sign up, Olga wrote, but they put off accepting him for a month on health grounds (he still showed traces of the pleurisy he had contracted in prison). While Olga's telling of the story only implied disapproval, Mischka's response—written within three days of receiving Olga's letter, a very quick turnaround for him—was choleric:

> I read with great astonishment, and then not with astonish-ment, of Jochen's decision. [Note the distancing use of the full German version of Jan's name.] In case he goes through with it, I would like to wish that he brings the necessary amount of commonsense—which actually is not so great—to bear, so as to hold out tolerable prospects for any future mutual life, which hopefully and probably will not suddenly be put at risk. As I said, hold out! And I also want my good wishes to be understood in this sense.

This I take to mean that if Jan joined up, his future relations with Mischka would be in jeopardy—expressed, for the sake of prudence in light of the postal censorship, in extraordinarily complex syntax and with maximum circumlocution.

In the event, Jan didn't join up. There was scarcely time, as the Soviets were at the gates and the Germans in retreat from the Baltics within weeks. Perhaps Jan's intention of join-ing the Legion—at such a late stage, and after evading call-up for so long—actually covered a hope of leaving Latvia for the West under military protection. The Soviet Army's attack on the Baltic states had actually begun in the summer of 1944, the immediate target being Lithuania but with some incursion into Latvian territory. By early August, Soviet forces were in occupation of the Latvian province of Latgallia, and by mid September they had pushed into northern Latvia. Riga was reoccupied without a struggle on 13 October.

'We're all looking in the direction of the West,' Olga wrote to Mischka on 20 May. Jan was at that point still in the hospital, but almost recovered. As for Arpad Jr, Olga seems to have had an earlier plan to get him sent to Vienna to study, which would have been difficult as he was not a university student and may not even have graduated from high school. Now she was focussed on getting him to Germany as a 'specialist', but nothing came of this either, though she wrote to Mischka in July that 'I hope soon, together with Arpad, to see you.' Only Arpad Sr, in poor health and close to sixty, had no plans to leave.

It was a very confused situation, with plans constantly being adjusted. In June and again in July, there are references in Mischka's correspondence to a possible trip home to Riga, and at some point that summer he evidently did get back to Riga, judging by his diary summary of his travels. But it must have been a short visit that left no other traces.

Olga's plan was to leave legally, on the pretext of moving her business to German-occupied Czechoslovakia. On 25 June, she wrote that she had to go to Prague, 'since I have a new order from the Wehrmacht (50,000 pairs), and for that I need quite different metal fittings than for the regular police'. Three weeks later, she had dispatched a consignment of her own things, including her private papers, to Mischka in Dresden via rail freight, clearly part of a permanent departure plan.

But there were difficulties: her health was giving way and her usual decisiveness was crumbling. Nerve pains in her legs were mentioned in a letter in May, and in June she wrote that she was trying to make plans for Arpad Jr, but 'everything is ruined by my immobility'. 'I don't know how I'll be able to make the final trip,' she wrote in July; she still wasn't feeling well, despite 'going for electric treatments five days in a row … I'm in a very bad mood, dreamy, disabled. I should long ago have got over these moods … Letting the soul wander in dreams doesn't make it stronger but transparent and friable, like the finest glass.' The letter ended on a note of appeal, with Olga invoking a childhood nickname: 'My dear Mauserl, write to me. Your Mama'.

It was a break in Olga's life with multiple significance. Not only was she preparing to leave home, but she had also separated from her husband definitively (or as definitively as she ever did) and was living alone in her workshop. Her married life, she reflected, had always been like a rocking horse, one partner up and the other down at any given time. 'Now it is my poor old husband who is begging for love and suffers.' But they were both unhappy, and they weren't going to grow old together. At the beginning of May, she made up her mind to take the final plunge and went to a lawyer to file for divorce. He wasn't home, however, and she resolved to go back in the morning—adding the rather ambiguous qualification 'If I should think differently about it in the morning, I would have to have changed a great deal.' She was trying without much success to convince herself that her personal unhappiness was a triviality in light of the world catastrophe in progress. Whether or not she actually got a divorce, or even filed for it, nobody in the family seems to know. My hunch is that she didn't. The last entry of her diary written in Riga is

'I am so sorry for my old husband. My husband, whom I loved so much and in such a complicated way.'

As of 13 August, with the Russians getting ever closer, they were all still in Riga, as Mischka's brother Arpad wrote to him: 'Mama will soon go to you in Dresden. We will go too. Whether it is to Dresden or somewhere else, we don't yet know exactly. For now we are still sitting in Riga ...' On 28 August, Olga wrote to Mischka from Riga that 'we have lived through a few exciting days here. But the big blows of events have temporarily fallen elsewhere, and so now we are again living calmly.' However, it was clearly time to get out before Soviet forces took Riga and the way was blocked.

Olga left on 1 October, a legal departure on a business trip. Her husband wrote a cautiously phrased letter to her with that date, signing himself 'The Old Man':

Dear Olga,

I came breathlessly to the steamer, you had telephoned that you were coming. I waited ... [sic] and was able to watch from the bank as the ship slowly pulled out. Then I went up and found on the table my torture photo. Perhaps it was an oversight, perhaps ballast or forgetfulness, chi lo sara [who knows] ... Anyway I am sending you my ugly mug as a present.

I got a couple of optimistic lines from A. [Arpad Jr]. I hope he handles himself properly ...

Perhaps we will see each other again under the 'hold fast' motto.

How strange that expression seems in the midst of this world chaos.

In line with our external environment I have developed something like rheumatism or neuralgia of the joints, so that from now on I can only (illegible—hobble?) rhythmically through life.

Until you come back to your country I will try to hold things together as much as possible, twiddle with the radio knobs, and 'read good books'.

Did you, poor life-wounded wife, get your clutch of young ones off?

Farewell, and to Mischi.

The Old Man.

I wonder if Olga showed Mischka this letter, with its absence of any final message to him. It looks as if the resentment was not all on Mischka's side. The expression 'life-wounded wife' (*Lebensinvalidenfrau*) touched Olga, and she would later quote it at the end of the diary of her marriage. 'Getting your clutch of young ones off', as Jan explained to me, meant getting him and Arpad off to Courland en route to an illegal departure by boat to Sweden. That was the plan, masterminded by Olga, and years later she was still reproaching herself for having left them to carry it out without her. But at the time of her departure, she thought it was going to come off. In a stop in Gotenhafen (Gdańsk) during her journey, she remembered sitting on a hill looking at the sea below and 'trying in the distance to discern the Swedish coast, where I thought both the young ones were'.

What happened, according to Jan's later account, was that the plan fell through because of Arpad Jr's thoughtless generosity. Jan and his new wife Balva were in hiding in Courland, on the western coast of Latvia, and the arrangement was that the forester with whom they were living would provide a boat to take the two of them plus Arpad to Sweden. This was supposed to happen on or around 1 October. Arpad duly arrived from Riga, but with four other people, which was too many for the boat. As a result, none of them left. Two weeks later, the Soviets reoccupied Riga and quickly closed the borders. This effort was the end of Jan's attempts to get out; he stayed in Riga and lived a long Soviet and post-Soviet life there. Arpad Jr made one more attempt, on 'the first day of peace' (presumably May 1945). Again, it was a ship to Sweden, but it never sailed because the Soviets came in and took everyone off. The crew were arrested but the would-be passengers were released and sent home—except for Arpad, who, out of goodheartedness, had been helping the crew load coal and was therefore taken for a crew member. He was arrested and ended up in Vorkuta in the Soviet Gulag, returning to Riga in damaged health three years later.

By 2 October, Olga was already in Reichenberg in the Sudetenland (part of the wartime Reich). This was her official business destination: she was supposed to be moving her workshop to the region, evidently with the help of her protector Dr Boening, who had an official position there. Reichenberg (now known by its Czech name of Liberec) was already within striking distance of Dresden, just 138 kilometres away on the other side of the Czech–German border, or four hours in the train via Prague. When she wrote to Mischka on 2 October, she said she was planning to go to Prague for medical treatment.

On 14 October, she was writing (again from Reichenberg) with some irritation at Mischka's not having written, asking why he didn't come there and whether her luggage had arrived or if he had received a letter from Papa for her. If Mischka could come to Reichenburg, Olga wrote, would he bring her dresses, and also the suitcase and her old diary (presumably the very one I now have), which was hidden under his mattress. One of her Riga workers, Nina Berners, had also arrived, bringing news of Arpad and Jan in Courland. Hidden in the middle of the letter were two heavy sentences: 'Today came the news on the radio that Riga has fallen. Thus we are now homeless. I want to hope very much that the young ones will struggle through.'

There is a break in the surviving correspondence for a month, perhaps because letters were not preserved or because the two had been meeting in the Sudetenland or Dresden. Olga and her 'crew' had barely set up shop when they were evacuated to another Sudetenland town, Tetschen-Bodenbach (now Děčín, on the Elbe, just inside the Czech border with Germany), and Misha later remembered making 'frequent weekend trips' from Dresden, despite the fact that the railway—the main line from Berlin to Prague—was often bombed and out of commission, making the trip much longer. Naturally there were bureaucratic complications connected with moving the business. 'My workshop is still not ready,' Olga wrote on 18 November. She had applied for her new licence, but Reichenberg and the neighbouring centre of Aussig [now Ústí nad Laben] were disputing about responsibility. As a result, Olga was constantly shuttling back and forth: 'I came in [to Reichenberg] on the slow train at 2 am. Next week I will go to Prague. This week I was in Aussig twice. I think a train conductor is not on the road more than I am.'

In the winter vacation of 1944–45, Mischka took off on a tourist trip, which he described to his mother as 'positive in the highest degree'. This is one of the small surprises of research, to find that in the middle of the war, just months before the Soviet Army crossed the German border, Mischka was calmly taking a holiday. He went to Munich, Garmisch-Partenkirchen and Innsbruck, fell in love with the mountains and found people in the south much nicer. On the way back, he swung through Vienna, called in on the Loefers and probably parked a suitcase with them. Leaving suitcases, and then later collecting them, is one of the leitmotifs of the Danoses' wartime experience—and not only theirs. When you have lost most things, it's very important where you left the rest; these are places where you have planted a small part of yourself, places that could be, or could have been, a home. Marlene Dietrich has immortalised this in her haunting song of the early 1950s, '*Ich hab' noch einen Koffer in Berlin*' ('I still have a suitcase in Berlin').

The Munich–Innsbruck trip was the end of Mischka's (comparatively) carefree wartime life in Germany, however. By this time, as Mischka told it to me, Olga and he were anticipating a relatively imminent German defeat, and Dresden, in the east of Germany, was likely to fall under Soviet rather than English-American occupation. The plan was to get themselves to Flensburg, close to the northern border with Denmark, and, if possible, over the border. Mischka's interest in Denmark was because of the physicist Niels Bohr in Copenhagen, but Olga, with her broad network of useful acquaintances, probably had some contacts there, as she did in Flensburg. They both started to pack up, the plan being to travel separately. (When I asked why they went separately, Mischka looked surprised and said it was obviously the best way: if one fell into misfortune, the other wouldn't be dragged in.)

Mischka had a room in a big, cold house in Dresden with a congenial landlady. He decided to give a farewell party on 13 February 1945, before setting out across Germany via Hamburg to Flensburg. That happened to be the night the Allies bombed Dresden and reduced the city to rubble.

6

The Bombing of Dresden

Nanni Schuster, 1945.
Photo enclosed in a letter
she gave Mischka as he left
Dresden after the bombing.

MISCHKA left two accounts of the Dresden bombing. One was in his diary, which he wrote up two months later, in April 1945, the other written for me as a musing half a century later. The similarity is remarkable, all the more as I am almost sure that Mischka had not reread the diary and indeed had forgotten about its existence (I found it in a box of his mother's papers after he died). In this chapter, I will let Mischka speak for himself as much as possible, inter-spersing the two accounts. (To distinguish them, the musing

is presented in a sanserif font, and the diary in a serif font.)
The musing is as he wrote it, with only typos and some idiosyncrasies of spelling corrected:

Around February I had decided that the time approached
when I will have to leave Dresden. The Russians made steady
advances, and who knows when and where the Allies would be.
Also, any occupation would be associated with at least artillery,
more likely also with air and tank assaults. We had talked with
my mother about what to do and had decided to 'evacuate' to
Flensburg, border town to Denmark.

No, or at most very little, war activities should happen there.
In preparation I decided to give a goodbye party. Indeed I invited
some 6 or 7 acquaintances, students all, to my place. As a treat
I made kissel [a Russian fruit jelly], I forget with which fruits
as the base. So, we were eating that stuff, when suddenly,
without any warning or reason the door, which was closed,
keeled into the room, it seemed quite slowly, but inexorably,
and remained on the floor in a horizontal position. That interrupted the party, and in fact ended it; we walked down into
the basement, where there already were the neighbors, with
distraught expressions on their faces, standing around and
not talking, but listening—which we also commenced to do,
and indeed some noise of explosions, distant, could be heard.
Then nothing further seemed to happen; so I went to the basement entrance and looked out, and saw 2 Mosquitoes (British
2-motor fighter-bombers, made of wood) passing overhead, but
doing nothing. After they left, nothing. A lull took over.

With the finality of that interruption the party disbanded,
and everybody started out for their homes. Having invited the
Karl May girl, I felt responsible for her safe return home, which
was diagonally across town, in the town section der Weisser
Hirsch.

Misha must have told me why he called her the 'Karl May girl', but I have forgotten. Most likely she was an admirer of the German writer of that name whose now forgotten novels, set in the American West, were immensely popular with German adolescents of Misha's generation.

So we start out, pass the Technische Hochschule [technical university], and reach the quite wide street leading to the Hauptbahnhof [main railway station]. But it looks ominous: flames emerging from windows on both sides of the street, the region around the Hauptbahnhof at the end of this street unclear. I decide to get an overview before continuing; behind the TH there are fields on the side of a hill; at the summit there used to be anti-aircraft guns, but just very recently departed. Indeed a clear overview: throughout the town here and there fires breaking through roofs; no direction seems clear. While contemplating the situation airplane noise becomes noticeable, and indeed as if the devil pokes: here and there in town immense fires erupt, sparks, flames, and everything: the explosives air raid commences. The sight is mesmerizing; I stand there hypnotized, a 20th century Nero. Soon incendiary bombs begin falling around us, then also explosive. Not far away one hits; I drag the girl along and drop into the bomb crater; that will provide protection against everything except for a direct hit. The girl starts to cry: I feel only immense tension, expectation, not fear. One hears the whistling of the falling incendiaries, ending with a thud when they hit ground, and the howling of falling bombs which end in an explosion. Is that whistling going to hit? How far—if at all—will the bomb fall?

The party was in Mischka's lodgings at Planettastrasse on the hill across the river from the central city. (The street, now

Elisabethstrasse, was renamed in Nazi times for Otto Planetta, a Nazi hero for his murder of Austrian Chancellor Engelbert Dollfuss in Vienna in 1934.) So if Mischka hadn't taken the Karl May girl home, he would have escaped direct danger. In the diary, the girl is virtually absent from the account, mentioned only occasionally as 'A.' It is as if Mischka were alone, with absolute responsibility for making the right decisions. On 13 April 1945, his first description of the fire, as seen from the heights before the bombing was renewed, is awed:

> I decided to go to the tower on the hill in order to get an overview of the strategic position. But from there the sight that presented itself was even more grisly and yet more splendid: fire everywhere. Accompanied, too—in spite of the distance of c. 0.8–1 km—by the appropriate music: the cracking of burning rafters, the roar of the flames, and now and then crashes as roofs fell in. Added to that there was also a wind, which, fanned by the fire, blew into it and only increased its fury. And to round it all off, a frightened dog, having probably been scared from the house by the onslaught, arrived on the scene and began howling in long, drawn-out tones.

'The picture was really gruesome,' he summed up, 'even gruesomely beautiful, but not horrifying'—or not yet. When the bombing started again,

> we lay down, there and then, on the spot. And then came the horror. Even if not yet in the highest degree and not in direct effect but just the very idea of it. Highly explosive fire- and fuel-bombs were being thrown higgledy-piggeldy over the areas that were not yet alight, and on those that were already burning. There was a confusion of firebombs

and explosive bombs being dropped, on to places that were
not yet on fire or already burning. More fire-bombs had
been thrown during the first attack; now the fires were
being thrown together by the bombs, as if they were being
stirred by giant pokers. And down there, within striking
distance, the Technische Hochschule was burning; at the
Elektrotechnische Institut the flames were already leaping
out of the windows of the top storey. And the whole time the
bombs were whistling and the fire-bomb canisters wailing;
they shatter in the air with a loud bang and dissolve into an
umbrella of individual rods of falling fire.

Here Mischka's account diverges briefly into an analysis of
his own responses—'Interesting, the reaction of the nervous
system: there was a sense of high tension, but surprisingly,
no trace of anxiety or fear'—before continuing with the
external scene:

> And all the time, more new combinations kept coming, and
> it whooshed and howled uninterruptedly, at first directly
> above us, and then further afield; actually, individual
> explosions could no longer be differentiated. And when you
> looked toward the city, mushrooms of smoke and flames just
> kept rising from the fire, and then after a while there was
> a more forceful explosion. These were the heavier chunks,
> like the ones that had already come down in our neighbour-
> hood. One can't really call them 'mushrooms', it looks more
> like a tree, with the undulation ...

At this point, the diary breaks off abruptly and resumes
some days later, on 18 April 1945. (He was in Hamburg by
this time, sitting in the Café Condi, which means that he must

have been coming down with diphtheria, although his prose gives no sign of this.)

One can't really call them 'mushrooms'. It looked more like a medieval watchtower, made up of a slowly growing and undulating melee of smoke and flames—after a while most of it has risen up into a sea of smoke and fire. And still it went on, non-stop. It seemed as though the force had hardly been alleviated, or at least had scarcely relocated to more distant parts of the city, when once again new combinations began to whir and the bombs began to hiss. The hissing was the most terrible, because of the uncertainty. And over all of this there was still a festive illumination, the luminescent parachutes; they hung like grapes in the air and came down very slowly. It was as bright as day from the fire and the 'Christmas trees'. But how the meaning of those words has changed! Almost symbolic. And it kept on hissing. Now it was already burning over in Kaitz [a suburb of Dresden to the south]. Just where we were, it was not burning because it was a field. More fire bombs now, fewer explosive fuel-bombs, because they were unloading those in areas that were already alight. And then suddenly it became quieter. It was still whistling at the other end of the city, but then it stopped there too. Then a couple of individual planes buzzed away over us, and everything went completely silent. Overhead, that is. Underneath, the fires roared and crackled; now and again houses tumbled down, sometimes a short time-fuse would explode, but otherwise all was calm. We stood up slowly, somewhat mistrustful of these unusual circumstances. The lower floor of the Elektronische Institut was burning now. Behind that, other buildings of the Technische Hochschule were also alight, and the annex to the High Voltage hall at the front. Only Chemistry remained untouched.

The 1996 account continues the story:

That whole thing took about an hour. It suddenly ended. I got out of the crater; there was the town; now an uninterrupted sea of flames. No way to get through. Also it began to rain. So I took the girl to the abandoned battery, found an open bunker, went in and lay down on the floor. Soon some survivors of the vicinity started to drift in, bewildered, and the bunker filled up, but not to overcrowding.

The diary has a lot more to say, in a tone of outrage, about the behaviour of those survivors:

Now the first bomb victims appeared. And what did they talk about? About their things. There was a daughter with her mother. They had been protected and had made their way out into the open through a neighbour's cellar and a shop. They were talking: 'Oh, my gloves! I've always had them with me before!' and so on. 'Mummy, I don't have my diamond ring with me!' (Mother): 'Just don't tell your father! I'll give you one of mine. I've still got enough.' And then on and on about the stockings and the rest. In the midst of this, but quite rarely: 'I wonder where Daddy is? He was at work of course. How I worry about him!!' and then back to stockings. Since then for weeks on end all I heard in Dresden was about stockings, underwear, dresses, hats and so on; I can't remember any other topics in connection with the raid. At most, someone would explain that he had been protected. Otherwise they all tried to outdo each other in listing their losses, but only their losses of underwear!

From which one has to conclude that those who had lived through worse things were either no longer living or silent. Horror had closed their mouths.

The next part, the morning after the raid, is the worst in both tellings. The musing recalls the scene that greeted them:

Then the morning lights came on and I surveyed the situation. The flames had disappeared, the fuel had been consumed. So I thought the best way would be to go through town; that would be much shorter than going around it. We start. The beginning was easy. Up to the Hauptbahnhof, on that wide street, we could simply walk. Some houses were semi-collapsed, with debris covering the sidewalk, and to some extent the street, but one could pass by. After the Hauptbahnhof, in the old part of town, the streets are narrower, and rubble begins now and then to cover the whole street. As the street continues to narrow, the rubble gets deeper, and one has to climb over it. Progress gets excruciatingly slow. If there should be now another raid— I dismiss that thought, suppress that thought is more correct. Climbing gets slower and slower—the pile of bricks is unstable; then there is visible the hair, the back of a human head, then again a leg sticks out, then again the bricks slide under the weight of a step, progress is almost imperceptible, no air raid, some further debris of the non-brick type, still no air raid—about here I notice that my receiver of impressions makes a click: it switches to semi-nightwalking [sleep-walking], no impressions, just climb, girl is crying, just drag her along, climb, the street could be traversed in 4 or 5 minutes, it must soon end, but the absence of buildings precludes knowledge of where we are, and indeed, the height of the brick mountain seems to diminish, some patches of pavement appear, the patches become larger and tend to merge, and then we see that we are out of the narrow street, even some buildings are still standing. Even a stretch of sidewalk is clear of bricks. Instead, there is a row of corpses, evidently extracted from the basement of the still standing building, uninjured, simply dead. Must have suffocated, as I now know, but then I simply saw that row, with no reaction. From then on streets are wide, no problem walking, damage to buildings decreases—we have left the old town, the Altstadt. By now all buildings are standing, seemingly undamaged, and then there is this 5 year old boy, next to the fence, lying face down, fresh as if asleep.

The diary story continues on 20 April with their renewed attempt to break through the next morning:

The streets were already full. People were moving about so strangely: for the most part they wandered slowly back and forth, seeming without any plan or goal, as if in a daze, almost like sleepwalkers. Only on the arterial roads was there a more uniform direction emerging: out of here! So we tried to get through. Nobody around had any information about how to get through. Everyone told us: 'No, you can't get through here! Try further along, over there' or 'Try back there!' Nobody knew what things were like in the city. We tried to get through at roughly the same distance as the Technische Hochschule sports ground from Zelleschet Way. But the smoke and the dust were so thick there that we couldn't get through. So we went to the next cross street and tried there, but that was just as bad … That's where I saw the first casualties, that is, the ones that could still walk, but whose eyes had suffered from the smoke and fire. First-aid men were looking after them; it was actually the site of a burned field hospital. This sight didn't encourage me in the least. But the futile search for a way through combined with the events of the previous night were gradually beginning to eat away at the nervous system; we had to start holding hands in order not to turn around, although so far the places we were in had only been fire-bombed. Finally we came to a wider street, where the No. 5 and 15 trams use to go up to Monerif [?]. This was where the fuel-bombed area began; clearly this made a much stronger impression.

The Karl May girl ('A.') makes a few rare, brief appearances in the diary story at this point:

A. was already losing her courage and wanted to turn back. I wasn't happy about that; wanted to go further; I wanted at least to get through the Grosse Garten and inspect the district there. We kept going. But now the brute, knock-out force of these impressions was building powerfully in its intensity. For here the bombs had fallen thicker and thicker. Whereas at first there had been only houses that were partly destroyed, here at the railway terminal and in Grosse Garten Street, every house had got a direct hit and had been burned out; most of them were still burning. And on top of that the smell of smoke and fire. The latter in particular has a splendid effect on the nerves. Subconsciously, the strongest impression of all was made by the people who were pre-sumably still under the rubble. And then slowly one became conscious of the fact that a further attack was possible, and of our absolute helplessness against it if that happened. But I still pressed on, as I hoped at least there would be some breathable air in the Grosse Garten, and then there would not be far to go. But the Garten looked different. This was the zone where the bombs had rained down at their thickest. Instead of the path I had unconsciously anticipated, there lay obstacles in the form of a tangled undergrowth of broken branches and trees, as well as craters. And now there came something that put paid to my moral bravado: the first corpses of the day. I had seen corpses before, after the battle in Riga in 1941, but these looked different. And coming on top of everything else, it was enough to make my courage collapse. Fear caught hold of me. Simple fear, fear of what had now become immediate horror, together with thoughts of a possible new attack. Out! Just get out of here! A. hadn't seen the dead bodies, but she fully agreed. I had lost all hope that the inhabitants of any place around had remained alive.

The chronology goes a bit haywire at this point, as Mischka digresses into fears about specific friends, including his new girlfriend Nanni, who later turned out to have survived.

This whole diary entry is unparagraphed in the original, written in small handwriting to cram in more, with the tension rising until it is almost coming out as a scream:

We started out again. And now came the horror, compared with which the previous morning was child's play. Through that, however, I had already been pre-schooled, and I knew that one only needed to notice, that is see, enough of something not to stumble over it … The main railway station. A row of charred bodies. I knew that my mother had actually had the intention to come to Dresden, and there was the possibility that she had come in just at the decisive moment; I made myself look over these rows, but didn't see the fur coat in question. Then we came to Prager Street, that is, the place where she had been earlier. Now it was just a heap of rubble.

Again, the diary account breaks off abruptly, to be continued without a break in the narrative on 22 March 1945:

You couldn't walk through it, you had to climb over stones and charred beams. Here and there, a sometimes charred, sometimes horribly lifelike body part was peeping out from the rubble. And you couldn't run away, you had to go forwards quite slowly. The only way not to pass out is, quite consciously, to let nothing affect you, not to think, just to press on, to turn all your thoughts towards where you are stepping, where you are going to climb over, to watch that you don't tread on a wobbly stone and get your foot stuck. The stones are still hot, and the steam is still rising everywhere. Otherwise, all around is silent, deathly silent; now and then, out of the stillness comes a sudden explosion somewhere, or a wall caves in; the only noise that accompanies you is the sound of your own footsteps, and even that is dead, losing itself without echo in the rubble. Keep going. Don't think about anything, don't see anything. Don't think about how it had looked just the evening before, how the art dealer had been here, the street corner or the cinema there … Keep going.

Finally, finally, the Ring Road appears. It is so wide that a path free of rubble remains down the centre. Here soldiers are carrying the bodies that are lying around and putting them all together in one place. No, not into one place, but on to the street that runs from Georg Square to the Elbe, where the No. 1 and No. 16 [trams] used to go to the main railway station. There is already a continuous row of bodies down to the bridge. A few people are going slowly along the row, looking at each one. There are not many. And there is the bridge. Hopefully at least the air will be more breathable. No, not really. There is only a gentle breeze blowing, and it brings with it dust and the smell of fire … We're walking along the Elbe in the direction of Waldschloesschen. Gradually, gradually, it is getting better. There are still dead bodies lying all around, and the bank is strewn with bomb craters, but the air is becoming cleaner. Now the craters are becoming rarer, and at Waldschloesschen everything is almost unscathed; not even all the windows of the houses are broken.

The 1996 version includes (as the diary does not) their arrival at the home of the Karl May girl:

> By the time we reach the house of the Karl May girl it is afternoon; the house is essentially undamaged; we get fed and I fall asleep on a freshly made clean bed.
>
> Next morning we had breakfast, the somewhat shellshocked family—mother and daughter, father [being], as essentially all males [were], absent, and myself. At a point where daughter is absent, the mother mentions that she has confidence in me and would trust me with her daughter. I don't know what to say, and accept her confidence. The time comes for me to leave; the mother asks whether I need something; I ask to be lent a suitcase, which is granted. I leave.

As Mischka told me this story orally, it was like a fairytale in which the hero is rewarded for his valiant deeds by being offered the hand of a beautiful princess but must continue on his quest—except that he didn't want her hand, had escorted her out of a sense of duty, and seems to have found her more irritating than a proper object of chivalry should be.

The journey home across the city, suitcase in hand, was not without incident, as the musing recalls:

> I retrace the path of yesterday, circumnavigating the Altstadt. As I reach the TH an air raid is sounded. I run to that field a few hundred m[etres] ahead. As I reach it I hear the noise of falling hardware, drop the suitcase and run toward the middle

of the field to get away from the trees—the sleeping boy of yesterday must have been killed by a falling tree limb. I drop to the ground; a number of small bombs detonate; some clumps of soil thrown into the air fall around and on me, I run towards the closest crater, but that is the end of the raid. I go back to pick up the suitcase, and there it is, on the rim of a crater, with a dent but not a hole. It remains usable.

The diary tells this story too, reiterating a point of personal scientific observation made several times in his narrative, that 'no fear or other embarrassing feeling was discernible'. By this time, Mischka had had enough of writing down the story, but he had one more remarkable sight to record:

What I saw, I don't want to go into further; it would be too much and there isn't enough space to tell it all. Just one thing, a more idyllic sight: across the street, in between the people—and without worrying about them, or about the cars bouncing over the holes in the bitumen—slowly walks a young giraffe. Without haste, her head held high, she disappears into the undergrowth in the Grosse Garten.

'*Ausgebombt, gesund*' (bombed out, unhurt) was the laconic message Mischka sent his mother in Aussig. 'Write post restante to the address you know in Flensburg. You go too!' This is one of the occasions when German efficiency astonishes: the medium was an 'express message' sent by telegram, explicitly marked as a notification of survival and thus probably free; and it arrived.

It was actually almost a month before he set out. First there was a romantic interlude with a young German woman, Marianne (Nanni) Schuster, whom he had met sometime the previous autumn, probably at the university. Nanni came from

Chemnitz in Saxony, and Mischka had evidently visited, or at least tried to visit, her family there, but they seem to have been friends rather than lovers until early in the new year. In the diary account of the bombing, his despairing feeling that nobody could have survived didn't last long 'because I was pleased, but not at all surprised to find a letter from MS waiting for me at home'. She had sat out the raid in the basement of her house, which, although 'located about 1 km from where the [dead] sleeping boy was', lay in the direction away from the Altstadt and had come through intact. The afternoon of his return from dropping off the Karl May girl, Nanni came over to Planettastrasse. The musing records that they decided to set off together to her family home, about 80 kilometres to the west:

> Packing just some minimum into the briefcase, ... off we went, to the West, essentially going from station to station to find a still functioning one. Indeed we got to such by the evening; a train was expected the next morning. We were sent to the chateaux of the local whatever, who provided a barn or such for refugees passing through town. There was straw on the floor, and a naked lightbulb hanging from the ceiling. We, together with the 50 or so other refugees put ourselves down, in the manner Vonnegut, in his book on the Dresden bombing, described as 'like stacked spoons'—even though it was only a family—in our case, two—at a time ... Next morning indeed a train appeared and later that day we arrived in Chemnitz; they lived far from the town, out of harm's way; the father, being a village doctor, had not been called up.

Mischka had left a message for his mother outside his Dresden lodgings—a piece of cardboard attached to a stick, as was the custom that had evolved during the war. His mother duly came up from Tetschen-Bodenbach to look for him, and in fact didn't see his message, but the neighbours told her he was all right. As promised in his stick-message, Mischka made his way to Tetschen-Bodenbach within a week (taking a roundabout route from Chemnitz, since you couldn't get through Dresden). In the next week, he went back and forth between Chemnitz and Tetschen-Bodenbach a few times, and he and Nanni made an excursion back to Dresden as well, going on their bicycles to pick up some of her things that had been left behind. All of this probably had its idyllic aspect for Mischka and Nanni—in a letter written two years later, when they were already divided by being in different occupation zones, Nanni referred to 13 February 1945, 'Dresden's death-day', as 'our birthday'—but horror was not far away. During the bicycle trip, they passed the main railway station, 'where the corpses were—still!—being extracted from the under-ground shelter'. In his diary, Mischka recorded that he 'had learnt to think over these things coolly and without getting upset, not letting them have an impact on me', but this was patently not the case. Of his later visits, he wrote:

I have seen the horrors and their traces. Now I am probably already immune. And at the same time not immune. But the horror remains in Dresden, it is still there. One month after the attack I stood at the main station: one track and platform were sufficiently repaired for the commuter train Pirma–Meissen to be running again. Prager Street had been cleared down the centre to allow the traffic through. Men were already working on further repairs of the main station. And yet: the horror of the city that had once been was still alive, and had everybody in its power. About 300 people were standing there, waiting for the train to Pirma. They weren't waiting for the train the way you usually wait, relaxed, impatient or frustrated, but with fear deep inside: will it come or not? Usually a crowd feels safe where an individual might break down; here even that didn't help ...

On top of everything else, Mischka had fallen in love. Now there was the question of whether his future was with, or without, Nanni. A diary entry for 27 February 1945, written in an extremely stilted and convoluted style, probably to prevent too much expression of distress, indicates that Mischka had asked Nanni to come with him to Flensburg (which presumably meant marrying him) but she hadn't been ready for the drastic step of leaving her home and family for the unknown. 'I played for a while with the thought to turn aside from my own path and to try to continue on not alone,' Mischka wrote. But there is in fact no indication that he ever considered *not* leaving for Flensburg; the 'turning aside from my own path' probably meant adding a personal commitment that might compromise his commitment to physics. But Nanni ('the case in question' in Mischka's agonised circumlocutions) 'disappointed me ... because she is staying at home, or, more exactly, because she has given up the struggle without actually really having begun it'. He had 'hoped that another result was possible', and even his mother, who had managed to make Nanni's acquaintance at this period, had been encouraging. But Nanni thought it was too much for her to handle, and perhaps, he concluded, this was the best thing for her. To sum up, naturally in quotation marks (I don't know from what piece of German romantic poetry): '*Du bist doch mein schoenstes Erlebnis gewesen*' ('You were my most beautiful experience').

On 12 March 1945, almost a month after the bombing, Mischka finally set off from Chemnitz to Flensburg. On the train, he opened the letter Nanni had given him on parting and found her photograph (he kept it in his diary, so it is now in my possession, and I have put it at the head of this chapter; a sweet, serious young woman, not spineless—but not a risk-taker either). 'What a strong impression a picture can make!' he wrote in his diary as he sat in the train. Opening the envelope and seeing her face, 'I got something like a blow to the chest.' The next day, he tried to make sense of the Nanni affair in his diary entry, comparing it with an earlier parting in Riga in September 1943, but got distracted by the thought that 'between 9.43 and 3.45, a year and a half has passed', including things that were 'quite alarmingly awful'. But 'perhaps that is going to change'. Half a century later, skipping over the parting from Nanni (whom he calls 'Blue-eyes' in this text), he concluded his Dresden musing with a bit of mathematician's number-play about his date of departure, which doesn't mean he wasn't in earnest: 'In my memory on the date 12345 begins a new chapter.'

7

Displaced Persons
in Flensburg

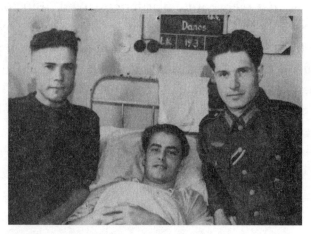

Mischka in Flensburg infectious diseases hospital, spring
1945. Nothing is known of the circumstances in which
the photo was taken or the identity of the orderly and
Wehrmacht soldier on either side of his bed.

TWO days after 12.3.45, Mischka was on a train en route
to Hamburg. His suitcase, containing some clothes and
twenty volumes of *Zeitschrift für Physik*, was wedged into a
rucksack made in Olga's Tetschen-Bodenbach workshop to his
own design (the suitcase could be opened without extracting
it from the rucksack). His spirits were buoyant, despite the
stresses of previous weeks. 'Now I am sitting in the D-train,

1st class, alone in the compartment, and waiting for the departure,' he wrote in his diary. 'Life is still beautiful!!'

A couple of weeks later, having arrived after many adventures in Flensburg, he took up the story:

> The trip was quite amusing. It began in the 1st class of the D train. So it went quite fine until Hanover, when they announced: All out, the train stops here. A D-train should have gone direct to Hamburg at 9.45 (it was about 7 am), but it went, as it turned out, absolutely not as far as Hamburg (just as the one before didn't go as far as Bremen), so I had the pleasure of hearing the announcement: Passengers travelling to Hamburg take the train to Celle. I got in and went to Celle. And then came the 'bombing time', in which Hanover was supposed to be destroyed. This circumstance, which was repeated relatively often, filled me with concern about my suitcase. But at midday a train went to Ulsen and at 2 am even further to Hamburg … I was at Hamburg main station by 5.

In Hamburg, he stopped off to deliver something to a Frau Neuendorf from Frau Bach (a friend of Olga's, so no doubt the commission came from her), checked that his suitcase had not been lost along the way and stayed two nights in a guesthouse. All this is related in jaunty style in the diary, despite the danger from Allied bombing, which hit Hamburg, with its docks and oil refineries, particularly hard. Actually he was lucky: having struck Hamburg on 8, 9, 10 and 11 March, the British bombers took a rest until 20 March. (Mischka was probably still in Hamburg then, but does not mention the raid.) In his guesthouse, he made the acquaintance of a fellow guest, 'a young woman from the other world' (can this be an American? a Russian? a fellow Balt?) whom he was eager to know better.

But then Mischka was struck by a catastrophe of another kind: he fell ill, which 'hindered me from greater activity, and also liquidated a greater interest [in the young woman]. So I didn't get as much from beautiful Hamburg as I might have done.'

The sickness turned out to be diphtheria, and that was serious. The diary glosses over the process by which, although sick, he managed to get on the train to Flensburg, but I remember what he told me about it. A sympathetic doctor in Hamburg diagnosed the diphtheria and told him that his official advice was to present himself immediately at an infectious diseases hospital, but his personal advice was to go straight to the station, before he got even sicker, and hope he made it to his destination. Mischka liked that kind of joke, even though it wasn't a joking matter. Somehow he got himself to the station at Hamburg, caught the train and, after a while, arrived in Flensburg. As far as I can remember, he said he was in bad shape by the time the train got to Flensburg and had to be helped off the train by fellow passengers. But the diary entry, written in hospital in a slightly dazed state, says nothing of this, simply reporting the saga of his admission to hospital.

Although it was after midnight (probably the night of the 24–25 March), registration at the Flensburg station medical point was surprisingly quick. An ambulance arrived within a quarter of an hour and took him off to the Flensburg City Hospital for admission to the infectious diseases ward. But then the whole efficient process broke down:

We came with the car into the courtyard. Then nothing happened. The driver got out and tried to ring in one of the buildings. He pressed various bells in front, behind. He tried to ring at the main building, but nothing happened; as sole reaction a dog in a kennel barked—then he came back and finally found a door where he was able to ring. Then a nurse came out, but only to give the information that this was not the right ward, and she didn't know where he could find the proper nurse. But no, after half an hour of standing in the courtyard a door suddenly opened and out came a nurse to take me to reception ... Then we came to the reception formalities, that they put me in a bed, gave me an injection and turned the light out. The thing I missed most was a bath. And then the first impression: a room, half dark, phlegm and spit in all corners; everyone was writhing in his place, groaning in various registers; a night light covered with a shade that had a relatively small opening, and all the time the groans and writhing—No! Out of here as fast as possible!

But that, obviously, wasn't possible, even though Mischka (perhaps slightly delirious?) seems to have examined the ventilation outlet in the wall and decided that while you could get in through it, you couldn't get out. So he stayed, and in the morning things seemed a bit better, though not much. He felt he had run out of 'spiritual energy' and was so tired that even making notes in his diary exhausted him. The doctor on his daily rounds aroused all his anti-authoritarian reactions and dislike of being treated as an inferior being:

When he examined me the first time, he found it necessary to look inside my mouth. As his command, 'Mouth open', did not produce a reaction of sufficient magnitude, he repeated his order very loudly and in a way that from a normal man could only be described as a scream.

As his condition improved, Mischka got to know some of the other patients and orderlies, two of whom are shown beside his bed in a photograph miraculously taken and preserved. He also encountered a prisoner of war and an *Ostarbeiter* (forced labourer from the East) in the hospital, the first in either category he had met face to face.

He scribbled a note in pencil to his mother on 25 March, giving his location and a very brief account of his illness and hospitalisation—'I had become a breeding ground for the diphtheria bacillus. The first impression (at night) was naturally not too cheerful, but now it's OK.' In the note, which may never have been sent, Mischka's narrative wanders all over the place, fretting about his suitcase, reporting on the visit to Frau Neuendorf, and finally almost apologising for having landed in hospital:

> I thought I had made a big mistake coming here, to a place I can't get out of so easily. But in the first place what else could I have done? The serum which I need as someone with diphtheria I couldn't get any other way, and to infect a camp is also not the correct thing. But it has to be emphasised that it's not so awful now, we're about seven people per room ...

Olga was already in Flensburg, and must have been beside herself with anxiety. It wasn't until 6 April that Mischka dispatched two identical postcards to Olga, one to Flensburg's central post office, the other to Olga's poste restante address at the Timm Kroeger School on Pferdewasser in the city, telling her what had happened. Even then, his concentration was a bit impaired: after having told Olga about the baggage problem ('The big suitcase is most likely sitting here at the station; I gave it in on my ticket in Hamburg. I still don't have any information about my things'), he added inconsequentially, and probably inaccurately, that in the hospital 'I occupied myself mainly with theoretical physics'. Then, after signing off, he noticed the physics remark came out of left field and added a postscript—'The second last sentence is illogical ... Verbal communication is easier'—before repeating the message about the big suitcase as if he hadn't already dealt with it.

Mischka remained in hospital for almost two weeks. At the end of the first week, he recorded his surprise at realising what had gone on in the world while he was temporarily absent:

> Yesterday evening I heard with the greatest astonishment that already this Sunday, that is, the day after tomorrow, it will be Easter. Palm Sunday has passed, without the Passion etc. And in this connection, it turned out that for the first time I started thinking about food. And what I thought about was Pascha [the Russian Eastern sweet] and the braised pork with red cabbage that is the great Austrian dish.

The lead-up to Easter wasn't the only thing Mischka had missed. He had also missed, and apparently still failed to notice, the lead-up to the end of the war. The Western Allies were across the Rhine and had taken Frankfurt. Austria, pork and cabbage and all, had been conquered by Soviet forces. The last great encounter of the European war, the Battle of Berlin, started two weeks after Mischka got out of hospital. On 30 April, Hitler killed himself in his bunker. On 2 May, German forces finally surrendered Berlin to the Soviet Army.

The war was over. A defeated Germany came under Allied military occupation. Mischka and Olga were now refugees, officially categorised as 'displaced persons'. These were momentous events, for the world as well as for the Danoses, but we know next to nothing about Mischka's and Olga's reactions. This is partly because, once the two were reunited in Flensburg, they no longer corresponded. They were not writing to anyone else, either, because ordinary citizens had no access to inter-zonal or international postal services for some months. Comment on world events was totally absent from their diaries. Olga, whose diary deals explicitly with the personal, made only one entry for the whole of 1945, in which she summed up her underlying state of mind for the year as 'ironic sadness'. Mischka confined his relatively few post-hospital entries in Flensburg to philosophy, physics and girlfriends.

Had he only been paying attention in Flensburg, there would have been a lot to write about. The Danoses had chosen Flensburg, a northern coastal city in the German state of Schleswig-Holstein, because it was close to the Danish border and they expected it would be quiet. But it wasn't as quiet as they anticipated. When Hitler killed himself at the end of April, he designated Admiral Karl Doenitz, Commander in Chief of the Navy, as Germany's president. As it happened, Doenitz's headquarters were in Flensburg, which thus became the site of the short-lived Doenitz government. It was from Flensburg, on 6 May, that the Doenitz government authorised unconditional surrender of German armed forces to the Allies and declared Flensburg an open city. Allied troops, led by Field Marshal Montgomery, entered the city without resistance on 6 May. On the eve of their arrival, someone on the British side had taken the trouble to tell the local radio station to stop playing Wagner.

Victory was officially celebrated by the British and Americans on 8 May, and by the Soviets on 9 May. This was only the first of many postwar disagreements among the erstwhile allies. Germany was divided into four military occupation zones: American, French, British and Soviet, with the capital, Berlin, similarly divided. Mischka and Olga found themselves in the British zone.

All sorts of people were flocking into Flensburg. For a start, there were high-placed Nazis on the run. Doenitz's government remained in existence until 23 May, but its last weeks were punctuated by suicides, flights and arrests of Hitler's top associates. SS leader Heinrich Himmler, who had at the end of April declared himself Hitler's successor but now accepted Doenitz's leadership, was in Flensburg briefly before fleeing in disguise and then, two weeks later, killing himself. Propaganda chief Alfred Rosenberg was in hospital nearby, being treated for alcoholism. Doenitz himself, along with Albert Speer, who had been residing in the nearby resort of Glücksburg, was arrested on 23 May, along with all the other remaining members of his government, who surrendered without a fight to the British.

A million German troops in the state of Schleswig-Holstein, where Flensburg was located, were in the process of being put into camps by the Allies as prisoners of war. Allied troops were arriving in droves, and so were refugees. Refugees had been coming to Flensburg by train and boat, and in horse-drawn wagons since the middle of January. By the end of May, the city had taken in 40,000 of them, raising its population (excluding soldiers) to 110,000. The majority of the refugees were Germans coming from the East, but they included 7500 foreigners, mainly Poles and Latvians. Food rations were officially set at 1200 calories a day but in practice were often less.

'The whole of Europe is mingling in Flensburg's streets,' the local newspaper reported in incongruously upbeat terms, as if the city were hosting a carnival, on 30 May 1945:

> One sees not only Russians, Poles and Danes but also Belgians, Dutchmen, Frenchmen, Greeks, Italians, Latvians, Lithuanians, Estonians, Luxembourgers, Serbs, Croats and many others walking through Flensburg's streets.—New troops change the city's character, the brown-khaki of the English, along with Canadian troops and [illegible] the US

army mingle in Flensburg. Never has our beautiful old city sheltered so many people as in these eventful days ...

Olga had got to Flensburg in the second week of April, three weeks before the German capitulation—a good time to arrive, as she was one of the early ones. She was billeted—presumably by German authorities, since the Allies had not yet arrived—in Glücksburg on the Flensburg fjord. This was the same place where Doenitz made his residence, though he was in the castle and she in a hotel. But from a refugee perspective, a hotel was a wonderful luxury; most found themselves in barracks and camps. 'Glücksburg—city of happiness!' Olga wrote on 14 April. ('Happiness city' is the literal meaning of the German name.)

> After two days of living in a camp, I have a big beautiful room just for me. My hotel is called Fernblick ['distant view']. It fits its name. I can see over the water to Denmark. I would like to stay in these parts and wait to see how things develop.

The trouble was that Mischka, recently released from hospital, wanted to go on to Denmark in the hope of studying physics with the great Niels Bohr in Copenhagen. 'For his sake,' Olga continued,

> I ought to try to get to Denmark. If everything goes well, I could let him go alone and remain here myself. But perhaps I am just thinking like that this evening because I am so tired of this life of trudging around. Perhaps my strength is not yet exhausted.

Why they didn't go on to Denmark is not clear: I have a vague memory that Mischka told me that by the time they had met up again and were ready to go, the British had closed the border. At any rate, they stayed in Glücksburg. The next six months seems to have been an empty time for both of them. In her summation in her diary of the year since she had left Riga, Olga described herself as 'Alone. The whole year' (she then conscientiously crossed out the last three words and substituted 'most of the year'; evidently there had been a lover around at one point). Mischka had no way of contacting Nanni because she was now trapped in the Soviet zone in the East, with no inter-zonal postal communication for civilians until October. His thoughts strayed back to Riga: 'Five years is not a long time, but all the same it's long enough. Have I changed since then? Who knows. What was going on then with Baby? Was that just childishness? I still have such a warm feeling when I think of it.' That's nice because, fifty years later, I took a liking to Helen, aka Baby, too. In August, Mischka met an Estonian nurse, but she petered out, and two weeks later he was musing wistfully that there ought to be a combination of Nanni and two other girlfriends identified only by initials, plus music. This last was a reference to the momentary spiritual connection he had felt with a music-loving man, a stranger to him, who came in and listened when he was playing the piano.

So there was a piano around already; Mischka usually located one pretty soon in a new place. The other thing Mischka always located was the local sports club, and sure enough, there are certificates from the Baltic Sports Society of Flensburg, dated 15 September, of his wins in the 400-metre race, the high jump and the 400-metre relay. That probably wasn't very high-level competition. Mischka was still feeling the effects of diphtheria, noting in his diary that he got tired very quickly and lacked the physical and mental stamina he had had before. One gets the sense that he was in recessive mode—'just the son of his mother', as he was remembered ten years later by one of Olga's male admirers, a local journalist working as press advisor to the military government. Possibly the mode was even actively antisocial. After Mischka had departed from Flensburg in the winter of 1945–46 to resume his life as a student, a comment in Olga's first letter suggests this, and perhaps also tensions between the two of them: 'It's true, God help me, that you are constantly working, even at the cost of your fellow men. That I can state under oath.' She hoped that after the move, 'you can finally get on a friendly footing with them [his fellow men]'.

When inter-zonal postal service reopened in the autumn, Mischka wrote a letter without an addressee (probably to Nanni) on his 'relaxing summer' at Glücksburg. This seems not to have been ironic, though with Mischka you never know. It was as if it were any old summer holiday at a seaside resort. No mention of war occupation, refugees, the dropping of atomic bombs on Hiroshima and Nagasaki (later a major issue for him) or even his own bout of diphtheria. The only other information that he gave about his life was that 'I worked this summer as a radio repairman for the occupation authorities, as a result of which I got rations—English Army rations.' That, of course, was worth noting in these hungry years.

Despite his diary's silence on the British occupiers, Mischka developed a dislike for them that coloured his attitude to England for the rest of his life. As he remembered in the 1990s,

> The Eisenhower edict was: 'no fraternization with the population'. The British forces stuck to that edict. The officers added to it arrogance, aloofness. They did not see the person standing in front of them; be that a German (the ex-enemy) or a DP, the so-to-say person liberated by them.

'So to say' is Mischka's sarcastic way of conveying that in the British officers' eyes, the DP was not a person. That was certainly true of some of the Western occupiers. The maverick US military commander General Patton made no secret of the fact that he regarded DPs as subhuman—particularly, but not only, Jewish DPs. As one official of UNRRA reported in 1946, 'formerly the DP was looked upon as a person unfortunate enough to have been a slave of the Nazis, but today he is generally considered primarily as a Blackmarketeer, a criminal or loafer, who does not want to return to his own country but prefers to settle into the easy existence of being cared for by the Army and UNRRA'. The Germans hated DPs, regarding them (especially the Poles and Russians) as a bunch of criminals and layabouts and resenting their privileged status with regard to rations. The DP was not a person you would want to marry your daughter or your occupation army son.

To be sure, DPs from the Baltic states were generally regarded as higher than the Slavs in the chain of being— 'splendid people whose camps are clean, bright and civilized', wrote one UNRRA official enthusiastically to the *Manchester Guardian*. But the downside was that they were also collectively more suspected than the Poles of having been Nazi collaborators. By the spring of 1945, Britain and the United States had decided that they did not recognise the Soviet absorption of the Baltic states in 1940, and hence did not regard Latvians as subject to mandatory repatriation to the Soviet Union, but many in UNRRA and the occupation governments retained a suspicion of them as Nazi collaborators who had voluntarily left with the Germans, particularly if they had served under German command in the Latvian Legion or Waffen-SS. Mischka was not in the latter category, though some of his Latvian friends like Bičevskis were, but it was also true that he and Olga did not fall into the 'victim' category of persons forcibly taken to Germany as slave labour. There is no indication, however, either in the contemporary documents or in subsequent retellings, that Olga and Mischka were ever even slightly worried about being sent back to Latvia, suspected of collaboration or deprived of UNRRA protection.

Although DPs were low on the social totem pole, the formal status of DP was greatly coveted because it carried good rations, guaranteed housing and medical care. The definition of a DP eligible for UNRRA care was someone whose displacement was the result of war and fascism. That excluded other categories of refugees, such as the millions of *Volksdeutsche* (ethnic Germans) streaming out of Eastern Europe, finding themselves, after the war, no longer welcome in the countries where their families had often lived for centuries, or Baltic Germans, like Baby Klumberg's family, who had responded to the Fuhrer's call to return to the homeland in the late 1930s and early '40s. (That's how it was in principle; in practice, Baby and many others seem to have merged with the general crowd of Baltic DPs who had left a few years later.) When, sometime in 1946, Mischka composed the apologia that he submitted to the British, explaining the circumstances in which he had come to Germany, noting his aunt's arrest by the Nazis and stressing that 'none of us three brothers has been a single day in the German Army', it was a possible suspicion of pro-Nazi leanings that he was implicitly refuting.

As time passed, and the Cold War gathered momentum, the working definition of DP changed and DPs came to be seen primarily as victims of Communism rather than Nazism (since the homelands they had left were either under or coming under Communist regimes). This made the question of wartime collaboration less relevant and was generally to the advantage of Baltic DPs because of their reputation for strong anti-Communism. In the late 1940s, when resettlement selection committees were vigilant on the question of Communist or Soviet sympathies, Mischka never had to defend himself against suspicion of pro-Communism because, as a Latvian, he was simply assumed to be an anti-Communist nationalist.

A DP registration card, number G21295530, was issued on 1 August 1945 in the name of Mikelis Danos and renewed on four occasions up to February 1946. It would be nice to present this as his definitive card of identity in the new life, but in fact two other DP cards in the 'G' series have survived, one in the name of Mikelis, the other in the name of Michael Danos. In addition, there was a fourth card, with the registration number A02054732 and in the name of Michael Danos, probably issued in the US zone, which we will come to later. DP life was full of identity documents and screenings, but this contributed as much to the multiplication of identities as to their clarification. For displaced persons—even honest ones like Mischka—nothing was set in stone: names and nationalities were fluid; identities were provisional, depending on demand.

As DPs go, Olga and Mischka were in a good position. Olga had arrived in Flensburg and found a niche there before the great influx of refugees from the East. They were Latvians, but not tainted by association with the Waffen-SS and Latvian Legion. They spoke good German and some English. They were a family unit of two active adults with no dependants. And, above all, they were in the British occupation zone, not the Soviet one, as they would have been had they stayed in the Dresden area.

Nanni, as a native German, citizen of a defeated country, had fewer advantages. In the first place, the fact that she was a German, not a DP, meant that she was ineligible for UNRRA protection, even if she became a refugee. In the second place, living with her parents, sister and brother and working in her father's medical practice on the outskirts of Chemnitz, she found herself in the Soviet zone, 'with all the joy of dealing with the Russians', as she wrote to Mischka in November. She and her sister had thought of fleeing to the American zone, but didn't, probably because of a sense of obligation to their parents and schoolboy brother. Life was hard, with food problems, coal shortages and transport interruptions; it was so cold that Nanni could only play the piano for five minutes at a time. She should have spent more time in Misha's Dresden apartment on Planettastrasse, she wrote sadly, to get in practice for freezing. If only there was some chance to play sport; if only she could continue her studies. It was a brave letter, but *if only* ran through it like a *basso ostinato*. In February, Nanni wrote again several times, mentioning hopes, which were later disappointed, that the Soviets would open the borders of their zone. When the anniversary of the Dresden bombing came round, she reminded Mischka that this was 'Dresden's deathday and our second birthday'. Mischka no doubt remembered this anniversary, but he also remembered that a couple of weeks later Nanni had opted to stay in Chemnitz instead of coming with him to Flensburg. When Olga asked about Nanni, as she periodically did in the months to come, Mischka's responses were reserved and his comments sometimes critical.

If Nanni was still trapped in Chemnitz, Mischka was about to make his escape from Flensburg back into real life, meaning life with a purpose. He was determined to resume his engineering studies. As Misha told me his life story in the 1990s, there was simply a gap—nothing worth reporting—between the events of February and March 1945 (the Dresden bombing and diphtheria episode) and his decision to leave Flensburg in October. The purpose of that October trip was to find a German university to enrol in. This became possible once civilian travel on trains was allowed again and universities reopened. He liked telling the story of this trip: it was back to the Dick Whittington mode, the young man with his knapsack on his back, off on the road again to make his fortune after a brief involuntary diversion. He was a person again, not just a displaced one. He was taking charge of his own destiny. And, on top of that, he was getting a bird's-eye view of Germany, from north to south to west (but not east) as it tentatively emerged from the ashes.

Mischka had done a year or so of electrical engineering in Riga and then another two semesters in Dresden, but he hadn't had time to finish. The universities had all been closed at the time of the Allied occupation in the spring and started reopening in the autumn, Göttingen being the first on 17 September. Starting in mid October, Mischka was scouring 'all the technical universities in the British and American zones', as he wrote to Nanni, to find out which was open and suitable. The chronology is hard to establish from his letters, but he seems to have arrived in Brunswick in the British zone in the last week of October. He reported to Olga that the technical university was in 'passable' condition, and that a professor there, the well-regarded high-frequency expert Leo Pungs, who knew Barkhausen, was willing to take him as a student. Mischka was obviously pleased to have established a rapport with this 'not unknown' (that is, famous) scientist who—although Mischka did not report this—had been a major figure in radar technology during the war. They spoke in Russian, suggesting a degree of personal rapprochement given Mischka's perfect German and the fact that Professor Pungs, though Russian-born, had lived in Germany for the past forty-five years.

For all Mischka's high regard for Professor Barkhausen, returning to Dresden to continue his studies was out of the question because it was in the Soviet zone. The institute had been destroyed in the Dresden bombing of February 1945, as Mischka had observed at a distance too close for comfort. Barkhausen and his wife had taken refuge with relatives outside the city after the bombing, although Mischka probably didn't know this. Unlike many other professors from the Soviet zone, Barkhausen didn't flee west but returned to Dresden in June 1946 to preside over the rebuilding of his institute, and remained there for the rest of his life. But the rebuilding came too late for Mischka, who would in any case not have contemplated relocating to the Soviet occupation zone. At one point, Mischka seems to have considered risking a visit to the East, to see Nanni and pick up a suitcase left with his Dresden landlady, but finally thought better of it.

He was not, however, confining his search for universities to the British zone, where he was registered as a DP. Early in November, he went to inspect Munich in the American zone. He had left some things there as well, evidently on his trip in the winter of 1944–45 and, as on the previous visit, was struck by the beauty of Southern Germany. 'If only the school were better,' he wrote to Olga, 'I would stay there despite everything, because it's beautiful.'

One of my most puzzling discoveries in Misha's papers is an UNRRA attestation to his residence at Zeilsheim DP camp in the American zone. It was dated 15 October 1945 and renewed on 31 December 1946. This is odd, not only because Mischka was never in residence there for any length of time but also because Zeilsheim, on the outskirts of Frankfurt, was specifically a *Jewish* DP camp, visited as such by Eleanor Roosevelt a few months later. The story got stranger when I found his name on a list of foreigners of Latvian citizenship compiled by the Jewish Community of Frankfurt. This 'Michael Danos' was a university student who shared Mischka's birth date (10 January 1922) and former home (Riga) but gave a Frankfurt street address (not the address of the Zeilsheim camp) and claimed to have been born in Pleskau (that is, Pskov, in the Soviet Union). This Michael Danos is not specifically identified as Jewish, but the purpose of the documents appears to have been to register Jewish foreigners. The date of the document was 21 June 1947, a time when Mischka was midway through his studies at Hanover Technical University in the British zone. What was he doing there?

I don't know how to explain Mischka's phantom two-year existence as a Jewish DP in the American zone. But in DP terms, it never hurt to keep your options open. Universities in the American zone were not excluded from his search in the autumn of 1945, and if he had ended up enrolling in one of them, he would have needed to be registered as a DP in that zone. Mind you, the timing is puzzling, since according to his diary, he wasn't even in the Frankfurt area on 15 October, though he passed through a couple of week later. My guess is that on his trip he met some old Riga acquaintances who were in Zeilsheim and signed up with them, just in case.

As for the subsequent maintenance of the registration, I suspect that Simon Mirkin, a survivor of the Jewish family Olga had protected in Riga during the German occupation, was a factor here. Initially brought to Germany by the Germans as a concentration camp prisoner in August 1944, he became a DP in the American zone when the war ended, working in Frankfurt for the Americans and the Jewish refugee aid organisation HIAS (Hebrew Immigrant Aid Society). Mirkin was officially registered as a resident of the Zeilsheim camp, though he actually lived in town. He had made contact with Olga in September 1946, telling her of his own survival and his father's death in Buchenwald, and promising to visit her in Flensburg next month. From that point he became a fixture in the Danos DP world.

Mischka's early November trip to Frankfurt included a stop off in Verden, a small town midway between Hamburg and Hanover. There seems no earthly reason for him to go there except that that was where the family of Mischka's old Riga friend Andrejs Bičevskis had regrouped as refugees after leaving Riga in the autumn of 1944. His diary notes the trip, but not its purpose or outcome (forty years later, he still had the characteristic of overlooking concrete practical details for a lofty overview). In this case, the loftiness had to do with falling in love, something I can scarcely complain about as he did it again with me decades later, but then it was a plane, not a train, and proved less ephemeral.

> I took my seat in the train; I had even reserved ... a place. Then various objects came flying through the compartment window: suitcases, packages, people. And suddenly a girl, extremely pleasant and simpatico. A ray of sunshine in the monotonous grey of the indistinguishable mass of travellers.

Mischka and the girl got to know each other over the ten hours of the trip, and he was still thinking about her four days later, when he wrote his unsent letter to her on the trip back. 'My peace is gone and my unstable equilibrium destroyed,' he noted anxiously. But things were looking up all the same, as he had reconnected with his old friend Andrejs Bičevskis— not, apparently, in Verden, but in Brunswick in the second or third week of November.

The Bičevskis family had had its own adventures. Andrejs had been called up by the Germans in 1943 to serve in one of the so-called 'Latvian' units that fought under German command. His elder brother was also called up and sent to the Russian front, where he was killed almost immediately. Andrejs was luckier. A first-class basketball player, he avoided being sent to the front because his team manager, serving as an officer with the Germans, pulled strings to have him assigned to a shipyard as a labourer. As the Soviet Army approached in 1944, Andrejs's brother-in-law lined up a fisherman to take the family to Sweden, but something went wrong—as with the Danos brothers' attempt—and Andrejs was left stranded. He was rescued again by his old team manager, who sent a motorcycle to pick him up and bring him to his unit, with which he retreated by boat to Germany in October 1944. The next months were spent with the unit, fleeing from the advancing Soviet Army in Eastern Germany, but by May 1945 they had made it to the Elbe, where Andrejs parted company with the Germans, crossed the Elbe with a group of Dutch concentration camp survivors and made his way, mainly on foot, to Verden, in what was by then the British zone of Germany, where he rejoined his sister, brother-in-law and mother.

The Bičevskis family was now living in the 'Rosalie' DP camp, where Mischka signed in as well, another apparent double registration (since he was already registered in Flensburg), which, as a bonus, brought him some new clothes from UNRRA stores. Mrs Bičevskis did his laundry, as he informed his mother. To find a friend again was an enormous relief, though Mischka would never have admitted it; the jaundiced attitude to his fellow men noted by Olga in Flensburg lifted. He even suspended his anti-nationalist principles enough to enjoy himself at a party celebrating the declaration of Latvian independence on 18 November (1918). Marjorie Broadhurst, an English UNRRA official attending the party, took a fancy to Mischka and Andrejs—it was their 'friendship for one another' that appealed to her, she wrote later, 'and, of course, your determination to get on'. They liked her too. 'She wasn't a deep person,' Mischka later wrote, 'but just positive and decent and even quite admirable.' She figures in Mischka's story, albeit briefly, as virtually the only occupation official who, in his perception, treated him like a human being.

Mischka and Andrejs both applied to the Brunswick Technical University, which was not yet in operation but was supposed to be opening soon. In the process, they met up with another old friend from Riga, Boris Bogdanovs. Mischka quickly located a newly opened sports hall and made himself useful as 'chief referee', though in what branch of sport I don't know. He also signed up, perhaps under the Bičevskis influence, with the Latvian committee in Germany, identifying his residence as Brunswick; his name as Michaels Danos (either a typo or an Anglo-Latvian compromise, 's' being the suffix for male names in Latvian); his profession as student; and his citizenship as Latvian.

Mischka and his friends were in the first wave of DP students clamouring to enter German universities as they reopened, and it took the authorities a while to regularise the situation. It wasn't until the summer of 1946 that UNRRA and the zonal authorities established some centralised control, forbidding DPs to apply except via UNRRA, banning inter-zonal movement except in extraordinary circumstances and doing their best to 'prevent flow of persons without authority into University towns' in the British zone. But by that time they had forced the Germans to accept a very generous quota of 10 per cent of all university enrolments for DPs (who were only about 1 per cent of population in the British zone) and had put them in the same rations category as administrative workers.

In the end, Brunswick didn't take Mischka and his friends, but nearby Hanover, which reopened in early January 1946, did; he and Bičevskis must have been among the first DP students to enrol. 'I am now living in Hanover,' Mischka wrote laconically to his mother on 15 January 1946:

I have finally been admitted. To Hanover [Technical University]. I like it very much here. Only I haven't yet got a permanent place to live … Hanover is a bigger city [than Brunswick]. Quite kaput. The technical university is also quite kaput. The whole organisation of my life is now somewhat thrown into confusion by this unexpected change.

Then, on 23 January, came a postcard about his 'strangely hard-working mood, which for the present threatens not to lessen'. This awkward circumlocution meant he was pleased with himself. The card gave Olga no practical information at all about his circumstances but meditated on his own capacity for single-minded concentration on a particular scientific question, regardless of contingent circumstances. He was 'surprised in the highest degree' by this burst of intellectual energy, noting with satisfaction that he was defying the old saw that in order to graduate from university, 'one must treat no issue or problem as anything but superficial, and do nothing except work assignments and protocols'.

Olga was a loving mother who believed in Mischka's genius, but even so, she must have been relieved when a more informative letter followed:

I am now living in Hanover. I will be studying here from now on at the technical university. Things are going very well, and it is also very interesting in that here the students are given a great deal of freedom and independence about doing measurements in the laboratory—probably the greatest in Germany. Thus I can understand why this TU is regarded as notoriously difficult. But it is a real joy to work here, and it is actually very easy if one isn't afraid to do some thinking. And then there is an electrotechnical specialist here who is really worth listening to …

On 12 January, Mischka received an identity card signed by the university rector in the name of 'Michael Danos. Student in the electrotechnical faculty, from Flensburg. Latvian citizenship.' So he was a student again, someone with a place and function in the world. Not on his own, as he had been in Dresden, but with a bunch of old friends around him (another of his old Riga circle, Dailonis Stauvers, soon showed up, along with Mārtiņ Kregŝde, in addition to Bičevskis and Bogdanovs). Mischka's university card didn't even identify him as a DP.

8

Olga, from Flensburg to Fulda

Olga with her sculptures (*Miami Herald*, 27 June 1954). The figurines at left and centre are probably earlier work, done in Germany; the bust at right, made in the early 1950s in the United States, is of her son Arpad.

O NE of the advantages of being a DP was that you didn't have to do anything: UNRRA, or later the International Refugee Organization (IRO), would look after you. Conversely, one of the disadvantages of being a DP was that there was nothing much to do. Olga was not someone to sit around with folded hands, so she looked for an occupation.

She started off, like any other educated, middle-class DP with artistic interests, thinking along cultural lines. She wrote a few poems, translated some fairytales and even once stood in for her sister Mary as a singer at a concert in Hamburg. Mary, who had survived the Nazi concentration camp at Ravensbrück and was living in a DP camp in Geesthacht, not far from Hamburg, had more serious professional intent as a singer: by the end of the 1940s, she seems to have re-established herself as a recitalist on the boundary of folk and art music. But Olga didn't see herself as a professional musician after so long away from singing, and her artistic activities were all make-work within the confines of the DP community. With the encouragement and financial support of the occupation authorities, DP exhibitions, DP journals, DP concerts and even DP universities flourished—but they were hothouse plants, catering to small, national DP clienteles, and essentially amateur, even when the artists and scholars involved were former professionals.

When the British zonal authorities sent round a questionnaire on DPs' former occupations and their trade and professional skills, Olga, with DP cunning, 'was silent about her tailoring capacities but listed my six languages', presumably in the hope that UNRRA would throw translating opportunities her way. But she was already investigating the possibility of re-establishing her tailoring workshop. Her future daughter-in-law, Helga Heimers, remembered Olga as a person with tremendous flair and energy for getting things started, though not so good on routine follow-up. The former qualities are evident as she bustled around setting herself up in tailoring. 'As you know,' she wrote cheerfully to Mischka, 'I have no money. But, as you also know, that is no big obstacle.'

The British started encouraging DPs to work from the spring of 1946, even trying unsuccessfully to make it mandatory. But the proportion of DPs with jobs remained low, and of those who worked, most had jobs within the camps, working for UNRRA. Olga's idea of setting up her own business *outside* the camps was so unusual that UNRRA's labour statistics for DPs didn't even have such a category.

It was complicated setting up a business as a DP. You needed to have German trade credentials (*Meisterbrief*), which DPs generally didn't possess. Olga was in a better position than most, in that she had gone through some of these hoops already in 1944, when she moved her business from Riga to the Sudetenland. 'I hope to keep the membership in the Artisan List that I already had in Sudetenland,' she wrote to Mischka, although unfortunately she had left her Riga Artisan Card there. Mischka got regular bulletins on her business activities. 'Things are still going quite bumpily with the workshop,' she told him in March 1946. 'In the first place with workers: there are not many of them, and those that are available are bad.' By the end of April 1946, however, she had two workers and an apprentice, and was anticipating adding to her staff.

At this point, the enterprise was evidently still based in a DP camp, probably the Geesthacht camp where Mary lived, whose UNRRA director had offered help and the promise of space. But Olga was already thinking of bigger things. 'A workshop in Flensburg is in prospect,' she wrote, 'and I will also get a workplace in Hamburg.' By late May, possibly earlier, Olga had moved her residence to central Flensburg (Jürgenstrasse 4), where she planned to set up the workshop, and wrote to Mischka that he should come and visit—'I have a good piano at home' (presumably she was a tenant and the piano was the landlady's). She was to have two rooms, one of them for the workshop, and 'am bringing two [sewing-] machines from the camp. Two very lazy women workers are already working, and on 1 June another three women, hopefully better workers, are coming on board.'

Her financial situation was precarious, and in retrospect she confessed a certain degree of anxiety: 'For a long time I was sitting here without a penny. I thought that if I died, there would be nothing to bury me with. But now things are going better ... Customers are taking their things [and presumably paying for them].' Olga, accordingly, was once again on a high. In a cheeky postscript to a July letter to Mischka, she suggested, 'If I have a workshop in both places [Hamburg and Flensburg], I should get a car too, don't you think?'

But the roller-coaster continued, and a month or so later she was writing that while she was still negotiating with UNRRA and the Hamburg authorities for the necessary permissions,

> it's not working out with the workshop. Now I have workers, I feed them, [but] everything is collapsing because I can only become a 'free-liver' [that is, a registered DP living outside the camps] if I get the workshop approval, and that is something no DP has done so far.

Part of the problem was living in the British occupation zone, which was more restrictive of small businesses than the American one. 'Should I go to the American zone?' Olga wrote to Mischka. But if she went there to establish a business, that meant leaving UNRRA care and giving up her status as a DP. This move—officially described as being 'discharged on to the German economy'—was still uncommon and purely voluntary as of the autumn of 1946, although the next year the British authorities started to encourage it to reduce the numbers in their care. It was a risk, and Olga wrote that she was at her 'wits' end, waiting for a decision to come of itself'. But by mid September, she had decided. She would give up her DP status and move out of the British zone in order to establish her tailoring business in the American zone.

This might have seemed a momentous decision, but even before it was made, the volatile Olga seemed to have lost interest. She was now 'almost certain to leave UNRRA', she informed Mischka in mid August, but 'that's not the most important thing'. The most important thing was that she was now launching a new career as a sculptor.

Back in the 1920s in Italy and later in Riga, Olga had dabbled in sculpture. Now she had taken it up again, making little porcelain figurines, some of secular subjects ('The Dancer'), others religious (a Pietà, a Madonna and a St Antony). This was becoming a passion, as she told Mischka in July: 'Can you believe it, my zeal for modelling is still to the fore. It's even as if I *have* to do it …' Early reactions from friends and acquaintances were mixed. One thought she shouldn't be making religious figures given that she was not a believer. Another thought that one of her little figures looked like a naked Frederick the Great, evidently not a compliment as she forthwith decapitated it, unfortunately breaking the torso and an arm in the process.

But then the wonderful moment of first recognition arrived. It came from a certain Dr Richter, 'whose father was a well-known sculptor in Dresden'. Having seen her figurines, he surprised her by asking to look at them again: 'After he had examined them in silence for a long time, he said, a bit abashed: "I admire and envy your muse. What other more famous sculptors wrestle with, you achieve easily. The last figure is really Greek …"' Olga felt that she had finally found her artistic vocation. 'It looks possible that a new period in my life is opening,' she wrote enthusiastically to Mischka.

On the more mundane level, she had to get the move to the American zone organised. Her chosen destination was Fulda, 100 kilometres or so north of Frankfurt in the state of Hesse. This was almost certainly because Simon Mirkin, her

Jewish protégé from Riga, had offered her a place to live there. Mirkin, who had survived the Riga ghetto and the Stutthof concentration camp to become a DP in the American zone, was grateful to Olga for saving his family in the early years of the war; in his first postwar letter to her, he related his father's last words before their separation (when Boris Mirkin was sent off to Buchenwald, where he died on 19 February 1945): 'My son, when some day we are freed, we must meet up at Frau Danos's house in Riga.' Working as an interpreter for HIAS and the US Army, Mirkin had substantially better rations and access to goods than the Danoses had in the British zone, and their correspondence in subsequent months periodically mentions food and clothing he had sent them. But, best of all, Mirkin seems to have owned a house in Fulda, presumably inherited from his businessman father. This house, at Florengasse 53, was his registered address as a DP until his departure for the United States early in 1947. After Olga moved to Fulda in the winter of 1946–47, it was to become both her residence and the address of her tailoring shop, now upgraded to the Olga Danos 'Fashion Salon, Bespoke Clothing to Your Own Pattern'.

But it wasn't the tailoring/fashion business that preoccupied Olga that winter—a time of record-breaking cold, though Olga never mentioned that in her letters and Mischka only in passing. Her budding career as a sculptor was the first thing on her mind. Shortly after arriving in Fulda, she wrote the most excited and buoyant of all her letters to Mischka about the remarkable way her sculpture prospects had taken off. She had 'plucked up courage' to call in at an art dealer's and offer to sell him one of her figurines for 250 marks. He agreed to buy it and gave her an introduction to a porcelain factory where she could get her figurines fired. As she walked home, an extraordinary thing happened, a bolt from the blue:

> [The dealer] appeared at my side, very animated, and wanted to talk to me again, this very day, even though it was late … He wanted to know how many [figurines] I could give him, and in what time frame. He would take everything from me, whether it was heads, arks or costumes. He offered to arrange exhibitions in Frankfurt, Munich and other places, and asked if I would also take official orders, whether I used a model, if there was anything else particular I wanted.

On his insistence, she went to the porcelain factory, where he showed her figurines to a group of about twenty people, including his son and the master artisan, who all raved about their artistry and tried to persuade her to work for them.

> They would put an atelier at my disposal; I could come and go when I want to, can produce one figurine in a week or five—it doesn't matter … It was very hard to stay calm and relaxed. They wanted me to sign a contract immediately. I said I had to think it over and would come back next week. But the director was to come in the next day, so I said all right. Could you come at 10? Yes, I can do that …

Olga was astonished, exhilarated and a bit frightened at the speed with which events were unfolding. She wondered if the dealer could have fallen in love with her, in a *coup de foudre*, since she couldn't imagine that 'the dead figurines could have such an impact'. (In a later letter, she wrote ironically of her disappointment in finding that it was her figurines he had fallen for, not her.) It's at this point that the reader of their correspondence becomes aware that something had shifted in their relationship. Mischka, now in his twenty-fourth year, seemed to have gained in authority, while Olga's requests for his advice had not only become more frequent but acquired an almost deferential tone. 'What will I do?' she wrote apropos of her negotiations with the art dealer about her figurines. She didn't understand half the legal language in the contract— terms like 'retouching', 'reproduction' and 'author's rights'. 'I'm afraid of making a fool of myself. Mischi, if only you were here!'

Mischka replied in measured and weighty terms, advising caution in business dealings:

On author's rights and so on, naturally you must establish clarity. In a restrained way you must also tell them what you want to get out of it, if others are making money out of you. I hope you didn't let yourself be caught unawares and make commitments … A name is also something to be paid for.

In the same rather ponderous, 'grown-up' tone, he encouraged her to value her art rightly, neither too high nor too low, and recognise that artistic success comes through 'mastery of materials' (in other words, no careless or slipshod work).

No doubt this was part of a genuine, spontaneous readjustment of relations as Mischka became fully adult. But it's also possible that the savvy and self-aware Olga was not just registering an adjustment but consciously encouraging it—in a sense tutoring him in his new role. In the early months of 1947, both of them seem to have been reflecting upon their relationship and even, uncharacteristically, discussing it overtly. Olga's special place in Mischka's heart had been evident before—for example, in the reflection in his diary that 'The highest thing in the world is a mother's love'. But in March 1947, he raised the question in a letter to her that he thought important enough to copy into his diary:

Dear Mama! It is a strange thing. When I leave you, I always feel bad because I have behaved ungraciously. And another strange thing: I am careful not to let any trace of warmth come into my voice and behaviour. So I jump to the other extreme. Why is this? Why do I put up these barriers? Even writing the salutation of a letter [to you] means overcoming some resistance each time. And yet you are the only Complete Person that I know. Only Arpad [his brother] can compete. Also you are not uncongenial to me ...

After a digression into other topics, including the failure of girls of his own age to live up to his ideal, he returns to the question of Olga: 'Your only "fault" is a lack of precision. That is the only thing that in the course of decades I have been able to observe.' The letter concludes with some elaborate circumlocutions about ideal types of women that I take to be a typically roundabout way of suggesting that Olga came close to his own ideal type.

Many mothers would have blanched at the difficulties of replying to the text, let alone the subtext, of such a letter, but Olga was up to the task:

My dear Mischutka! You don't need to feel bad when you leave me. I know exactly how you feel about me, much better than you express it. I respond to your inner attitude. I think that with regard to your behaviour to me, it's my own fault, that is, the fault of how I brought you up [that is, with the emotional distance discussed above] ... Now that unsentimental way of behaving towards each other has become internalised, and we keep it up, even as we know what we are to each other.

Olga's response continued with a cheerful reassurance that she could always see through him anyway. It was always quite obvious to her, from various little 'signs that you are not conscious of', how he really felt at a given moment about her or things in general. She wouldn't tell him what these signs were 'so that you don't hide them'. But the implied comparison with other women set off some alarm bells. She didn't like his tendency to compare his girlfriends with some 'ideal type' and then find them wanting, she wrote brusquely. He 'shouldn't try playing this kind of theatre with your wife, when you have one. That can have bad consequences, and deservedly.'

Adding a bit of introspection of her own in a subsequent letter, Olga reflected on her upbringing of her sons, particularly her efforts to maintain some emotional distance:

> I didn't shower you with tenderness, but treated you in a comradely fashion. I never kissed any of you on the mouth, always only on the eyes. When you were still little, you were for me, I could almost say, even if it's not quite right … sacred, [meaning] that one instinctively feared to profane. Later I intentionally did nothing, I was afraid of awakening your sensuality as young boys too soon.

Whether Olga had succeeded in her aim of discouraging her sons from falling in love with her is open to debate. She may have been more successful in bringing them up to be proud, with a strong sense of their own dignity: 'I never asked you [her sons] to beg pardon—politely saying sorry is something else. It could make me really angry if Iantschi [Jan] did this on his own initiative, and [I] forbade him to do it.' Mischka didn't need instruction on these lines. Olga might tease him in her letters about being a bad correspondent ('Write soon, dear lazybones!'), but he never started his replies with the conventional apology. I was interested to learn of Olga's part in developing a trait in Misha that was very familiar to me, but hitherto a bit puzzling. Misha was generally an easygoing man, but he never apologised for anything, large or small. The reflex 'Oh, sorry' that punctuates most people's everyday interactions was quite absent from his. If he saw that he had done something that annoyed me, he would, without comment, simply avoid repeating it.

At this period, Olga was undoubtedly the most important person in Mischka's life, and he in Olga's. That, of course, didn't mean that they lacked separate private lives. Mischka often wrote to Olga about his; she sometimes wrote (but more briefly and in less confessional vein) to Mischka about hers. When describing business relations with men, she might indicate that business did not exclude flirtation, on one or both sides. She would occasionally give an ironic report of a suitor, like the Englishman (probably an officer with the military government or UNRRA staffer) whose love letters kept comparing her to other women, always with the conclusion 'You are so different, so different' (Olga quoted this phrase in English).

When Olga's two German admirers from Riga, Herren von Koelln and Seeliger, showed up again in Germany, Olga passed on the information to Mischka. Von Koelln (or Koellner) was in Wiesbaden and had got a job as a hotel porter. Paul Seeliger, the former commandant, had resurfaced in Flensburg, making contact not only with Olga but also with Mirkin, his former charge in the ghetto. Mischka met Seeliger too, and later told me that the former camp commandant had then

> already been imprisoned, de-nazified and released; the latter in a large measure because of the statements of support from some Jews of the Riga ghetto who had survived and made it to New York—they had on their own initiative sent letters about Seeliger to the de-nazification authorities in Germany.

While there is a letter in Olga's papers that strongly suggests that she and Seeliger had an affair at some point (whether in Riga or in Germany is not clear), no hint of this appears in Olga's and Mischka's correspondence. In other words, she would tell him about suitors she was not interested in, but not those she was. Mischka, for his part, either did not know or did not choose to know about any lovers in Olga's life.

Olga felt the loss of her Riga family keenly. Two of her sons, as well as her ex-husband, were trapped in the Soviet Union, with its closed borders and restricted contact with the outside world. She knew through the DP grapevine of Arpad Jr's arrest and banishment to Gulag and couldn't bear to think what might be happening to him. Even with Mischka with her in Germany and Jan probably relatively safe in Riga, she wrote in her diary that 'life seems to have lost much of its point for me':

> What strange fate has left me making my way in the world like a gypsy. Like a comedian, a buffoon. Smiling and smiling. Very often merry, just as often sad, but always smiling … Once I had a family. Five people, for whom I was the fulcrum. For these people I learnt to bear hard things lightly. For them I learnt to have an eternal smile. And now I am alone …

Olga's sentiments, as expressed in her diary, often have a theatrical quality. When she wrote to Mischka, the tone was less exalted but the sense of loss equally strong: 'Almost every night I dream of Arpad or Ianschi, sometimes also of Papa.' She had an 'out-of-control yearning' to see her two absent sons and was making 'impossible plans' to go to Riga herself, she told Mischka in January 1946. These plans did indeed seem impossible, given the closed border. But Olga was always a spinner of schemes, and this one surely tapped into the romantic sense of herself that is central in the diary—no doubt she knew the 'heroic exploit' genre of émigré memoir exemplified by Princess Volkonsky's story of crossing the border in disguise after the Russian Revolution to snatch her husband from the clutches of the Cheka. Olga was still thinking about such an exploit several months later. 'Do you know, Mi, that I am giving serious consideration to fight[ing] my way through to Riga. But first I have to make sure of the Swedish side. I have got things underway with the Swedish church in Hamburg.' (What this reference means is unclear, but presumably the Swedes had established connections in Latvia, probably covert.)

When international postal service reopened for civilians in Germany in April 1946, Olga and her sister Mary both wrote to Sweden and Riga, hoping to find or get news of Arpad and Jan. Some news came in six months later—a postcard to Mary from the Jewish neighbours who had lived in the apartment below hers in Riga, had spent the war in Russia and had now returned. The neighbours were mainly concerned to recover furniture from their apartment that had been moved to Mary's after they left, but they had got Mary's address from Arpad Sr—which meant not only that he was still alive, probably living in the old Danos apartment in the same house as Mary's, but also that he had information about their whereabouts. This must have been a blow to Olga's increasingly fond recollections of her ex-husband: he could have got in touch, or at least sent a message, but he hadn't. 'Probably he can't write,' she commented when passing on the news to Mischka. Actually it seems that Arpad Sr had fallen in love with a young singing pupil and planned to marry her. But Olga, of course, didn't know that.

Since she started to keep her diary in the early 1920s, Olga had always regarded it as 'the book of my marriage'. In an entry in the spring of 1946, she expanded this definition to make it 'the book of my marriage that no longer exists, of my family that has been destroyed':

> I can't help thinking of my poor awkward old husband. I see him always sitting in front of the radio, straining his ears, or reading a book. I haven't made any of the people who loved me happy. My poor husband. Probably he still doesn't understand why I left him.

She thought of Arpad Jr ('my best friend') too; and with the approach of St John's Day (Johannistag)—in Germany a workday like any other, but in Latvia a holiday—she thought of Jan: 'Oh, Jantschi! Are you still alive … Jantschi! … Where are you, my darling? In Latvia? … Is Balva with you? Are you in Russia? Siberia? Are you a soldier? Oh, Jantschi!'

Olga kept trying to make contact with her son and ex-husband in Riga through any means available. In March 1947, a strange woman knocked on her door in Fulda, looking for shelter for the night. She turned out to be a DP preparing to repatriate to Latvia and promised to try to find news of the Danos family. 'Perhaps she will do it. I am both happy and fearful at the prospect.'

Then, in 1948, out of the blue, a letter came from Arpad Jr. He said he was back in Riga (though without explicit reference to his Gulag spell and release) and working for the time being as a labourer on bridge construction. He probably also gave the news that Jan and his wife Balva now had a child, since Olga learnt of it at about this time. Reassuring though this was, his letter caused Olga and Mischka as much anxiety as relief.

The letter's text, in Latvian, has unfortunately not been preserved; all we have is some worried correspondence between Olga and Mischka that includes quotations, whose underlying meaning they were trying to understand. They were worried, in the first place, because they suspected that Arpad had been encouraged or even forced by the Soviet authorities to write the letter and, in the second place, because the letter evidently asked them to come home. Such letters were often sent to émigré relatives—some personal, some dictated and formal, and others in between—because the Soviet state, as well as their families, wanted them back. They knew Arpad had written the letter because they recognised his handwriting, but a close analysis of his corrections suggested that he had a censor, real or imagined, breathing down his neck. Mischka referred to the letter as having the character of an 'article' rather than a personal communication, which suggests that Arpad had not only written in an official style but may also have expressed some conventional Soviet-patriotic sentiments. The Arpad they knew had not been pro-Soviet, though who knew what Gulag had done to him.

In fact, Gulag had left Arpad damaged, the result (so the later family story went) of his having intervened in a fight to protect a woman and been badly beaten up for his pains. It would not have been unlike the Arpad I knew decades later to have written something like an 'article' to his family, since one of the characteristics of his condition, which seemed to me to be a kind of autism, was precisely his habit of addressing people as if reading out an official text rather than having a personal conversation. The first time I met Arpad, in the early 1990s, he almost ignored Misha, although he hadn't seen him for years, and thrust on me, as a Russian reader, an elaborate Russian typescript of a draft law for the reform of marriage, the topic that was currently obsessing him. It was beautifully done, both in terms of style and presentation, and if Arpad hadn't said he was the author, I could have accepted it as a genuine product of the Soviet Union's utopian moment back in the 1920s. But an 'article' obviously wasn't what Mischka and Olga expected from Arpad in 1948.

The Soviets were eager to repatriate their citizens, including those like the Danoses and other residents of the Baltic states whose citizenship was very recent and tenuous. But Soviet repatriation had a bad reputation in the West because of the forcible return of some millions of former POWs and other DPs in the immediate aftermath of the war. Now the Soviets were no longer forcing people to repatriate (with individual exceptions when their hush-hush security services captured suspected war criminals and collaborators in Europe), but the DP community and the Western Allies remained highly suspicious, fearing that even voluntary repatriates would be arrested on their return. Olga's unexpected repatriating visitor the previous year was one of a comparatively small number of DPs who took up the Soviet invitation.

Mischka and Olga had no intention of going back to Riga, but they were worried that their failure to do so might cause trouble for Arpad, all the more because of his vulnerability as an ex-prisoner. Arpad's letter urged them to write, as well as urging them to return, but they were not sure if this should be read at face value or, Aesopianly, as its opposite. The issue was whether they should reply and, if so, what they should say. 'It's clear that one must write,' Mischka wrote to Olga. 'In my opinion the most important thing is that Arpad knows that we have received his news, so that he is not unnecessarily worried. Then we will see how things go. It must be better [for Arpad] to receive as little mail as possible from abroad.' Olga did in fact write, probably twice, but no further letters came from Riga, and she later felt guilty about having taken the bait in case it had caused trouble for her sons.

Mischka's advice was expanded in a later letter, after he had consulted his Latvian student friends Bičevskis and Stauvers.

They thought 'it wouldn't hurt to write a letter saying something like that we would be happy to return, but have to stay
here for a while'. In other words, to convey the idea that they
were not planning immediate repatriation without explicitly
ruling it out, so that Arpad couldn't be blamed for having
anti-Soviet relatives. Only the minimum of information about
themselves should be offered; after all, Arpad knew they had
survived. 'Exact information on my doings is not appropriate,'
Mischka wrote sternly to Olga. 'And not about yours either.'

In the same year, Olga received worse news from Riga:
her husband, Arpad Sr, had died. The family information on
this is that Arpad's marriage plans had fallen through, and
after the singing pupil had left the city, he started neglecting
his health and not taking insulin for his diabetes. The woman
then changed her mind and came back to Riga, but it was too
late: he was dead. Jan and Arpad attended the funeral. But
this backstory was probably unknown to Olga and Mischka for
another decade, when correspondence from within the Soviet
Union became easier and Jan and Arpad Jr made contact. It
is not clear exactly when Arpad Sr died, but the news had
reached Olga and Mischka by June 1948.

Unlike Olga, Mischka gave little conscious thought to the
family back in Riga, although a diary entry in 1945 notes that
he often dreamt of them. His father's death was a trauma that
he quickly and rigorously suppressed. I thought at first that it
went totally unmentioned in his correspondence and diary but
then realised that it must be what he was writing about in two
enigmatic entries reporting some unidentified shocking news
in the summer of 1948:

It is remarkable, but probably commonplace [this word
in English] that it seemed somehow empty of content, it
doesn't take root in my consciousness; it is really as if I

haven't grasped it. That 'no longer existing' is somehow so alien, calling forth something like fear, a sense of pure strangeness. Since Herr W [his landlord] has cheerfully turned the radio on, I absolutely can't concentrate anymore.

This unwillingness to state the fact of a death, or even to use the word, remained characteristic of him throughout his life: 'he ain't no more' was the odd way he would inform me in the 1990s that someone he knew was dead, and one felt that even that was being dragged out of him. The next day, 6 June 1948, he made another entry, even more clearly indicating the depths of his distress: 'I see myself forced to do again something I already did once, that is again to go so far as to seek an analysis, although at the moment I don't feel myself capable of it'. When or where this earlier analysis, evidently by a psychologist or psychoanalyst, took place is unknown, but Misha all his life had a respect for the discipline that I found surprising (and wrongly, as I now see, attributed to the influence of American popular culture in the 1950s). I doubt, also, that he carried out the analysis plan on this occasion, as if he had, it would probably have been mentioned when he started having panic attacks the following year. Insofar as I can make sense of the next sentences of the second diary entry, he thought news of his father's death had had a 'catalytic effect' that might enable him, in the course of an analysis, to bring his feelings to the surface and make it possible for him to express them. Yet even half a century later, Misha spoke only unwillingly and tensely about his father's death.

Olga probably told Mischka of the death face to face; at any rate, there is no mention of it in their surviving correspondence, other than a sad reference in a letter from her in the summer. Her main confidant about the death was her diary.

She recorded the news on 2 April 1948, noting that this would be the last entry in 'the book of her marriage':

> I can scarcely see for tears, but I have a duty to write in it. You, to whom the highest feelings of my life belong, lie under the earth. Dead, like my mother, without my being able to lighten their last hours. No, much worse, abandoned by me, left alone, unhappy. I sob, as I have heard women sob, take myself in hand and then burst out in a long loud sob. Now that I have written it out, I am calm. I will not weep any more. All the tears of my life have now been wept for you, and for me, I again wept at your death as I wept often in so many pages of this book. The last time I saw you was as the ship sailed away … As the ship turned, I came to the prow and saw you walking away. Slowly like an old man, supporting yourself with a stick. You didn't turn round again, and I watched as step by step, slowly, tired, you walked and disappeared round the corner. You went home, quite alone, to remain quite alone … That hurts so deeply, even though I had long ago inwardly freed myself from you … I feel so tired of life, so old. Arpad is dead.

In fact, it was not quite the last entry. Four pages were left in the diary, and for her husband's birthday in May, Olga filled them with a postscript, beginning with a careful transcription of Heinrich Heine's lyric 'Im wunderschönen Monat Mai' ('In the Wonderful Month of May'), which Robert Schumann had set to music. It was the song Arpad had sung when they had first met and he had singled her out as his future bride. On that occasion, his friend had told her that if she married him, she would need courage. Now, she wrote, 'that life, requiring too much courage, is now [over]. And in the end I came to the end of it too. The end of my courage.'

In summation, Olga offered a poetic eulogy:

Somewhere stands a hill. Perhaps your daughter-in-law—
our daughter-in-law—has planted some flowers. Perhaps it
is forgotten, since time has forgotten you ...

'And that is all.' So sounds the last of my thoughts
devoted to you. The page lies before me. Your hand wrote
those lines. And now it's impossible to grasp that this hand
is no more.

Arpad Danos, Paul Sakss and their five children (late 1920s). In the back row, from left, are Ariadna Sakss, Vera (friend of Olga's), Arpad Danos Sr, wife of Professor Bamburg (no information on the Bamburgs, who are presumably friends of the adults), Paul Sakss and Professor Bamburg. In the front row, from left, are Michael, Jan and Arpad Danos, and Jogita Sakss.

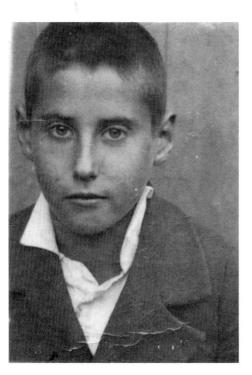

Michael Danos, aged ten, 1932.

Jogita, Mary and Ariadna Sakss, early 1930s.

Riga: revelry on the beach, 4 July 1943. Misha is kneeling on the right.

Olga and Michael Danos in Riga, early 1940s. I like to think that Olga is wearing one of her own fashion creations.

Michael Danos, aged twenty-one, 1943.

Michael Danos, pole vaulting, early 1940s.

Olga at the wedding of Michael Danos and Helga Heimers, Hanover, 1949. Olga is in a dress of her own design; a very decorous Heimers aunt is standing behind her.

Michael and Helga Danos at 31 Rohrbacher Street, Heidelberg, circa 1949. Helga and Mischka sit on either side of the artful arrangement of branches with which they decorated their new apartment.

Michael and Helga Danos in bed with Stauvers, Heidelberg, circa 1950. On the bed is the 'beautiful big down quilt' that Mischka and Helga wanted to take to America. Photograph by Dailonis Stauvers.

Hans Jensen with Maria Meyer, early 1950s.

Michael Danos and Helmut Steinwedel at the blackboard, Heidelberg, circa 1950. Mischka is on the left. Steinwedel, on the right, was a student of Jensen's who was both a guest at Mischka and Helga's first dinner party and the co-author of Mischka's first published article.

Ariadna Sakss with her children, 29 July 1956. The children are Neraida (aged nine), Egons (six) and Paulis (three). This photograph was enclosed by Ariadna in a letter to Olga re-establishing contact after her return to Riga from exile in the Soviet Union.

Olga with Johanna and Tamara Danos, 1956.

Olga with two-year-old Johanna Danos and Martha Heimers, Florida, 1955. The photograph has details written on the back by Martha Heimers.

Michael Danos, with daughter Johanna under his arm, mid 1950s.

Michael Danos and myself, Washington, DC, 1996. I think the turbulent water is the C&O Canal (usually very calm) near our house in Washington, with the Potomac River behind. It was probably taken during the 1996 floods. Photograph by David Fitzpatrick.

9

Student in Hanover

Student friends in Hanover, outside the flying school
(c. 1947): from left, Dailonis Stauvers, Boris Bogdanovs,
Andrejs Bičevskis and Mischka.

IN the photograph taken outside the flying school that was
their official residence as displaced persons, Mischka and
three fellow students, friends from Riga days, look on top
of the world. They are good-looking, upstanding, even well
dressed; who would think they were DPs? Bičevskis had happy
memories of their student days in Hanover. He and Mischka
and their friends hung out together and told a lot of jokes,
Bičevskis told me; they were committed to not taking life too
seriously. They didn't dwell on the past or think about what
had been lost during the war. They were enjoying the present
and looking forward to the future.

At first glance, that doesn't seem much like the Misha I knew, who took life seriously and, moreover, felt this was a human obligation. It isn't exactly the Mischka reflected in the correspondence and diaries of the Hanover period either. There is a lot of philosophical musing in these documents, and a lot of anxiety—about his studies, his health, his girlfriends—which is sometimes addressed in oblique philosophical terms. And yet I can more or less believe in the Bičevskis version. Along with the essentially serious Misha, there was always another Misha around, someone who enjoyed company and flourished in it. It can't have hurt, back in Hanover with his Riga friends, that he was the best-looking of the bunch (surely this is an objective judgement, not just my prejudice) as well as the brightest. That was the person his first wife, Helga, remembers meeting in 1948. Half a century later, I knew him too: the impromptu Misha, who was always ready to go out to celebrate nothing in particular or, if we stayed home, might dance me round the dining room table on the way to make dinner. Very early in our acquaintance, before I knew all this about him, I was surprised to find that Misha was in his element at parties, 'drifting around', as he would put it, with a relaxed half-smile on his lips, talking easily to everyone (or at least everyone but any *Prominenz* or self-important person who happened to be present, to whom he would also talk, but in a more challenging and less friendly way).

Misha kept many photos from the Hanover period, small, unlabelled black-and-white shots of him out on country walks with various unidentified girls, in groups at the university, running and pole vaulting at sporting meets. We can even document the fact that Mischka, as well as Misha, was capable of clowning around, because there are some photographs of that as well. Of course, the face we present for a casual snapshot with friends on a day out is different from that of the diarist, writing alone in the evening, and who knows which face is the 'real' one. In the photos, unlike the diaries of this period, Mischka comes across as happy.

Hanover in 1946 was not everyone's idea of an earthly paradise. The British zone was the most highly populated in Germany and had contained much of Germany's industry. But by the end of the war, its industry was largely destroyed and its towns devastated by bombing and flooded with refugees. The region's own agriculture was nowhere near strong enough to feed the influx, and the supply of agricultural products from other zones was unreliable to say the least. In the cold winter of 1946–47, the food crisis in the British zone's cities, including Hanover, was bad enough to produce strikes and street protests that continued into the spring.

Hanover itself had been a 'disaster zone' when Allied troops first entered it in the spring of 1945, looking 'like a wound in the earth rather than a city', as one British war correspondent remembered: 'I could not recognize anywhere: whole streets had disappeared, and squares and gardens with them, covered over in piles of brick and stone and mortar.' Allied bombing had levelled the centre of the city and destroyed or severely damaged most of the houses, as well as knocking out electricity, water and sewage systems. When the British established their occupation regime, Mischka was not the only person to find them arrogant. 'They were the new *Herrenvolk* and lived a life tantamount to apartheid,' a historian writes. 'The officers kept separate from the men, the Army from the Control Commission, and everyone from the Germans.'

The British approach to the universities, as they gradually reopened between the autumn of 1945 and the spring of 1946, was relatively laissez-faire. Denazification kept some professors in limbo for a while, but the technical universities (*Technische Hochschulen*) were less affected than the universities proper.

As for the student body, Wehrmacht veterans came flooding back into the universities, causing the British anxiety about rising Nazi sentiments. To counteract this, and punish the Germans, the Allies required that German universities accept a DP contingent of up to 10 per cent of the new enrolment in 1946. This was a huge target, never reached and soon lowered, but it served its purpose for the fairly small group of DPs like Mischka and his friends who were actually qualified for university study.

University students were the most privileged of DPs. They were mainly 'free-livers', which meant that although they were registered in a DP camp, they actually lived elsewhere, usually in town. ('Free-livers' is UNRRA's terminology; it was a category of DPs for whom they remained responsible but about whom they knew very little.) Living *privat*, which is what Olga calls it in her letter, meant renting a room from a landlady, often a war widow, and paying in cigarettes (the DP cigarette ration was four packs a month, according to Stauvers's recollection; cigarettes were essentially currency in Germany in the period before the *Währungsreform* in 1947). Student lodgers would also be expected to help with heavy lifting round the house, and also sometimes contributed food from their DP rations, which their landlady would cook. Landladies often had books, pianos and pretty daughters. This was the way Misha had lived as a student in Dresden in 1944, and the way he and his friends lived as students in Hanover from the beginning of 1946.

There were more than a thousand DP students from the Baltic states in German universities in the British zone in 1946–47, with Latvians the largest group, probably in the range of 650–750. Hanover Technical University had more than a hundred DP students among its total of more than three thousand students, perhaps forty of them Latvians. Fifteen of them—including Mischka and his friends Stauvers, Bičevskis, Bogdanovs, Mārtiṇ Kregŝde and Aleksandr Kors—were studying engineering. Among Mischka's Hanover photos, members of this group appear often, separately and collectively, and he kept in touch with most of them for many years. The photo at the beginning of this chapter shows Mischka and his three closest friends outside the building of the former cadet flying school (Fliegerschule-Herrenhausen) in a suburb of Hanover, now the DP camp in which they were officially registered. They could have lived in the camp—which had rooms with four beds, with shower and lavatory along the corridor—but preferred to live outside in lodgings close by, all on the same street, Bičevskis remembers, but in different houses. (Stauvers fell in love with his landlady's daughter.) They used to go to the *Fliegerschule* sometimes, though, to collect their rations, for lunch with table tennis or billiards afterwards and, in Misha's case, to play the piano.

It was a great bonus for DPs who got into university to live outside the camps among Germans; it made them feel halfway normal, a Polish Jewish DP student remembered, able to believe in a future. That almost certainly applies to Mischka and his Latvian friends too. But in the case of these German-speaking Latvians, finishing their education in Germany was something they might well have done—and, in Mischka's case, firmly intended to do—regardless of war. It was easy for them almost to forget that in actual fact they had landed at university in Hanover as wards of UNRRA whom war had forcibly displaced.

Hanover Technical University had come through the war without too much damage, other than to its buildings. But Mischka's first impressions of the intellectual level of the institution—no doubt based on comparison with Barkhausen at Dresden—were not altogether positive. He wrote uneasily to

Olga in May 1946 that he was feeling a bit as he had done back in Riga when he had had to transfer from his classical gymnasium to an inferior school: then, he 'hadn't wanted to go to school any more because it was just a way of passing the time', and now 'I have the unpleasant impression that the TH has nothing more to give me, nothing fundamental ...' There may indeed have been problems, especially in theoretical physics, since some of Hanover's theoretical positions (viewed with suspicion by the Nazis) had been filled by experimentalists. But a few weeks later, Mischka had discovered that there were actually some good (if not top) physicists in Hanover, 'so perhaps something positive will come out of this semester'.

Although he was still studying electrical engineering, physics was what was on his mind. He reported almost reverentially to Olga on a talk by the great German theoretical physicist Werner Heisenberg, from Göttingen, one of the founders of quantum mechanics:

> Heisenberg is an unimposing, surprisingly young man [he was in his mid forties] with an unimposing voice [who gave] a paper completely without showmanship, absolutely unadorned, simple, clear and transparent. Conclusion: the more complicated a thing is, the more simply must one think. Heisenberg is one of the top people in the world.

This was an early indication of Mischka's lifelong love affair not just with physics but specifically with theoretical physics. To be sure, in Dresden, Barkhausen had pulled him over to the experimental side, but as one of his Latvian friends commented at the time, that was something new for the 'theorist' Mischka had been in Riga. Mischka and Bičevskis seem to have briefly contemplated moving to Göttingen to work with Heisenberg and Otto Hahn (one of the discoverers of nuclear fission, who had won the Nobel Prize in 1944) before committing themselves to Hanover. Reflecting in a letter to Olga on the possibility of comparing human achievements in the natural sciences to those in philosophy and art, Mischka gave Heisenberg the edge over Goethe, if not over Beethoven.

Clearly Mischka had a commitment to science far beyond that of the run-of-the-mill student. But that didn't mean that things were necessarily easy for him. Mischka liked learning, but he liked doing it in his own way. He was often resistant to being taught, and his teachers, accordingly, didn't always appreciate his talents. All his life he had been very sensitive to what he called 'the problem of academicism, of a teacher's authority stifling independent thought'. In science and maths, he liked thinking up his own approaches and could be downright suspicious of those who tried to teach him standard techniques, which he suspected might compromise his sense of the whole. In Hanover, as earlier at the University of Riga, he tended to skip lectures and, in exams, insisted on working out his own proofs from scratch instead of reproducing the proofs that had been given in class. Nor did he always show the automatic respect for professors and the professorial status that was normal in German universities. No doubt, he wrote to a girlfriend ['F.B.'] in 1946, he could become 'a not so bad professor in high frequency technology' (the area he had worked on with Barkhausen in Dresden), but he wasn't sure that it was what he wanted: 'I hate ordinariness and yearn for independent thinking.'

In science, Misha often had an instinctive understanding of phenomena, which he saw in pictures rather than words. It was a perennial issue for him that his mind operated differently from other people's, and he was never sure whether his idiosyncratic way of approaching scientific problems made him intellectually inferior to other people or superior.

This self-doubt was simultaneously assuaged and intensified by his mother's unwavering belief in his genius. It was a problem all his life, as witness the musing on the topic he sent me early in our marriage: 'First, I know—but better not admit!—that I am top. [But at the same time] I know that it is not true, that actually I am a fraud. By not admitting the first, I can keep also the second under wraps.' Misha was a mature physicist with a solid reputation in his field when I met him, but it quickly became clear to me that some physicists saw him as a genius while others—probably the majority—ranked him lower or simply couldn't understand him, and that this disparity of reactions worried him. Communicating his insights to other physicists was not easy, and my sense was that he did best when working with a collaborator who could act as a mediator. I experienced the communications problem at firsthand when he tried to teach me some physics: not only was it hard to understand him, but it was particularly hard when he thought he was making it completely simple.

In the Hanover period, things were complicated for Mischka by difficulties with concentration and memory that were evidently after-effects of the diphtheria or perhaps of wartime trauma in general. His concentration was 'absolutely not good enough for anything theoretical, not even for having an idea, let alone working it out'. He could only study for about two hours before losing focus, and his brain 'seemed like a tough mass, where an impression can be let in via a pinprick, which then closes up; it is somewhat comparable to paraffin on tar. God knows when it will be normal again.'

His first exams at Hanover in May 1947 were a misery to him—in letters to Olga he reported poor memory, sleeping badly, anxiety dreams and inadequate preparation, lamenting that 'stupidity is now my normal condition, and that moments of a little clarity come only as an exception'. Not surprisingly, he ended up with what was in effect a C grade average ('quite good', which was second from the bottom of the German four-tiered system of passing grades). It was no better in the exams in October, when one professor actually gave him the lowest passing grade ('satisfactory') in electrotechnical theory, a subject in which he ought to have done well. He was outraged about this grade and tried to challenge it or at least get the professor to justify it, but to no avail.

The exam results didn't give the whole picture, however. Even as one professor was giving him a low grade for electrotechnical theory, another was so impressed by his work in a related field that he invited him to deliver a paper at an important colloquium attended by 'the big men of the university and in industry'. 'I am a bit out of place in this company,' Mischka reported to Olga with satisfaction.

As a budding scientist, Mischka had another string to his bow: his contact with Fritz Sennheiser, who had arrived from Berlin to take up the chair in high-frequency physics and electro-acoustics. Mischka encountered Sennheiser in the lab in his first months at Hanover and was taken on as his assistant, apparently on the basis of what Sennheiser had heard of his work with Barkhausen in Dresden. One would think this would have pleased Mischka, but his account in a letter to Olga on 20 July 1946 doesn't give that impression: he got the job 'without having wanted it', he writes, and seems, in this letter and all subsequent references, to view Sennheiser with a certain suspicion.

Sennheiser was in the process of setting up a high-frequency electro-acoustical business that was soon to become spectacularly successful, and another person in Mischka's place might have welcomed the chance to get in on the ground floor. But Mischka seems to have thought Sennheiser was trying to pigeonhole him as someone who could solve technical problems, whereas he was already aspiring to the theoretical side of physics. Perhaps, in addition, he simply didn't much like the man. In the course of denouncing the professor who had given him the 'satisfactory' grade in a letter to Olga, he noted in passing that Sennheiser belonged to the same species— 'a learned man, but no *Persönlichkeit*'. *Persönlichkeit* is defined as 'personality' according to the dictionary, but in Mischka's usage it conveys something between individuality and depth of character. I take it that he found Sennheiser (whose later publicity photos radiate genial bonhomie) rather shallow and uninteresting as a person.

At this point, Sennheiser certainly seemed to like Mischka, or at any rate to think highly of his abilities. Indeed, given Mischka's prior experience at VEF and with Barkhausen, he was a lucky find. Very soon after their first discussion in Hanover, Sennheiser took Mischka out to his other lab, part of his electro-acoustical business, in the village of Wennebostel outside Hanover (it had been moved there during the war to be safe from bombing) and immediately asked if he would be interested in taking a job there after graduation. Mischka's answer was that after graduation he wanted to go to Göttingen to study physics, which Sennheiser accepted. As Mischka remarked to his mother, at least 'I have already got a guarantee of a job if I should want to get married.' It's a surprise to have marriage suddenly coming into the picture, but this may be connected to his relationship at the time with the unknown 'F.B.', to whom he also reported the job offer. He had been expecting the offer, he told F.B., and it 'would have guaranteed a quite viable, professionally not uninteresting future for me'. But 'I turned it down, of course, without the slightest hesitation. I must not bind myself, limit my development.'

Sennheiser was still in the picture at Easter 1947, when he 'had the tactlessness to set a date for 31 April', thus preventing

Misha's planned trip to his mother's for the holiday. A year later they had a reasonably successful conversation about some work that Mischka had given Sennheiser to read: Sennheiser 'made quite an impressive impression', he wrote, the awkwardness of the phrasing suggesting his uneasiness about the man, despite the unusually positive evaluation. A few months after that, Mischka went to talk to Sennheiser about supervising him in a possible doctoral thesis on acoustics, indicating a major shift in their relations, at least from Mischka's point of view. But the conversation went badly. Sennheiser didn't fully understand the problem Mischka was proposing to investigate and thought of it as experimental rather than theoretical. He also seems to have been steering Mischka to a possible job as an experimental physicist with Northwestern Radio Hamburg. This, or perhaps Olga's positive reaction to the idea, very much annoyed Mischka: 'A job like that would be just killing time … The things that interest me to work on in the long term don't need any Hamburg Radio. I can do them at my writing desk.'

Mischka gave up the idea of specialising in acoustics and doing a doctorate with Sennheiser. In their final conversation, he had discovered 'something that is not surprising and quite natural: Sennheiser doesn't like me'. It may not have been surprising, given that Mischka didn't particularly like Sennheiser either, but it obviously hurt. He used to mention him sometimes to me (though I then had no clear idea who he was), and there was always an edge in his voice. Sennheiser had shown himself to be in the category of scientists who didn't appreciate and were perhaps even jealous of Mischka's special insights and instinctive feel for physics, or at least recognised them only on the technical and experimental level, not the theoretical. 'So much for Sennheiser,' Mischka ended his report to Olga. But perhaps a feeling of disappointment or missed opportunity remained. The Wennebostel lab was the basis for the Sennheiser Electronic Corporation, founded in June 1945, which was to grow into one of the world's foremost developers and producers of audiotechnology: voltmeters (the first product, probably what they were working on when Misha first went), microphones, headphones, telephone accessories and so on. The company is still flourishing today, according to the web, and Sennheiser is remembered as 'a legend in audio'. Ten years older than Mischka, he outlived him by more than ten years, dying at the age of ninety-eight in 2010.

German professors are quite frequently mentioned in Mischka's letters, German students hardly ever, or at least not the males. The DP students and the native Germans didn't mix much, apparently: there was a tinge of condescension on the German side, according to the recollections of Mischka's friends Bičevskis and Stauvers, perhaps related to the fact that a substantial proportion of the Germans were former active or reserve officers in the German armed forces, often overt or covert Nazi sympathisers.

A new note of anti-Germanism is evident in Mischka's letters of the Hanover period. His adolescent pro-Germanism had completely disappeared, and his tone when he wrote of Germans, individually or collectively, was often critical. Writing to Olga, he described a potential landlord as 'a typical German [the word being given in Latvian, thus invoking unfavourable stereotypes of Baltic Germans]—pigheaded, thick-skinned and easygoing', though 'withall polite and obliging'. Mischka had a tendency to describe Germans that he encountered casually almost as ethnographic specimens: exhibit A, an 'idealistic Nazi' whose patriotic education had been so perfect that he didn't even realise that was what he was; exhibit B, an upper-class German manager met on a train who was 'naturally a Communist idealist' (that 'naturally' is typical Misha, conveying his ironic appreciation of the predictable unpredict-ability of the world at the level of individuals and atoms).

On the rare occasion that he met a German he liked, it was flagged as an exception. 'Even among Germans there are some positive people,' he wrote of his meeting with the international-minded Professor Erich Obst, who held the chair of geography at Hanover and was planning to set up an International University in Bremen. I did a bit of research on Obst and discovered that he doesn't look all that positive in retrospect: he was one of those German colonial geographers whose geopolitical bent made them, initially at least, sym-pathetic to the Nazis, but could be reconfigured after the war as internationalism. The trouble with doing research, however, is that one may end up knowing more about the subject than Mischka did. From his point of view, Obst was a non-nationalist German whose 'youthful enthusiasm' and humanistic-philosophical bent were appealing.

The other thing that was appealing about Obst was his friendliness. Evidently viewing multilingual Mischka as a potential teacher at his International University, Obst invited him and another student out to his house for tea—a most unusual gesture from a German God-Professor to students other than his own—and, in parting, urged them warmly to come back. It wasn't often that Mischka encountered such gratuitous friendliness in Germany, and it moved him, perhaps disproportionately. I remember that kind of overreaction from my own foreign-student days in England, and I wasn't even a displaced person. Mischka and Bičevskis reacted similarly to the kindly interest of Miss Broadhurst, formerly of UNRRA, who, after moving to Canada at the end of her posting, unexpectedly wrote the two of them a friendly letter: they were 'moved almost to tears', Bičevskis remembered, as they composed their reply.

If Mischka and his Latvian friends didn't have much to do with German men of their own age, the situation was quite different with regard to young (and even not-so-young) German women. Presentable young German men were thin on the ground because of war losses, and healthy, educated, German-speaking DPs were consequently in great demand. Bičevskis was too shy to take advantage of these opportunities, according to his own report, and after a few years met and married a Latvian girl. At the other extreme in the little group of friends, Boris Bogdanovs was the Don Juan—a good dancer who went in for dancing competitions and had multiple affairs with war widows (who gave him their husbands' clothes and shoes). One girlfriend, the daughter of a very rich German business family, wanted to marry him, but the family disapproved and sent heavies to scare him off. Bogdanovs was always relieved when his syphilis tests came back negative, Bičevskis recalled, but his friends were more amused by his exploits than judgemental.

Mischka, however, took the whole question very seriously, and agonised in his diary about whether the Bogdanovs approach to women was permissible. But it was himself he was judging (or deciding not to judge) rather than Boris. Mischka was neither as promiscuous as Boris nor as lighthearted and open about affairs, but he too was not short of offers, both of sex and marriage, from German girls.

One such sexual offer that Mischka evidently accepted came from an 'experienced woman' with a child from a former relationship. Given the prevalence of rape by soldiers as well as the general breakdown of social norms at the end of the war, a whole cohort of German women were undoubtedly sexually experienced, not necessarily by choice. Mischka did not reflect on the circumstances in which his temporary partner had acquired her experience, but he judged her for it. She would be 'ideal company for Boris', he wrote in his diary at the beginning of their acquaintance; moreover, she was a person without depth or independence of mind, an 'absolute average', as one might expect of a German. Not to mention calculating and materialistic. But it would do him no harm to 'go through a training in superficiality' through an affair with her, Mischka reflected, and the inevitable eventual parting wouldn't particularly hurt her as girls 'don't take it so tragically, if one doesn't take it so tragically oneself'. This, of course, implies that Mischka was going against the grain of his own habit of 'taking things tragically'. But it's still uncharacteristically mean, even if slightly mitigated by the fact—revealed in a letter to Olga, though not in the diary—that the experienced woman had ultimately found a better marriage prospect and dumped him. (I don't know what Olga thought of this story, but I thought it served him right.)

In Mischka's diary, there are several drafts of letters in which he earnestly explains to German girlfriends why he is not interested in marrying them. One explanation was that he didn't feel ready for marriage, and saw it more as a restriction on his future development than something positive. The other explanation was that he was in love with someone else, but she had been locked up in the Soviet zone and therefore inaccessible since the end of the war. Undoubtedly both these things were true: Mischka was too honest to lie, even about such awkward matters. But of course there were contradictions here: if he was in love with Nanni, he should be actively trying to get her to come out and marry him, which he wasn't; and he shouldn't be having affairs with other people, which he was. For someone like Mischka, these contradictions were painful, a pain he passed in varying degrees to Nanni and his German girlfriends in the West.

Nanni, his 'great love from Dresden', had been being kept 'in reserve', as he explained in one of these letters, but now

(January 1948) 'might be flying the coop' (getting out of the Soviet zone). She 'might be his future', he wrote—although in the same paragraph he expressed his general reservations about marriage.

Since the end of the war, Nanni had been working in her father's medical practice in Chemnitz. She had suspended her university studies in 1944, perhaps involuntarily: the disruption at universities in the Soviet zone was more profound than in the Western zones, and a ruthless purge of Nazi sympathisers among the professors, together with mass flight to the West, left only a quarter of the old professoriate in place when the universities reopened in 1946. To complicate matters further for a 'bourgeois' student like Nanni, the universities were also required to practise affirmative action in enrolment on behalf of working-class students, who should constitute at least 30 per cent of total enrolment. Still, whether it was Nanni's fault or not, Mischka's letters to her have an underlying motif of dissatisfaction on his part both at the 'lack of independence' that kept her tied to her family and at her lack of initiative on the question of finishing her university studies.

Their correspondence continued, but with obvious tensions. In the autumn of 1946, when Mischka heard from Nanni that she was enrolling in a local trade school, he hit the roof, denouncing trade schools root and branch as a form of anti-enlightenment whose effect was to suppress the faculty of independent thought, and expressing his great personal disappointment at her decision. In reporting this to Olga, he noted that his letter in response might have been a bit 'shattering' to Nanni, as indeed it might, but that it was really appalling that Nanni should have taken what even she admitted to be a step backwards: 'the disappointing thing, which is actually so typical … is the recidivism: back home again, straight back into the old pattern'. A few months later, Nanni wrote with anxious whimsy that 'one has the impression that Hanover wants to break diplomatic relations with the state of Saxony, particularly Lichtenwalde [the suburb of Chemnitz where her family lived]. Lichtenwalde awaits clarification on the part of Hanover-Weitenhausen'.

Travel between the Soviet zone and the West had been risky in the first months after the end of the war, but then became reasonably easy, though you were supposed to get an official inter-zonal pass from the Soviet authorities. Nanni could therefore have come to the West without too much difficulty at any time in this period, if she had felt it possible to leave her family. But by mid 1947, regulation of inter-zonal travel was tightening up again, as the Cold War took hold and Germany moved towards permanent division into two successor states (the Federal Republic of Germany, based on the postwar American, British and French occupation zones, and the German Democratic Republic, based on the Soviet zone). It was beginning to look like a now-or-never situation for those who, like Nanni, had some inclination to leave but had not previously made up their minds. At the same time, the call of family responsibilities on Nanni was weakening. Her younger brother Roland was about to finish school and would probably leave home to go to university. Her sister Lilo crossed the border in May 1947, visiting Mischka in Hanover before settling somewhere in the West. And then, in June, it was Nanni's turn to make the trip.

Travel from the Soviet zone was already becoming hazardous by the summer of 1947, with persons caught crossing without permission liable to be interned or sent to work in the Saxon uranium mines. Nanni escaped this, but her trip wasn't a success. It was bad timing as far as Mischka was concerned: his affair with the 'experienced' woman was still either on or very recently over, and the reunion with Nanni clearly went badly. Whatever her original intentions, Nanni went back to Chemnitz after about a week.

The return trip was miserable, with an overnight stay at the border at a primitive barracks ('pigs in their stalls have cleaner conditions than people sleeping there on straw that hasn't been changed for at least a month'), and Nanni was clearly rattled by the whole experience. In a long letter written quickly in pencil after she got home, she implicitly reproached Mischka for double standards in having his fun with other women while she was shut up in Chemnitz, and moreover (this accusation was a bit more deeply buried) treating her as damaged goods because of her lack of 'purity'. While this was all expressed in abstract terms in the guise of a philosophical discussion of man–woman relations, it naturally caught Mischka on the raw, and he fired off a priggish and angry letter harshly rebutting the implicit charges as well as correcting her understanding of the philosophical issues involved. (Poor Nanni. Assuming she was not naturally philosophically inclined, as the bulk of her correspondence suggests, she had made a big effort to meet Mischka's standards with her painstaking references to Kant and Schopenhauer.) He couldn't imagine what in their conversations in Hanover could have given her the impression he regarded her as tainted: 'What I was talking about was the horrifying and disappointing cheapness of people, girls and young men alike, who give themselves away for a couple of Reichsmarks.'

Nanni must have been sadly discouraged, but she still did not want to break off the relationship. In August, she sent Mischka greetings from Berlin, and in September a jocular letter to her 'dear faithless tomato', followed three days later by a less jocular plea that Mischka break his 'icy cold silence' and let her hear from him. But apart from the quarrel and the guilt, the bottom line was that they could no longer pretend that their separation was involuntary, something neither of them could change. Nanni, it was clear, could have decided, and still could decide, to leave her home permanently and come West. Mischka, for his part, could have urged her before her visit to come and marry him (which there is no indication he did); he could have repeated his urging after her visit instead of telling her off. But neither of them was ready to risk it. Mutual inaction left both of them feeling injured, unloved and increasingly distrustful.

Mischka's other passion was sport, and it still mattered enough to him half a century later that he told me a lot about it. It was the unproblematic part of his life, I gathered, something he was good at and enjoyed that carried no guilt and relatively little anxiety. His Hanover sports club (Turnklub zu Hanover) was the centre of his social life and, incidentally, the place where he met most of his German girlfriends (the 'experienced woman', for example, was a world-class long jumper). Locating the sports club—which in Germany was always open to everyone—was always the first thing he did in a new city, and he felt at a loss when he went to America and found out that it wasn't so easy there. As we once happened to walk past the New York Athletic Club in Manhattan, he related his chagrin at showing up on its doorstep shortly after his arrival in New York, to discover that it was an exclusive, membership-only social club, formally inaccessible to women and informally to Jews, blacks and penniless foreign immigrants.

Pole vaulting was Mischka's main athletic event in Germany, though he ran in 800-metres races and did some high jumping and long jumping as well. Bičevskis described him as 'typically fearless' as a pole vaulter, which you needed to be in the days of bamboo poles and landing on hard ground. Actually Mischka was already looking for a replacement for the bamboo pole that, along with his knapsack full of physics journals, belongs to my Dick Whittington picture of him in 1944–45. It was before the days of flexible fibreglass poles, which started to come into use in the 1950s and greatly improved performance, but Mischka experimented briefly in 1946 with one of the new aluminium poles, acquired with the help of a sympathetic UNRRA official, which, however, turned out to be too short.

He had started to analyse his pole-vaulting style in order to improve his performance, and this no doubt explains the profusion of small black-and-white photos of Mischka in flight, sports pants flapping, like a large and rather ungainly bird. Bičevskis said the analytic approach didn't actually improve Mischka's results—but then, as a top athlete himself, member of a basketball team that competed in Paris in May 1947, Bičevskis had high standards. Mischka's results were good enough to make him the winner at the British zonal championships in August 1946. These were DP competitions, but Mischka was hoping to compete at the German national and international level. According to the story he told me, he was in line for selection when the German team decided not to accept DPs, even though on form he was better than the German who ultimately won the pole-vaulting competition.

Olga probably read the frequent and detailed discussions of sports events and preparations in Mischka's letters in much the same indulgent but not deeply interested spirit that I later did. On philosophical discussions, however, she did better. In Mischka's letters, philosophy rivalled sports, study and girlfriends as favourite topics, and Olga's replies were reliably interested and encouraging, if not always fully comprehending. I, on the other hand, was tempted to skip them altogether. My low tolerance/lack of aptitude for philosophical generalisation was well known to Misha, who tolerated it as a *déformation professionelle* of historians. I felt guilty, even so, as I flipped through the closely written pages of philosophical argument (all in German, and handwritten), but the problem was that when it veered off into philosophy of science, I could barely understand it. When, as happened with about equal frequency, it involved abstract discussions of men–women relationships, I just wanted, in my empirical historian's way, to know which specific relationship of his own he was really talking about.

There is a whole section of his papers, probably dating from 1947, devoted to an article on nihilism by one Manfred Büttner, which had recently stirred up controversy. Mischka's contribution—neatly typed out, headed 'A Response' and signed by Michael Danos, student in electrotechnics, Hanover—was very likely published, though I don't know where. For a long time, I avoided reading this essay carefully because I thought he was off on his man–woman/ Bogdanovs-sex musings again. So when I finally read it, I was pleasantly surprised to find that it was not about sex but rather a Nietzschean reflection on the plight of man without God, which clearly had practical significance for Mischka, a lifelong atheist:

> From the nihilist standpoint, a correct life leads to the same results as one built on 'Christian truths', but it demands incomparably more strength to carry through, since you have the responsibility to bear it all alone, and there is no control over your actions except your own. It is no wonder that this burden may finally be too heavy, that so many people turn off this road and find themselves some support. The beauty of nihilism is that life lies unrestricted before you, that you stand alone in the storm. If one takes this position, then one grows and gains a strength whose potential would otherwise be unthinkable. But one can also be destroyed.

If Mischka still felt himself to be standing alone in the storm, his worry about being destroyed as a scientist by trauma-related failures of concentration and memory was starting to recede by the time he took his final exams at Hanover in the spring of 1948. Already in the autumn of 1947 he had started to notice an improvement in intellectual stamina: 'It seems as if I might be getting back to normal again. My memory is getting ready to want to return.' A few months later, he was more, if not completely, confident: 'The gap seems to have closed.' He could once again plumb the depths of Beethoven's *Moonlight Sonata*, which he had thought irretrievably lost after his sighting of the Jewish graves in Riga in 1943. He now felt that 'there was a possibility of regaining all that I once possessed, meaning also concentration and the ability to grasp problems precisely and finally see a way of solving them'. Olga had never doubted that this would eventually happen, he noted, but he had, and such doubts still sometimes plagued him. 'But there is *no doubt, the gap has been closed.*'

Die Schlucht scheint sich geschlossen zu haben. That phrase jumped out at me from his diary. *Geschlossen* was what he kept saying in Washington DC in August 1999, after the first of two strokes that a week later killed him. He had lost his English, and I, with my poor German, was struggling, as in a nightmare, to understand him. I thought he meant by *geschlossen* that something was shutting down on him, despite his stubborn efforts to keep it open. But there was remarkable consistency over the years of Mischka's way of thinking, so now I surmise that it was really the opposite: he was saying that a gap had opened up (as when he stopped reacting to the *Moonlight Sonata*), but he was doing his best to close it.

Whatever he meant, it was typical Mischka to treat a stroke as a scientific problem to be solved by his own, rather than the doctors', efforts. If not for *geschlossen*, and the awfulness of not understanding what he was trying to tell me, I might not have spent the 2000s trying to improve my German. My story was that I was working on German in order to write this book, but actually it was magical thinking à la Joan Didion: next time Misha urgently needed me to understand his German, I would be ready.

Along with Mischka's renewed confidence in his mental powers in 1947–48 came a growing sense that he was getting the hang of quantum nuclear physics. As always with Mischka, that meant that he was beginning to understand it well enough to see anomalies in the conventional wisdom— that is, to strike out on his own. He had noticed that one of the standard axioms 'doesn't seem to work', as he wrote to Olga in March 1947, and 'the exciting thing is that the thing that doesn't seem to fit is a universally acknowledged fact'. Eighteen months later, he reported with pleasure that he had independently arrived at the same conclusion about one such anomaly that had just been reached by three of the great phys- icists—Heisenburg, Max von Laue and Wolfgang Paul—at a seminar in Göttingen.

Mischka graduated from Hanover Technical University in May 1948 with the same 'quite good' grade that he had got in his exams the previous year. But it no longer mattered much, since he had found a mentor who recognised his abilities. This was the theoretical physicist Hans Jensen, whose courses in atomic (that is, nuclear) physics Mischka had taken since the summer semester of 1946. Jensen, though young, had made his name during the war with work on the separation of uranium isotypes; he had taught at Hanover TH since 1941 and had recently been appointed professor, though not the top grade of *ordinarius*. There are only occasional mentions of Jensen in Mischka's correspondence before his graduation, although in his diary for July 1946 he notes, in the midst of a lot of *Sturm und Drang* about his personal life, an epiphany in the middle of Jensen's seminar on atomic physics: when he came out onto the street after the seminar, 'the sun shone so beautifully that I felt really happy'. The next year, he reported that Jensen had encouraged him to work on a problem whose solution had the potential to be 'an event in the field'.

Straight after his graduation, Mischka started work as Jensen's assistant in the Hanover Institute for Theoretical Physics. It was his first real adult job. *Assistent* is more like a young right-hand man to the professor than a teaching assistant or tutor in Anglophone universities, and Mischka was almost awed by his new responsibilities, including standing in for Jensen in classes when he was out of town—'it's something quite strange, having such independence as a substitute'. His excitement at moving into the world of theoretical physics did not prevent him noting 'another joke of world history', namely that after a period of dearth as far as girlfriends were concerned, he had just taken up with a young woman from the sports club by the name of Helga Heimers. (New girlfriends didn't usually get identified by their full names, so Olga was meant to take note.)

The association with Jensen brought a new direction and purpose to Mischka's life that was to prove lasting. Mischka already knew about the 'the overwhelming probability' that in the winter semester Jensen would move to the University of Heidelberg to take up the position of *ordinarius* professor of theoretical physics there. The move was firmly decided by the autumn of 1948, by which time Mischka, in addition to working as *Assistent*, was also enrolled as a PhD student under Jensen. Jensen was going to Heidelberg in January of the new year. And his scientific assistant and PhD student, Michael Danos, aged twenty-six, was going with him.

10
Physics and Marriage in Heidelberg

Wedding of Mischka and Helga, 1949.

M ISCHKA arrived in Heidelberg to take up his new job with Jensen on an early summer evening in May 1949. As he walked up the hill along Philosopher's Way to the Physics Institute, his rucksack on his back, the river lay on his right hand and the old town beyond it. Heidelberg, a beautiful medieval town, was one of the only German cities not damaged by Allied bombing. Arriving there after Hanover was a shock in itself. But what made the moment transcendent for Mischka was that, as he climbed the hill, music came wafting down from the institute. It was the Beethoven *Violin Concerto*, played by Fritz Kreisler.

Misha told me the story in the 1990s, when we visited Heidelberg together. As always with Misha's stories, it was related with such immediacy that it might have happened yesterday. He undoubtedly could have told me which movement of the Beethoven he had heard, if I had only thought to ask. In a letter written to his new girlfriend, Helga, back in Hanover, he told essentially the same story—another instance, like the Dresden bombing, of Misha's unusual ability to keep his memories intact and unedited over half a century—but with less emphasis on transcendence and a few more technical details. It was '10.30 pm (22.30)' when he arrived, he told Helga, and the Kreisler record was being played in Jensen's room on an electric (not mechanical) turntable that was 'not bad at all'.

Jensen greeted him hospitably, producing 'the remains of the roast potatoes he had had for lunch' for Mischka's supper:

> Then we sat down and started to talk … It got later and later: we had already once decided to stop talking and go to bed, and I was already standing at the door, but then we relapsed … and the [conversation] went on for an hour and a half (until 1.30) …

Mischka was bowled over by this. He knew Jensen already, of course, but not in a personal capacity. Hans Jensen was a great man in physics, if not quite of the stature of Heisenberg. During the war, he had been a member of the famous Uranium Club, led by Heisenberg and the physical chemist Paul Harteck, and he was also close to the Copenhagen physics group around Niels Bohr.

For Mischka, this evening arrival at the Heidelberg Physics Institute felt something like the pilgrim's arrival in Mecca. But it was also the beginning of a friendship with Jensen that was of the greatest importance to Misha as a person as well as a physicist. Jensen, who remained a close friend and mentor until his death in the 1970s, played many roles in Misha's life. He was his *Doktorvater*, the supervisor of his dissertation, who brought him into a particular area of physics and set him off asking particular kinds of questions. He became a family friend, particularly close to Helga but also on good terms with Misha's second wife, Vicky. With his frequent visits to America after the Danoses moved there in 1951, he was a bridge between Misha's new life and his old one.

One of the things that happened to Mischka in Heidelberg, as a result of joining Jensen's theoretical physics group there, was that he came to see himself as part of a great tradition. He defined that great tradition in physics as international when I knew him, and so it was. But all the same, much of it took place in Germany, and Misha's apprehension of it and sense of belonging came via Jensen and the (mainly German or German-trained) physicists who, as Jensen's friends and collaborators, were habitual visitors at his institute in Heidelberg. Misha knew so much about the history of physics, and talked about it to me so often, that it came as a shock to realise how little of it he had known before he went to Heidelberg. Of course he knew about Heisenberg ('one of the top people in the world') as well as a few luminaries like Max Planck, Arnold Sommerfeld and Albert Einstein. But until his second year in Hanover, he hadn't even heard of the notorious school of 'German physics' whose battle with 'Jewish theory' before the war had received Nazi patronage: he wrote to Olga that he had just

> read with astonishment in [the American journal] *Physical
> Letters* what a hair-raising thing the Nazis had allowed, even
> in relation to theoretical physics: they tried to put a German

physics in its place, not being embarrassed to write lampoons on Heisenberg, Sommerfeld and even Planck, the Nestor of German physicists.

That 'German physics' episode was remarkable, but even more remarkable were the developments in physics in Germany around the time of the First World War to which it was a reaction. The publication of Einstein's relativity theory in Berlin inaugurated a period of breakneck advances in atomic and nuclear physics in the interwar years. The process was international, or at least pan-European, with the theoretical and experimental discoveries that led to nuclear fission and ultimately to the atom bomb coming in a brilliant sequence that leapfrogged national boundaries, starting in Ernest Rutherford's laboratory in Cambridge, going through Göttingen, Copenhagen and Enrico Fermi's laboratory in Rome, and culminating in Otto Hahn's and Lise Meitner's demonstration of nuclear fission, which won the Berlin-based Hahn a Nobel Prize in chemistry in 1944. But, international though the community was, Germany was in the vanguard, and its contribution was particularly strong in the theoretical realm. In the 'beautiful years' for physics from the turn of the century until the early 1930s, Germany produced a string of Nobel Prize winners: Wilhelm Röntgen, Philipp Lenard, Max von Laue, Max Planck, Johannes Stark, Albert Einstein, James Franck and Werner Heisenberg. With the exception of three experimentalists—Röntgen, the discoverer of X-rays, and Lenard and Stark, who would become the key figures in 'German physics' in the 1930s—all were theoretical physicists.

But then came the Nazis. They were against Jews, and Einstein and many of the other German theoretical physicists were Jewish. On top of that, they were against cosmopolitan theoretical 'Jewish physics' and in favour of experiment-based

'German physics'. Experimentalists like Philipp Lenard, who held the chair at the University of Heidelberg, were particularly offended by ambitious theorising like Einstein's relativity theorem, which lacked immediate experimental demonstration; they thought of it as pure speculative fantasy that would take physics away from its true path. You didn't have to be Jewish to come under their condemnation: the young (Aryan) German Werner Heisenberg, a pioneer in quantum mechanics (almost as objectionable as relativity theory), was berated by Nazi periodicals as a 'white Jew'.

The result of the Nazi assumption of power in 1933 was that about a quarter of all German theoretical physicists in university posts were dismissed because they were Jews, and a large emigration of physicists followed. Einstein led the way, publicly condemning the Nazi regime and becoming the number one villain in Nazi eyes, his property being seized and eventually a price being put on his head. Berlin, Göttingen and other great centres lost their senior physicists and a whole cohort of the coming generation, including the young Edward Teller and John von Neumann, who would later join the Manhattan Project in Los Alamos and work for the United States on the production of the first atomic bomb.

The heyday of anti-modern, anti-theoretical 'German physics' was in the mid 1930s. By the end of the decade, it had become clear even to the Nazis that if they wanted to remain in the game of developing atomic energy, they couldn't afford to dismiss modern theoretical physics. The nuclear fission effect identified in 1939 by Otto Hahn and Lise Meitner (now, as a Jew, exiled in Stockholm) opened up the way to the production of huge amounts of energy, once scientists had worked out how to produce and control chain reactions. This was the task of the informal group known as the Uranium Club, of which Jensen, still in his thirties, was a member.

Another key participant was the somewhat older Walther Bothe (born in 1891), who was Professor of Experimental Physics at the University of Heidelberg when Mischka arrived there in 1949.

As war loomed, the Uranium Club's activities were naturally of great interest to the German military and supported by them, but never on anything like the scale of the Manhattan Project in the United States, and without the short-term objective of building an atomic bomb. The Uranium Club physicists—whose lack of drive to invent a bomb probably reflected some disinclination to trust Hitler with such a weapon, even if less than they later claimed—focussed on building a 'uranium machine' (that is, a reactor) and got tied up with some false leads and technical problems along the way. On a wartime visit to Denmark immortalised in Michael Frayn's play *Copenhagen*, Heisenberg tried to tell Niels Bohr in a roundabout manner that Germany was *not* making a bomb, but succeeded only in appalling him by the idea that it perhaps could. The young Jensen had a walk-on part in this story too, because it was he who, after a subsequent wartime visit to Copenhagen, made his colleague Heisenberg aware for the first time of the intensity of Bohr's reaction. The Americans, meanwhile, were convinced that Germany, that world centre of nuclear physics, was well on the way to making a bomb and would naturally be trying to do so. It came as a shock at the end of the war to discover how far from the truth this was.

While 'German physics' was on the wane elsewhere, in Heidelberg it remained ascendant. Lenard, the experimentalist founder of the institute that Mischka entered in 1949, had held the chair at the university since 1907 and had criticised Einstein's relativity theory as early as 1910; his antipathy to modern theoretical developments in physics predated his Nazi sympathies, which arose out of a sense of German national humiliation in the First World War. A local hero in Heidelberg, Lenard's influence remained great even after his retirement in the early 1930s, and he insisted successfully that 'only a master of experimental physics' should be appointed to the chair, rejecting the candidates initially proposed as too 'theoretical' and one-sided. Walther Bothe was the compromise candidate, a distinguished experimentalist who, however, was not averse to modern theoretical physics. But Lenard's supporters made Bothe's tenure so uncomfortable that after two years, he retreated into the more congenial surroundings of Heidelberg's Kaiser-Wilhelm Institute for Medical Research, where he built Germany's first cyclotron.

Thanks to the efforts of some ardent Nazi disciples of Lenard's, the Heidelberg Physics Institute was already so *judenfrei* in 1933 that, in contrast to the rest of Germany's physics institutes, there was no need for a purge. The main Nazi activist was a former student of Lenard's, Ludwig Wesch, who became a lecturer professor of technical (applied) physics at Heidelberg in 1943. It was said that one of the reasons for Bothe's precipitate flight to the Kaiser-Wilhelm Institute was that Wesch was in the habit of organising military drills in the loft above the office where he was trying to work. Though not of the same stature as a physicist as Lenard or Bothe, he was nevertheless a real scientist rather than a charlatan on the lines of Trofim Lysenko (the opponent of genetics in the Soviet Union), working primarily on defence-related radio technology during the war. But he was and remained a staunch opponent of modern theoretical physics.

For Jensen and his fellow members of the Uranium Club, the war's end was a dangerous time. Agents of both the Soviet Union and the United States were running around scooping up nuclear scientists they thought might be useful for work on the bomb. The British whisked a group of Uranium Club leaders, including Heisenberg and Harteck, off to a secret holding place in England, Farm House, to try to find out the real story about the (non-existent) German bomb. The Farm House contingent were released and returned to Germany in the spring of 1946, Heisenberg becoming director of the Kaiser-Wilhelm Institute (renamed for Max Planck, like other Kaiser-Wilhelm Institutes, after Planck's death in 1947) in Göttingen. Jensen in Hanover and Bothe in Heidelberg both remained at liberty, though they had to go through a not very rigorous denazification process.

For the former 'German physics' proponents, the outlook was bleaker. Heidelberg was in the American occupation zone, where denazification was more stringent than in the British zone, and Lenard and Wesch were in any case notorious for their Nazi connections. The Americans decided not to prosecute Lenard because of his age, and he died, a free but embittered man, in 1947. Wesch, on the other hand, was one of the few to be convicted as a 'major offender' in denazification proceedings and dismissed from the university. The Physics Institute was left in a shambles, partly because towards the end of the war Wesch had removed a lot of equipment for safekeeping in a village some 70–80 kilometres away. The whole university was closed when occupation forces came in at the end of March 1945, and even when it reopened, the Physics Institute led a ghostlike existence, almost empty of furniture, equipment and personnel and without heat. Its last Nazi-era director, the experimental physicist August Becker, a close colleague and friend of Lenard's, had his own house in Heidelberg confiscated by the military government and was dismissed from his position in February 1946. Bothe's cyclotron was seized by the Americans as well, though as scientific booty rather than punitively; he didn't get it back until 1949, the year of Mischka's arrival.

It was Bothe who had the job of getting the university's Physics Institute back on its feet, moving back from the Kaiser-Wilhelm Institute to the position Wesch and his acolytes had forced him out of before the war. But it was tough going at first. He had to get the building running again, heat and furnish it, organise the return of the institute's scattered scientific equipment and, at the same time, hire new staff, trained in modern physics, and get rid of the Lenard/Wesch legacy. This was only partially achieved by the summer of 1949, when Mischka showed up. Memories of the Lenard era were still vivid in Mischka's time, and he had a stock of Lenard anecdotes to prove it, mainly heard from the institute's mechanic, a survivor of several changes of regime. One of the stories concerned Mischka's own office in the institute. Under Lenard's reign, it had housed a lecturer in theoretical physics whom Lenard couldn't get rid of, but as Lenard hated theory, he had instructed that 'Theoretical physics apparatus' be painted on the door. That sign was still there when Mischka arrived—he was tickled by the idea of being a piece of apparatus.

Jensen, selected in 1948 as the new professor of theoretical physics, was the key appointment, and it was after his arrival at the beginning of 1949 that things really started humming. But as a modern theorist, he met considerable opposition. Some of the Lenard group remained in Heidelberg, fighting to get their old jobs back, and there were still many in the Heidelberg university and social establishment who sympathised with them. With the establishment of the German Federal Republic in 1949, enthusiasm for outcasting and punishing former Nazis quickly waned. Becker, already of retirement age, successfully petitioned for emeritus status (which carried a pension) in 1951. Wesch, now working in industry after serving a prison term, got his 'major offender' conviction reduced to 'minor offender' on appeal and spent more than a decade agitating to get his university job back (he was turned down for a second time in 1956 after both Jensen and Bothe's successor in the experimental physics chair threatened to leave if he were reinstated).

Postwar Heidelberg physics was surrounded by such a golden aura in Misha's memory that I found it hard to judge how it stood, objectively, in the history of nuclear physics. Perhaps that didn't matter for my story, but it niggled away at me. I read the classic accounts, but they are all written in terms of a teleology that leads to Los Alamos and the making of the bomb—in other words, a German–American competition to make the bomb that the Americans won. In this story, Germany loses its good physicists in successive waves of emigration, mainly to the United States. The world centre of physics moves from Europe to the United States. Once the Americans have the bomb and Germany loses the war, physics in Germany drops out of view.

All this makes a lot of sense, but teleologies tend to smooth out any deviations along the way that don't fit the big picture. I think that's what probably happened with postwar German nuclear physics, at least up to the mid 1950s, when another wave of emigration took yet more physicists (including Misha) to the United States. It looks to me as if Misha wasn't deceiving himself, and there really was a minor golden age for theoretical nuclear physics in postwar Germany, with Heidelberg one of the most lively centres. The ten years after the Second World War were not a peak period of Nobel Prizes being awarded to Germans, which scarcely comes as a surprise. But then, when Germans started winning Nobel Prizes for physics again, Heidelberg scooped the pool. Walther Bothe, the Heidelberg cyclotron man, won a Nobel in 1954, and a Heidelberg-trained spectroscopist called Rudolf Mössbauer won in 1961. In 1963, Mischka's mentor Hans Jensen was joint winner, along with the German-American Maria Goeppert-Mayer, for work on the nuclear shell model they were doing when Mischka was his student.

The excitement of those years was recalled by one of Mischka's contemporaries, Berthold Stech, who was also Jensen's student. Stech's arrival in Heidelberg actually preceded Jensen's, and he remembered the shock of Jensen's appearance on the scene, which put them 'suddenly in contact with modern theoretical ideas and approaches':

> It was challenging. Jensen was unconventional ... [He] managed to make Heidelberg a leading center of nuclear physics in experiment and theory ... Of course it was the high time of nuclear physics and the shell model. We students were witnessing an exciting period with hot and lively discussions. But even more important, we experienced the outstanding scientific and social atmosphere created by Bothe and Jensen which extended to the newcomers and students. Besides scientific competence, there was also heart. Coming back from years of war the institute became our home where we spent all day and half the night.

The centre of it all was the Tea Colloquium (*Tee-Colloquium*), lovingly remembered all his life by Misha. He walked in on his first one, evidently having just arrived from Hanover, when the colloquium was already in session and was admitted by Jensen's senior assistant, Helmut Steinwedel:

> There around a long combined table sat the professors, Jensen, Bothe, [Heinz] Maier-Leibnitz and some more who I did not know, the assistants Steinwedel and others, and graduate students. Steinwedel announced my name and I sat down. Suddenly, unexpectedly, I was served a

chemical beaker (100 cc) with tea, and the general discussion continued. After a while a graduate student went to the blackboard and commenced to report on a paper from a recent *Physical Review*. Quite soon he was interrupted by questions and comments from different people, including myself. I found that whole situation exceedingly stimulating, and interesting, and informative.

Including myself is a nice touch: here was Mischka jumping in to discussion with the great men, his bags not yet unpacked and the ink still fresh on his PhD diploma. That was unconventional but in local disciplinary terms not outrageous: democracy of discussion between professors and students had been an important part of the Göttingen tradition in physics before the war too. Obviously Mischka, like Jensen, enjoyed flouting hierarchical conventions. Even in the Tea Colloquium, there were some conventions relating to seniority, but Mischka ignored them:

The traditional rule was that the newest member of that circle was supposed to prepare and serve the tea. I was blithely unaware of that and found out about it only after a new graduate student appeared and took over these duties. I felt a little uncomfortable about not having done my turn and told it to my predecessor, who said that it is perfectly OK, since I was a theorist. In fact I was quite happy about my ignorance.

Scientific life was a lot livelier in Heidelberg than in Hanover, Mischka wrote more than once to his mother: 'Since I came here, I have got a whole lot cleverer.' The best part was the Tea Colloquium discussions, where every aspect of the topic was clarified by 'comments and questions, even mini-lectures' by members of the audience in an atmosphere that was 'light and free' but, as far as the underlying intellectual issues were concerned, dead serious. 'It was by far the most important learning experience I encountered throughout my career,' Misha wrote later. The greats of the German nuclear physics world—people like Heisenberg and Fritz Houtermans from Göttingen and Hans Suess from Hamburg—would turn up at the Tea Colloquium and present their latest work. Jensen and Bothe, working hard to end Germany's international isolation after the war, persuaded even émigrés reluctant to revisit Germany to come to Bothe's sixtieth birthday celebration in 1951. Jensen's collaborator Maria Goeppert-Mayer and the now US-based Hans Bethe, Eugene Wigner and Enrico Fermi were among others who visited the Heidelberg Institute in this period.

Young physicists were scarce on the ground, the war having wiped out a large part of Mischka's age group in Germany, and no doubt they were the more valued because of it. When Mischka had been around in Heidelberg for a few months and got friendly with Steinwedel, Jensen's senior assistant, they had a discussion one night about their prospects. Their conclusion was that 'we are too old to come up with a discovery of the magnitude of Einstein, Heisenberg, Schrödinger. They were all 25–26 years old when they did it. We are 27, and as far from that kind of discovery now as anybody else.' It was characteristic of the Heidelberg atmosphere that they should think in such ambitious comparative terms; probably, despite their stated pessimism, they all secretly hoped to win Nobel Prizes themselves one day. Actually none of them did (except the spectroscopist Rudolf Mössbauer, who was a bit younger than Mischka and arrived in Heidelberg after he had gone), and I think Mischka at least always felt that to be a bit of a failure. But there are cycles in science, and the great age of

Nobel Prizes for German physicists was coming to an end. By the time Mischka's cohort got into their stride for the competition in the 1960s, the buzz had moved out of their area of nuclear physics. Hans Bethe, the Sommerfeld-trained German émigré who relocated to Cornell and who won in 1967, was the last of the line.

The question of physicists' past Nazi affiliations was naturally a matter of interest. In Hanover, Mischka had never paid much attention to it, but once he got to Heidelberg, that changed. Jensen had been a party member, though after the war Heisenberg had vouched for his lack of enthusiasm in one of the attestations of political harmlessness known as *Persilschein* (after the laundry powder) that were part of the denazification process in these years. According to a memoir by Berthold Stech (one of Mischka's Heidelberg contemporaries), Helmut Steinwedel and Mischka, when they arrived successively from Hanover, 'told us about Jensen with great admiration, his attitude during the "Third Reich" and how he managed to survive inhuman times and still do interesting physics'. This probably came mainly from Steinwedel, who had been closer to Jensen in Hanover and had known him longer. But the question of Jensen's Nazi past was one that Mischka gave a lot of thought to in his first months in Heidelberg. He and Jensen talked about it, at least obliquely. Quoting Jensen in a letter to Helga, Mischka set out his argument:

> If you see over and over again that people whom you have trusted have thrown in their lot with the party and actually become addicted to those nationalistic resentments, and you are always being pushed against the wall, then you think: to hell with this rubbish, let's leave, go far away from here, go to Australia; then one can at least be a free man again. But then after a while you get back your courage and start

pushing back against it again. That is all you can do. So he [Jensen] didn't go to Australia, Argentina or America.

In the same letter, Mischka assured Helga that 'I have not the least grounds to assume, but rather all grounds against assuming, that [Jensen] was ever a Nazi ... He was in the party, of course. But to put it even more strongly, it can be claimed with a probability bordering on certainty that if anybody ever joined because there was nothing else to do, that person was Jensen.' With Mischka, such rather awkward formality of style often conveys uneasiness. But in this case it may also reflect the fact that the question of Nazi membership and general German guilt were closely linked in Mischka's mind, and he was writing to a German girl he was proposing to marry. The big thing to understand, Mischka instructed Helga, was that Jensen, although a German, is 'primarily a human being (*Mensch*), thus a cosmopolitan [first] and only secondarily also a German'. This made him even better than Obst, the German intellectual Mischka had met and briefly admired in Hanover, because with Obst it was the other way round: German first, and only then cosmopolitan (*weltbürgerlich*). Moreover, Jensen had the proper critical attitude towards Germans—'shares the opinions of my mother and myself', as Mischka put it to Helga—that Helga herself needed to adopt. Germans are arrogant because they feel inferior. They claim Germany is *the* country of poetry and philosophy, but this (whatever the teenage Mischka may have thought back in Riga) is actually completely unfounded. He quoted Jensen's categorical dismissal of the claim: 'there is one superior thinker who was an East Prussian: Kant. Otherwise the rest are no greater than their French or English counterparts.'

Helga Heimers was the other thing on Mischka's mind. Five years his junior, she was the daughter of a solid Protestant,

North German family (her father was director of a school for the blind). In terms of athletics, she was a sprinter as well as a hurdler and long jumper. At first Mischka didn't pay any particular attention to her because she looked so young (his previous girlfriends from the sports club were older and more worldly and experienced). Helga, for her part, had already taken note of him as a lively and popular member of the club, admired for his personal qualities as well as his excellence as a pole vaulter (within the sports club, evidently, his being a DP was not a social handicap). Helga was surprised and flattered when Mischka turned his attention to her. It happened on a bicycle trip, probably in the summer of 1948, to Hamburg, Lübeck and the Baltic coast. The person she fell in love with, as she later remembered, was light-hearted and fun to be with, the life of any party. He was also unconventional, which was both appealing to Helga and sometimes embarrassing, and critical of German formality, including that of her family. The qualities in Helga that Mischka stressed in his letters to Olga were her youth (and, by implication, her innocence and impressionableness) and her appreciation of music and paint-ing. She had the same hatred of German rigidity as he had, he told his mother optimistically: she just hadn't previously realised, for lack of experience of the wider world, that this rigidity was a specifically German trait. The other good thing about Helga, conveyed to Olga by Mischka in particularly convoluted prose, was that she loved him.

Mischka seems to have made up his mind to marry Helga in the early spring of 1949, perhaps in response to her plans to go to England as an au pair for a year (on in January, cancelled late April or May). Like all his major decisions, as he wrote in a letter to her parents, the decision to marry was made suddenly, but on the basis of 'earth that was already ploughed'. He took Helga to meet Olga around Easter. This seems to have been only a qualified success. Helga wasn't sure that Olga thought she was good enough for Mischka and felt envious of, and no doubt excluded by, the close understanding between mother and son. She wasn't altogether happy when, in Olga's next letter to Mischka, she sent her greetings to 'little Helga' (*die kleine Helga*), which Helga took as a bit of a putdown. (Olga switched to a different diminutive, Helgalein, after Mischka passed that on.) As Mischka's move from Hanover to Heidelberg came closer, he informed Olga, without further elaboration, that 'the probability that I will be taking the young lady (*Jungfrau*) with me continues to grow'—that is, that they were planning to get married. Olga replied slightly tartly ('If I understand you rightly, you want to take the young lady with you') with an abstract disquisition on the difficulties of choosing the right life partner, ending with the observation that

> at least one of the two partners must have their eyes open [*sehend sein*]. In your case, it must be the wife, so that you can live up to your talents and bring them to fruition. For both your sakes I hope that Helga brings enough strength to the task.

By extraordinarily unfortunate timing, Mischka's decision to marry Helga coincided with Nanni's long-delayed departure from the Soviet zone to the West. I found it hard to read her increasingly less hopeful letters to Mischka without wincing, but it wasn't only Nanni I felt sorry for. The first mention of a planned departure is in a letter from Mischka to Olga, evidently written in August or September 1948, where he reported that 'Nanni was here' and that 'she has become independent and wants to move to the Western zone'. (The approving tone suggests that at this point he was not yet in too deep with Helga.) As of January 1949, however, she was still sitting at home in Chemnitz waiting impatiently for departure to become possible (the nature of the obstacles are not spelt out), congratulating Mischka on his new job and urging him to work hard ('Genius equals hard work [*Fleisse*]. Otherwise you'll never get to America!'). By the beginning of April, she had reached Göttingen in the British zone, after a traumatic two-week imprisonment in the Soviet zone en route, and with rather forced cheerfulness suggested that if Mischka found himself in the area, he might come and see her; she couldn't come to him in Hanover just yet because she had no money, and anyway 'it doesn't behove a woman to visit a man'. She was working as a housemaid, but that didn't matter: 'in America lots of people start off washing dishes'. If he heard of any work for a chemical technician, he should let her know. But above all, he should write. He didn't, so on 14 April she wrote again, this time without sending greetings to his mother as in the earlier letter, and signing herself formally 'Marianne Schuster' instead of Nanni. 'No doubt you have so much work that there is no leisure for private life. Should it be so, you are forgiven … If it's a woman that is the obstacle, you are forgiven as well. But you could let me hear from you anyway, I won't be jealous and would only rejoice in your happiness, or do you begrudge me that?'

Mischka did reply to that letter, evidently sticking to a light tone and steering clear of awkward topics or too many specifics. In her reply on 9 May, Nanni commented rather acidly on a joke (recycled from an earlier letter to Olga) about his landlady and daughter constituting '1.5 women', hoping that 'you are having a lot of fun with your 1.5'. She was in Reutlingen in the French zone by this time, intending to go on to the Swabian university town of Tübingen. Mischka must have emphasised his (long-term) emigration plans, perhaps to indicate non-availability, because she wished him well with them, adding that she herself preferred to stay in Germany where she had the credentials to finish her education—and 'in any case', she added, 'I am a hateful "German"', thus ineligible for the IRO resettlement available for DPs. She hoped that in his next letter he would 'express himself somewhat more concretely, since it sometimes remains a riddle to me'.

Mischka must finally have promised to come to Tübingen to see her, for she wrote again on 16 June discussing possible dates. As far as I can tell, this meeting never took place. Instead, Mischka had some kind of nervous collapse that brought Helga hurrying to his side and had her parents sending him off to a 'nerve doctor' to determine if his health was sound enough for him to marry.

The specific episode, a 'mild fit on waking up', occurred when he was away on a sports trip in the middle of June. In contemporary terminology, he seems to have been suffering from panic attacks. Helga remembers that he sometimes had to get off a crowded tram to recover from such an attack, and at her parents' place had had fits of uncontrollable shaking when he had to lie down, frightening himself and the Heimers. Since he had arrived in Heidelberg, he had been prone to get 'nervous' in the evening when he was tired, expressed in 'a feeling of light internal shaking'. Describing his symptoms to the Heimers' Dr Malkus, evidently a psychiatrist, he referred to 'the mistrust of myself' and sense of insecurity that occurred at such moments, 'in which I am frightened by this anxiety and become more anxious'. Mischka attributed this to 'nerves', which he had to try to strengthen. He was shocked when, in response to his question about whether there was any impediment to his marriage, Dr Malkus failed to provide the expected reassurance but instead suggested waiting for a month to see how his condition developed. After the month had elapsed, he evidently gave the go-ahead, and Mischka wrote to Helga on 27 June to say that, being confirmed in his opinion that his symptoms were just 'nervousness' in a basically healthy person, he saw 'no ground why we shouldn't get married as quickly as possible'.

Olga, meanwhile, had reacted with a mixture of reassurance and astringent commonsense. 'I know these gentlemen,' she wrote. 'Nerve doctors are the biggest charlatans.' To make Mischka wait for a month before passing him as fit for marriage was 'unforgiveable rubbish—what difference would a month make?'—and could have no result but to upset the patient:

> You have been assessed as having sensitive nerves. You had scarcely emerged from puberty (and one doesn't know how long the afterlife of that is) when you were hit with a mass of [upsetting] experiences ... and you had to deal with them with weakened bodily capacity for resistance. So the nerves were under ever greater strain, until finally the tension was continuous, if also not always consciously, and it was not possible to relax. If tension becomes too great, there is going to be a moment when control weakens and they give way. In yourself, you are a healthy man and what can stand in the way of your marriage? I would even expect there to be a certain nervous tension, along with spiritual wellbeing, associated with being together with the person you love ...

She recommended long walks, breathing exercises, more sleep and a better diet (more butter).

It looks as if Mischka, untypically, hadn't yet told Olga about Nanni's reappearance, no doubt because the whole subject was too painful. But after a while he did, and he also gave her a wry paraphrase of Nanni's response when he finally informed her (probably after the fact) about his marriage to Helga. Nanni's letter was 'very decent', he said. She gave

him the slightly barbed advice that being unfai
wife was the main potential danger, but otherw
to assume that I possessed in reasonable measur̲ ̲.̲.̲.̲ ̲o̲t̲h̲e̲r
qualities necessary for a successful marriage'. Olga replied
staunchly that Nanni (whose side she was not going to take
against her son, even if she liked her) had not got it quite right:
'You have *all* the qualities to make a happy marriage.'

On the eve of his marriage in August, Mischka sent his
prospective in-laws a statement of his qualifications as a
husband and his attitude to the marriage. It started off ordi-
narily enough with a survey of his current position, salary and
prospects. The path to an academic chair (highly prestigious
in Germany) lay open before him, and although 'I have not
firmly decided that I will necessarily be a professor,' he would
probably take it. Science was his life, and he had pursued it
systematically, even if from the outside his course might seem
to encompass a number of quantum leaps. Marriage to Helga
was another of those quantum leaps, but as he stated in one of
his favourite negative statements of a positive, 'I am not very
sceptical about Helga's and my life together'. Conceding that
people tend not to be sceptical at the beginning of a marriage,
he cited his own powers of 'objectivity and self-criticism' in
support of his non-scepticism (optimism?) about the marriage
and concluded that for it to break down, 'both parties would
have to behave stupidly, or one party would have to behave
very stupidly'. There was nothing in the letter about being a
DP and a foreigner who was likely to take their daughter away
from Germany.

Whether or not the letter was reassuring for Helga's parents,
they accepted the inevitability of the marriage and put a good
face on it. On 4 August 1949, the scientific assistant and engineering graduate Michael Danos, of the Orthodox faith, born
in Riga, Latvia, on 10 January 1922, married the student Helga

orothea Helene Luise Heimers, of the Lutheran-Evangelical confession, born on 14 June 1927 in Hanover. The church marriage followed an earlier civil ceremony in Heidelberg (chosen over Hanover because the Americans required less documentation than the British). The Hanover wedding was largely a Heimer family affair, but of course Olga was there, cutting a fine figure in a dress she had made herself. Judging by the photographs, not only was the bride beautiful and blushing, but so was the groom. Herr and Frau Michael Danos had made their debut.

11
Olga's Departure

Olga with Simon Mirkin on her arrival in New York, November 1950. Contemporary press photo, courtesy of Barry Mirkin.

OF Mischka's old friends from Riga and Hanover, only Dailonis Stauvers was at his wedding. The rest had scattered to all corners of the earth or would soon do so. Bičevskis had gone to Australia; others were off to Canada, Chile, Venezuela, Boston and New York. Stauvers himself was probably already planning his departure to the United States, which took place in 1951. The exodus had started two years before Mischka's marriage, and the Danoses' correspondence now regularly contained news of friends departing or planning to depart to Brazil, Holland, South Africa and Palestine.

Simon Mirkin, Olga's Riga protégé, was one of the first to go, leaving for the United States in mid 1947. He was able to get in early because he worked for the Jewish refugee organisation HIAS and the American occupation authorities. Olga's sister Mary was also putting in an application for the United States, the most popular of all destinations for DPs, as were her former husband Paul Sakss and his new wife. Some people had problems with visas and selection by the country of their first choice. But, inexorably, the transient DP communities established in the wake of the war were starting to unravel.

These mass departures were made possible by a new Allied approach to solving the DP problem. The mission of the old international refugee authority, UNRRA, had been to repatriate as many DPs as possible, while looking after those remaining in Europe who were unwilling or unable to repatriate, until someone could work out what to do with them. Political motives were usually cited for the DPs' unwillingness to return, although undoubtedly many from the East, with its historically lower living standards than Western Europe, had unspoken economic motives as well. The 'non-repatriables' included most of the DPs from the Baltic states, Olga's and Mischka's compatriots, who did not regard the Soviet Union as their homeland. With their shattered economies, Germany in particular and the European nations in general were not in a position to absorb more than a small proportion of the DPs. The doors to the United States, where many DPs wanted to go, remained largely shut during UNRRA's reign, and Britain was trying to block movement of Jewish DPs to Palestine, another favoured destination. So for several years after the war, the ultimate fate of the non-repatriated DPs was uncertain.

The IRO (International Refugee Organization), which replaced UNRRA as custodian of the DPs in 1947, had a new plan. This was in effect to give up on the idea of repatriation and move swiftly towards mass resettlement of DPs outside Europe. In 1948, the US Congress passed the Displaced Persons Act providing for large-scale entry, albeit with a complicated system of preferences and restrictions and the requirement that DPs have a local sponsor. Australia, Canada, Argentina and other Latin American countries with labour shortages indicated a willingness to take their share. The system was that DPs recorded their resettlement preferences with IRO but then had to apply to the individual countries and pass a medical, occupational and political vetting by their selection committees. The political vetting was initially to prevent entry of Nazi collaborators and war criminals, but as the Cold War took hold, blocking Communists and Communist sympathisers came to seem equally important.

Olga and, from 1949, Mischka were off the IRO's 'care and maintenance' list as a result of 'going on to the German economy', but they were still eligible for IRO resettlement if they cared to take up the opportunity. Whether they wanted to leave Germany and resettle was the first question they had to decide. If the answer was yes, the next questions were where they wanted to go, and which countries were ready to take them.

As Latvians, Mischka and Olga ranked relatively high on the preference list of the resettlement countries, which tended (like the Nazis) to prefer blue-eyed Northern Europeans to Poles and other Slavic groups. Australia, for example, put Latvians right at the top of its mass resettlement scheme, and the United States regarded them as desirable too. The potential problem for Latvians was suspicion of wartime collaboration, particularly by those who had volunteered to fight with the Germans in the Latvian Legion or the Waffen-SS, but the Danoses were not in that category. On the other hand, the preference of most of the receiving countries for young, healthy manual workers did not favour the Danoses. Young professionals and 'brain-workers' among the DPs were in less demand as immigrants, even if they had finished their education in Germany courtesy of UNRRA; if they got through the selection, they couldn't count on getting jobs that fitted their qualifications, and some found it advisable to fudge their biographies and present themselves to the selection committees as builders' labourers or domestic servants. Older professionals, especially those in less than perfect health, were often shunned by selection committees, along with sufferers of TB and syphilis and the disabled. Most selection committees favoured a cut-off age of around forty-five for DP immigrants, which was a potential problem for Olga, who turned fifty in 1947. Fortunately, she had had the forethought to misstate her date of birth from the moment of her arrival in Germany, and managed to lop off a few more years from her IRO documents.

Olga and Mischka, particularly Mischka, belonged to the relatively small number of DPs capable of supporting themselves, currently and in the future; for them, remaining to make a life in Germany, or perhaps elsewhere in Europe, was a plausible option. You might expect that they would have considered this seriously, particularly in view of their linguistic skills, Mischka's marriage to a German girl and Olga's unwillingness to accept the separation from her sons in Riga as final. Yet there is no sign that either of them did so.

This is a bit of a puzzle. Once he moved to Heidelberg as Jensen's assistant, Mischka's best chance of a future as a physicist, particularly a professor of physics, lay in remaining in Germany. We have no direct evidence of his attitude to the Federal Republic, established the year he went to Heidelberg, but he thought very highly of the currency reform (*Währungsreform*) of 1947 that paved the way for West Germany's rapid economic recovery, and continued in later life to cite it as a rare case of dramatically and instantaneously successful state economic intervention. As he remembered,

> Before the Währungsreform, trains, trams incredibly overcrowded, like in India; people were pushy, impolite, crude, aggressive, thin-tempered, etc. ... First day of DM [Deutschmark]: after getting my DM-s, I invested in a month tram-pass, which was indispensable for getting around: to school and to sports club. It was a reasonable fraction of my capital. I entered the tram. Surprise: nobody pushed, no foul language; instead: everybody polite, soft spoken, civilized. Seats available. Strange. Same on street: instead of milling, jostling crowds, polite pedestrians; instead of store windows yesterday empty and bleak, same today filled with goods with prices attached, and prices reasonable, even though nobody actually could buy much, except perhaps somebody representing a large family. Within some days, as more and more people got their salaries, the economy began moving, and that was the beginning of the Wirtschaftswunder [economic miracle].

To be sure, arguing against remaining in Germany was Mischka's new anti-Germanism, which led him to write critically of the German national character, refer to the country and its occupants as 'Germanium' and 'Germanen' (not with the German words '*Deutschland*' and '*Deutsche*'), and to say later that he couldn't have stayed in Germany, for all the appeal of Heidelberg's Tea Colloquium, because of his feeling of 'pressure' there. This pressure evidently arose from a sense of constraint and tension; he expressed it to me later as not being able to breathe. This was a physical description, not a psychological one, but when pressed on the psychological basis, he invoked something like the theory of 'authoritarian personality' popular among postwar American social scientists, including psychiatrists sent to work in the American zone of Germany to uncover 'Nazi personalities' as part of denazification. 'The German alternatively commands and scrapes,' one of these psychiatrists explained; 'this is obvious in the family, where the father, dominating his wife and children, no sooner leaves the house than he bows to his superiors.' Fascist personality traits were to be expected 'among children with stern, often physically abusive fathers and distant, frightened, and unaffectionate mothers'. Misha's 1995 analysis runs along similar lines, with the addition of his favourite epithet for German behaviour, 'rigidity', and inclusion of the tendency to watch for and officiously correct non-conformist behaviour on the part of others.

Olga did not express anti-German sentiments in her letters, though Mischka assured Helga that she shared his strong hostility to German nationalism. Given her firsthand experience of the problems of small business, she may have been less sanguine than Mischka about the future of the German economy. On the other hand, she was not at all confident about her personal prospects elsewhere, especially in the United States, imagined in Europe as 'a big factory populated with heartless robots'.

Perhaps the basic reason the Danoses felt, more or less unquestioningly, that they had to leave Germany was psychological. It would have been hard, even for such independent thinkers, to stand confidently against the tide that was pulling hundreds of thousands of DPs out of Central Europe, especially as the pace stepped up dramatically in 1949. By mid 1949, more than half a million had gone (out of an original million or so DPs), and a year later the number of departures had almost reached 800,000. Moreover, assisted departure was not an option that was going to last for ever. The IRO, mainly US-funded, was expected to get the job done within a few years and go out of business, and the US Congress was becoming impatient. In fact, the IRO stayed in operation after several deferments of closure (Olga and Mischka periodically exchanged anxious news of the latest developments), but the prospect of its imminent demise, along with the organisational help and free passages it offered, created its own pressures (*What if the last boat goes without me?*). By the time the IRO actually ceased operation at the end of 1951, only a 'hard core' of fewer than 250,000 DPs remained in Europe (not just Germany, though the largest group was there). While a minority were employed, like the Danoses, in the German or Austrian economy, the majority were rejects—persons with 'paralysis, missing limbs, or a history of TB', along with convicted criminals and the elderly—left at the mercy of the new Federal Republic and charitable organisations because no country would take them.

If departure was on the agenda, the next question was where to go. Olga's original preference was for Latin America, and she registered Argentina with the IRO as her preferred destination in 1948. She already had contacts there, probably from earlier DP departures, and thought the language would be easier to master, since she knew Italian. Earlier, back in the Hanover days, Mischka had not been wholly against the Argentinian option, going so far as to ask Jensen if he had any contacts there (Jensen did, at the National University of La Plata in Buenos Aires, and said he would write to recommend Mischka). But by mid 1948, Mischka was categorical in his support for the United States option and opposition to Latin America. 'I still see no substantive grounds for your desire to go to South America,' he wrote brusquely to Olga, adding that he regarded the language as a minus, not a plus (admittedly, his Italian was not as good as hers) and learning Spanish an unnecessary complication. (He was, in fact, increasingly focussed on improving his English, practising it in his letters to Olga—'I do not need any mony [sic]. And do not bother about me!' is an early effort.)

Olga had another go at explaining her reasons, with no more success than before:

> Look, Mischutka, I am simply frightened of the US. Life there demands too much shoving for my taste. And I don't see the remotest possibility of remaining independent, just maybe working in a factory. South America is not so feverish, and I hope there to have a chance to establish myself.

At this point, Olga was so set on Argentina and hostile to the United States that she was willing to contemplate their emigrating to different destinations, writing that 'if you go to the US and see some possibility for me there, then I could always move. But perhaps I would also be able to do something for you in Buenos Aires.' As late as September 1948, Olga was still thinking in terms of Argentina and saving her money for an application to the Argentinian consulate in Frankfurt: she was so fed up with Germany that 'if it had been possible, I would have jumped on an aeroplane and flown to South America'. Still, she was hedging her bets to some extent, encouraging Mischka to put his name on a new register of DPs qualified for university jobs in North America and urging him to 'please, really please, do everything that I don't know but you do to make your scientific work accessible and transportable'.

Regardless of destination, Olga was becoming increasingly dissatisfied with her situation in Germany. The high hopes she had had for her sculpture when she moved to Fulda seem to have been disappointed, at least until shortly before her departure. Although in a later interview with an American newspaper she described her occupation in Germany before her departure as 'mending religious figures from bombed out German churches in Frankfurt-am-Main, Wiesbaden, Bremerhaven and other cities', there is almost nothing on this subject in her letters of 1949. Much more space is devoted to discussion of her tailoring business and money troubles.

The tailoring business looked good on paper, but in her letters it comes across mainly as a burden. There were reports of trouble with angry customers when she was ill and couldn't summon the energy to finish a job (it is not clear why she was doing the sewing herself, but it was possibly alterations on work done badly by her employees). There were also indications that the tailoring connected her with a grey barter economy: early in 1949, she reported visiting a general's wife in Wiesbaden who gave her some material to make up but also took $10 and two cartons of cigarettes from Olga in exchange for a man's jacket (for Mischka). Problems with tenants in the house she was living in also feature quite prominently in her correspondence; it looks as if she may have been in charge of supervising the house and letting other apartments on Mirkin's behalf. When she fantasised about flying away to South America, it was because 'I wanted money so much, to earn a lot of money. Perhaps a more normal time will come sometime.'

Fulda didn't feel like a proper home, she wrote to Mischka. Apropos of the question of emigration destinations, she commented:

> However it comes out, I would like to get away from Fulda. It is odd that even though now I have a house, I can't settle down. When I would get back from my trips to Flensburg, Glücksburg, even my hotel room in Reichenberg, I felt as

though I were coming 'home'. But not here. Often I tell myself that I will probably end up having to stay here—just for that reason.

Olga came down finally in favour of the United States. Her only direct statement on the decision was written years after, when—in still fractured English, so probably not too long after her arrival—she recalled that 'after long hesitation I had given in my friends and his wifes repeated persuasians, to come to America'. The friends were probably Simon Mirkin, newly settled and employed in New York, and his new wife Ilse, also a DP. What seems to have tipped the scales for Olga was Mirkin's offer to sponsor her. The United States, unlike most other resettlement countries, required immigrants to have a sponsor even if they came in under the DP Act of 25 June 1948, which authorised the admission in the next two years of 200,000 DPs for permanent settlement. This sponsor might be a charitable, religious or ethnic organisation (Mirkin's own sponsor had been his employer in Frankfurt, HIAS), or it might be an individual. No actual invitation from Mirkin survives, but he identified himself as her sponsor in a statement to the press on her arrival, and explains his sponsorship as an act of gratitude to her for saving his life. There is documentation of his subsequent offer to sponsor Mischka. By the end of 1949, in any case, Mirkin's involvement in Olga's departure plans are taken as a given in her correspondence with Mischka. She now thought she might get to America quicker than her sister, who had applied earlier, since 'Mirkin is sending me the work contract'.

Right up to the moment of departure, however, Olga showed little positive enthusiasm for her chosen destination, or even for departure as such. Her mood in 1948–49 was depressed, and this showed, rather uncharacteristically, in her letters to Mischka as well as her diary. 'Mischutka, I'm getting old,' she wrote in July 1948. 'Since I heard of Papa's death, I look backwards more than forwards.' The next winter, around the time that Mischka was making up his mind to marry Helga, her mood was even lower, at least judging by a letter written to him but never sent. Having started by thanking him for a letter ('You can make someone so happy with a few words'), she plunged immediately into a demonstration that his letter had not, in fact, had this effect:

> You are one of those I love most [but] we shouldn't stay together ... No, we shouldn't. I mean to let you go. All the people who depended on me, I brought them unhappiness. I will not at any cost give you advice. Everything I have done has been bad. I can't get rid of the thought that the two letters I wrote to Riga [after receiving Arpad's letter] have brought misfortune to the young ones [Arpad and Jan]. All my efforts to turn my thoughts in another direction don't help the pain. If it could help, I would kill myself. But I don't believe in that kind of magic ... Dear, dear Mischutka, I won't send this letter. But I'm going to pull back from you all the same, doing it so that you don't notice. I have to spare you that at least. What a flood of nonsense is pouring out. It's nothing but egoism ...

I was quite upset when I read this letter (late in the game, when I had already written the first draft: it was a fragment in untidy handwriting that looked hard to decipher). *No*, you didn't bring unhappiness to Misha, I wanted to tell her. On the contrary, you were a lifelong support and inspiration to him; if only everyone had such a mother. But this would have been a message from Misha's wife rather than his biographer. Of course Olga was too sensible and too protective of Mischka to send her anguished letter; she kept such emotions for the diary and the drawer. And, being the resilient person she was, she coped.

It's tempting to speculate that one of Olga's strategies for coping with a partial loss of Mischka through marriage was to find a substitute. Daniel Kolz, a young pianist about Mischka's age, first appears in the correspondence in a rather strained and arch letter to Mischka and Helga about the wedding, which it appears Daniel had attended, though not officially as Olga's companion. In this letter, Olga makes much of the remarkable resemblance of Mischka in his wedding photos to Daniel, which she and Daniel had marvelled at. Thereafter, Olga's letters regularly contain news of Daniel's career, and Mischka's letters include friendly enquiries about him (Mischka and Helga also kept in touch with him for years after they had all moved to America). Olga was still an attractive woman, and whether Daniel was just a protégé or also a lover is open to question. At the time, Helga recalls, it did not occur to her that they were lovers, though in retrospect she thought they probably were. If it occurred to Mischka, no trace remains. In any case, Olga and Daniel provided each other with support, emotional and practical, and evidently enjoyed each other's company. The most buoyant letter in Olga's whole correspondence in the Fulda period describes a celebratory dinner with other friends that Olga and Daniel had organised on the spur of the moment after some success of his. 'You have a really young mama-in-law!' was her final cheerful comment to Helga.

Kolz was also no doubt partly responsible for the growing prominence of music in Olga's and Mischka's letters. They had always exchanged occasional reports of music they had heard in concerts and on the radio, but in 1949–50 the frequency and seriousness of these reviews became such that they might have been professional music critics. Probably it wasn't only

Kolz's arrival on the scene but also Helga's that produced this result: music was the main thing the four of them had in common. But they weren't the only ones in Germany to whom classical music mattered. It mattered so much to the German population as a whole that even the Allied occupiers noticed. 'If ever the beasts of war are tamed, it will be music which will grant us the strength of heart and soul to do it,' as one official of the American military government put it.

Hoping to bring out the Germans' better side, all the occupying powers, including the Soviets, competitively encouraged live performances and supplied more on their zonal radio stations. Naturally there were some political complications, particularly with regard to performers: the Nazi leaders had also liked music, as long as it wasn't modernist and degenerate. The pianist Ellen Ney, a Beethoven specialist and sometime favourite of Hitler, was on the blacklist in the American zone until 1948, her concertising limited to 'atonement' concerts for American troops, POWs and DPs. The great pianist Walter Gieseking had problems too. He had not been a Nazi party member but, because of his visibility as a performer in Nazi times, was widely regarded as a collaborator. The Americans had him on their blacklist until early 1947, although the French allowed him to teach and perform freely in their zone. When he went to play Carnegie Hall in New York in 1949, immigration officials swooped in, following noisy public protests, and he had to leave the country swiftly under threat of deportation.

The Danoses both went to Gieseking's concerts in Germany that same year, Olga in Frankfurt and Mischka in Heidelberg. They went to those of Ellen Ney, too, as well as a whole string of other pianists and string quartets, all thoughtfully reviewed. Neither Olga nor Mischka showed any sign of being interested in the political controversies; they went to

Gieseking's and Ney's concerts for the music. So, incidentally, did my father and my eleven-year-old self when Gieseking came to Melbourne in 1952 (there was controversy about the visit in Australia too, but my civil libertarian father was against boycotting musicians for political reasons). Olga was a bit critical of Gieseking's Debussy (the composer was some- thing of a Danos specialty, his art songs being prominent in Arpad Sr's repertoire) and so, I must admit, was I, when he played all twenty-four *Préludes* at one sitting in Melbourne, putting me off Debussy for decades.

Mischka had splurged a back-pay windfall to buy a Philips 'Philetta' radio 'with very good sound quality' to listen to music. He had it on while writing a letter to Olga, and his attention was suddenly diverted to a broadcast of Bach's *Chromatic Fantasy and Fugue*: it reminded him how extraordi- narily modern Bach was (he offered a brief technical analysis); there was nothing like it again until Hindemith. Mischka, but not Olga, quite often mentioned Paul Hindemith in his com- mentaries on music. His exposure to Hindemith—a German modernist composer who had emigrated in the 1930s—was no doubt thanks to OMGUS, the propaganda arm of the US occu- pation forces, which was pushing modern music and abstract art on the Germans on the slightly bizarre premise that as the Nazis had labelled modernism 'degenerate', it must have some intrinsic connection with democracy.

When Olga first started taking serious steps towards depar- ture in the summer of 1948, she was still thinking in terms of Argentina. She went through her IRO screening for emigra- tion eligibility at the end of July, and was planning to go off to Frankfurt to register with the Argentinians as soon as she had enough money. Her emigration number came through early in 1950, with the United States replacing Argentina as her destination. But there was a problem with the birthdate registered in her papers, of which the police had informed her a few weeks earlier. In April she wrote to Mischka that her papers were going through IRO, but she was so fed up with all the problems that the night before, on the eve of the final submission date, she had 'toyed with the thought of having to give up the whole emigration'. The main problem seems to have been that her documents showed an earlier birthdate than 1905, and she was insisting on a correction with as much outraged determination as if she had actually been born then, and not in 1897. In the end, by going over the head of a junior official to a senior one, she had her way. These arrangements were evidently all being coordinated with Mirkin in New York, but that correspondence is lacking. Once Olga had been approved on all sides as an immigrant to the United States, control left her hands for the time being: she just had to sit and wait until the IRO told her to proceed immediately to the transit camp prior to embarkation on such and such a vessel.

But then came a new complication: Olga fell ill. There was a sore spot on her stomach, and she booked in for an X-ray. She was worried about the cost of the medical visits and treatments, however, so when the doctor wrote her an expensive prescription, she ignored it and went to a homeopathic medicine man. Surely it would soon get better—but in the meantime, things were 'very bad in terms of my mood, and so it's a blessing that nobody from my nearest and dearest is around. I don't know how to put up with being sick with elegance—I mean spiritual elegance.'

It turned out that she had to have an operation. 'I was bleeding uninterruptedly for almost a month and waited to go to a doctor until it stopped. Some days it was so strong that I could scarcely stand.' When she finally did go to the doctor, he insisted on putting her in hospital; 'it would have been better to put it off', as she wrote to Mischka, '[but] I have to let them cut my belly open, and better soon than later. I have already made arrangements with the butcher and now am just waiting for some money that should come through in a few days.' The operation took place in the Herz-Jesu Hospital in Fulda around the third week in June, and she expected to be in hospital eleven days. She woke up from the operation hearing snatches of Beethoven and thinking it was her son Arpad bending over her. As she reported to Mischka and Helga, 'the scar is over the whole belly. I think he must have pulled my entire innards out ...'

Not only was this operation incredibly badly timed, since she was likely to be summoned for emigration any day, but it was also a major blow financially. Olga had been trying to save up to cover departure expenses, but all that was gone, and Mischka was called on for an urgent contribution. Even that didn't cover all expenses for the hospital stay and medical treatment, and Olga had to persuade the surgeon to allow her to send the final payment later from America.

Her summons to the transit camp in Butzbach (north of Frankfurt, about 100 kilometres from Fulda by road) must have come not long after she got out of hospital, or conceivably even earlier. She was in Butzbach by 31 July, arriving by train and then walking to the camp. On the way, she sat down on a hillside overlooking the forest and remembered how seven years ago (surely six, in fact) she had sat on just such a hill in Gotenhafen and looked over the sea to Sweden, where she wrongly thought her sons Arpad and Jan had found refuge: 'Today I have nothing to look for.' She was 'miserable as a dog', she wrote to Mischka. 'I don't know why I have to go to America. And yet I am going to do it. Without inner conviction but out of some kind of [illegible word—*Muk*?]'. Perhaps it's appropriate that that key word is illegible. Was it courage (German *Mut*) that was driving her on? Or torment

(Russian *muka*)? Or something between fatalism and a stubborn determination to finish something she had started?

Before embarkation she spent a couple of months based in Butzbach in a remarkable whirl of activity. She seems to have been almost constantly on the road, attending to urgent business, and wondering why, in her life, everything always had to be done at the last minute. Fortunately, her health held up, so that she could write bravely to Mischka in mid September that

the stomach wound has healed well and peace reigns in my intestines. Now fortunately there is no discharge. The only thing is that my resources are at this moment only half a [Deutsch]Mark. It's also a bother that I have to travel so soon after such an operation … Things are better with me again. Who could take this joke [i.e. the illness and operation] seriously!

One set of last-minute business was of a legal and financial character, some of it evidently connected with the settling of affairs with regard to Mirkin's house in Fulda. The outcome as well as the substance of the matter (or matters) are unclear: in an undated letter probably written in August, she rejoiced that after 'endless correspondence' between Fulda, Kassel and Frankfurt (where the lawyer was), the affair had been settled in her favour and 'I have finally become rich'. But evidently she spoke too soon, since the next month there are references to 'my Kassel disappointment' and the fact that Helga's mother had been kind enough to offer her a loan, 'which I accepted with great relief'. In any case, it's clear that with regard to the business matters, she left a lot of loose ends still dangling, which Mischka and Helga had to tidy up after her departure.

Some of her pressing business was related to emigration. Despite her efforts to postpone it, she had to go through medical inspection in August; rather surprisingly—you would think a recent major operation might have hit alarm bells—this went without a hitch. She was running around various local and American commissions and the Fulda police collecting and delivering documents. And on top of that, she was constantly trying to find time to get to Heidelberg for a final visit, though it looks as if she never managed it.

The most remarkable aspect of Olga's departure was that in these last months in Germany, her activity as a religious sculptor suddenly went into high gear. In mid September, she wrote to Mischka that with perhaps two weeks remaining before her departure, she had begun some sculptural work for the church in Fulda and was now trying desperately to finish it. If only the priest would let her work late into the night, but unfortunately he slept just above the church cellar in which she worked. So she was having to stay on for some extra days but hoped to be able to leave on 22 September. 'You can imagine that I absolutely must finish my big "Work".' Art experts, including the sculptor Richard Maur, with whom she had had some contact back in Riga in the 1920s, had come to see her figurines, notably a St Antony holding the Child Jesus in his arms, and praised them. Olga was pleased by their positive reactions, but even more (she said) by the fact that when she told Maur that she had described herself to fellow Latvian DPs as his pupil, which was not strictly true, he had said she had every right to do so and he would be glad to be seen as her teacher.

Mischka was drawn into the last-minute appraisal of Olga's figurines too, and sent a remarkably detailed critique, noting a fault in one of the pleats in St Antony's sleeve and that the Child's face was too grown-up for his body. Olga was still working hard, especially on the Child (she had sculpted him naked but was now, perhaps in response to Maur's suggestions, clothing him). On the eve of her departure for the embarkation camp, she was thinking almost exclusively about her sculptures, dashing off a note to Mischka and Helga defending her vision of the Child as ageless in terms of Catholic tradition. She was sending the figurines (evidently St Antony and the Child) to them in Heidelberg and regretted that she couldn't send them her Holy Family as well—they would find Joseph 'particularly amusing', she thought; the figure was a bit stiff, but she was just going to have to leave him like that. 'Despite all the mistakes ... I am satisfied in the highest degree that I have made him.' In a final postcard sent off the next morning, she was still obsessing about the sculptures, tormented on her last night by dreams that she had done St Antony's pleats wrong.

She had received her embarkation notice on 13 September ('the thirteenth: is that a lucky or unlucky number?'), with instructions that she would be departing in eight days. Meanwhile, there was another mishap: she fell when getting out of the train in Butzbach and injured her leg. She hoped this would get her an extension, and indeed she was able to add in a postscript: 'Extension until 28 September. On the way to Frankfurt. Oh-oh-oh-oh! Such anxiety!!!'

Olga's actual embarkation date was Sunday 22 October 1950, so her ship's sailing date was probably postponed at the last minute. The next we hear from her is a letter from the middle of the Atlantic Ocean en route to New York giving a rather harrowing, though unself-pitying, account of the trip. She was on a troop ship filled with DPs, allocated a top bunk— just under the light and the ventilation, which Olga reports as a positive—in a corner in a hall accommodating 500 people in tiers. The IRO had given each passenger $1.50 to spend at the PX on board, and Olga had used it to get stamps to send her letter from Halifax, their first North American stop.

Shipboard conditions were obviously awful, with fetid air, and pushing and shoving at meals, and vomit in the gangways. On deck, there were seats for only about fifty people; when it rained, the only shelter was under the lifeboats that were hanging up. Nevertheless, after a terrible twenty-four hours of intense seasickness during a storm in mid-ocean, Olga spent most of her time there, if not lying and writing in her bunk: 'I always stand at the railing or—if it is frosty, sit on the rolled-up rope ladders and look for hours at the water and the sky,' wearing two jackets and her fur coat.

As the ship approached New York, the passengers were allowed to stay on deck all night to get a first sight of the city, but Olga went to bed, rising on 1 November at four—half an hour before breakfast—to see the Statue of Liberty—or rather, not to see it, since it was obscured by 'night and cloud'. It took an hour for the tugs to pull them in, in which time New York's skyscrapers became visible. She was one of the first through medical control, and as she was waiting for immigration to open, Mirkin appeared. He had promised to meet the ship, but still it was a big relief to see him—'he didn't look so ugly any more', as she commented in her report of the arrival sent to Germany. She didn't enjoy it, however, when he insisted on parading her before the crowd of reporters and photographers gathered to write their DP stories. Instructing her to leave the talking to him, 'Mirkin gave them a whole novel (*Roman*)' about her and their past connection, Olga wrote wryly to Mischka and Helga. This is how the *Spokane Daily Chronicle* reported Mirkin's story:

A 29-year-old Jewish refugee paid a debt of gratitude to a Christian woman who sheltered and befriended him when the Nazis overran his native Latvia.

The story began in Latvia in 1941.

Simon Mirkin, his young sister and their parents were clapped into a German slave labor camp for Jews near Riga. During a trip to Riga on a labor project, Mirkin met Mrs. Olga Danos, 44, Russian Orthodox, who made her living as a dressmaker for the wives of Nazi officials.

Mirkin said that, through a bribe, Mrs. Danos arranged for him and his family to live with her. They were released from camp and made their home with the dressmaker for two years.

After the war Mirkin married and came to the United States. But he never forgot his benefactress. Today, Mrs. Danos arrived by ship as a displaced person—sponsored by the Mirkins, with who [sic] she will live.

'I want to return to her just a little of what she had given me by helping her to start in the United States,' Mirkin said after greeting Mrs. Danos at the pier.

This was indeed a touching and uplifting story, though perhaps one shouldn't take it too literally, given Olga's comment on Mirkin's 'novel'. Since the Danos family knew very few details about Olga's activity saving Jews, I had always hoped that if I could ever track down some Mirkin descendants, they would know. And finally I did track down Barry Mirkin, thanks to Olga's noting the name of the toddler who damaged one of her letters to Mischka shortly after her arrival in New York. He did indeed know about Olga and how grateful his father, recently deceased, had been to her for saving him. He sent me the press cutting and the photo of the two of them together on her arrival. In crossing emails, each of us eagerly asked the other for details about exactly what had happened in Riga and just how Olga had saved Mirkin and other Jews. Alas, neither of us knew. Now, I suppose, nobody ever will.

12
Mischka's Departure

Departure, 1951. Mischka (in hat, third from left) and Helga (in coat with fur collar) are sitting on their luggage waiting to depart, probably from Bremerhaven, for New York.

MISCHKA'S and Olga's relations were necessarily different after his marriage to Helga. 'Perhaps I write less often now,' she wrote to Mischka some months after the marriage, 'but it is because I know that you won't miss it. You also know what my attitude to you is, how happy I am about that [presumably the fact that he was no longer alone].' This clearly represented the 'pulling back' that she had privately decided upon—distancing herself from him, but in such a way that he wouldn't notice. Whether Mischka noticed or not, he was at pains to convey his own belief that when people talk about 'losing a son through marriage', they are thinking of situations when the connection is in any case weak or one-sided, whereas in the case of himself and Olga, 'it is superfluous to explain that [the connection] has only increased over the course of the last twenty years'.

After the marriage, Olga was careful to include a special message for Helga (Helgalein) in her letters. Initially a bit artificial because they didn't know each other well, the tone became increasingly relaxed. Some of Olga's communications with Helga were practical, like her instructions on how to make the Russian paskha, of which Mischka was so fond. Increasingly often, Olga addressed her letters to both of them—'Dear gang', 'Dear children', 'My dear little family'. Once Olga was in the United States, according to the normal pattern of young married couples writing family letters, Helga became as frequent a correspondent as Mischka. Olga usually signed off as 'Your Mother' or 'Your Ma' ('Mi' and 'Ma' had become the standard usage in Mischka's and Olga's correspondence), while Helga wrote to her as 'My dear Mama'. Olga also established good relations with Helga's parents, Willy and Martha Heimers, whom she evidently visited in Hanover on more than one occasion: after getting out of hospital in July 1950 and in the throes of hectic preparations for departure, she wrote to Martha imagining herself 'in my favourite chair under your lamp, in Willy's peaceful presence and with your always friendly face nearby'.

While Olga was clearly fond of Helga, and apparently vice versa, she remained uneasy about whether Helga really knew what kind of man she had married. Just after her arrival in New York, she wrote anxiously:

Living with Mi is particularly difficult, dear Helga. He is an exceptional man. What kind of talent is in him he himself did not realise for a long time. I think he doubts sometimes if he can absolutely do something. He doesn't belong to those with a well-balanced nature, who systematically work towards a goal, cool and considered. He is a pure artist (his science is pure art) and, as such, sensitive, subject to moods, eruptively creative. He *needs* a wife who believes in him and his abilities, even when they are apparently not at their top, to keep him in good shape. It lies in your hands to give the world a great man ... That you have a fine sensitivity for various things I have observed several times with great satisfaction. Mi has told me that you have above the average capacity for loyalty (which is only a gift of the heart). But whether you have correctly recognised Mi's great, rooted and deeply hidden talents—that I don't know. Whether you will train in yourself that strength to become his spiritual torch I also don't know. But I believe it because you are sensitive and have the gift of love.

Helga didn't see Mischka the same way Olga did. It was the man who interested her, not the scientist, and she thought Olga's emphasis on his genius overblown. (Olga was the same about Daniel Kolz, Helga told me: she thought both of them were bound to be the equivalent of Nobel Prize winners.) In the two years that Helga and Mischka lived together in Heidelberg, learning to function as a couple and play the wife and husband roles were major preoccupations. Mischka even took to describing his domestic environment in some detail in his letters to his mother, albeit with a certain self-consciousness. After he and Helga moved in November 1949 to a new and slightly larger apartment on Rohrbacher Street, he described how they had removed the pictures provided by the landlady and hidden them behind the cupboard, as well as hanging a curtain across one corner of the room and putting an artistic arrangement of branches gathered in the forest in front of it: 'now it is really pleasant'. 'There are signs that our married state is making progress,' he wrote to Olga. 'We have even got somewhat used to the fact that in public we properly belong together. Only the "Frau Danos" is still always a bit strange ...' 'Frau Danos' was, of course, a name that had hitherto belonged only to Olga.

Mischka was no longer formally a DP, having gone off IRO maintenance and 'on to the German economy' when he moved to Heidelberg and started earning a salary. He was now living like a German—or a German bourgeois, to quote his own description of a 'leisurely bourgeois Sunday' (but note the tongue-in-cheek reference to their late rising, surely not a German bourgeois habit):

> After we had got up at 11 or 12 and eaten lunch, we had to hurry not to miss the performance of Beethoven's *Missa Solemnis* that began at 4. That's why we got up so early ... Then we came home and made ourselves comfortable; we made cocoa and wanted to hear the broadcast of a symphony concert from Stuttgart when suddenly the power went off and we sat for an hour in the dark (by candlelight).

Quite uncharacteristically for Mischka, clothes became a topic in his letters of 1949–50, with much correspondence about the making of a corduroy suit. He felt that he and Helga had made a good showing at a little party at the institute to which wives were invited, noting, however, that this was no surprise: 'We had expected nothing less than to be the best-dressed family, at least with regard to the feminine part.'

At their first dinner party, with Mischka's colleague Helmut Steinwedel and his wife as guests, they were running late when the Steinwedels arrived, and Mischka was never able to change into his good trousers. Mischka gave Olga a cheerfully ironic account of all this, but Helga thought it was no laughing matter and added her own postscript:

> I don't think it's very nice of Mischka to have written to you about our mix-up and not being ready. It was very embarrassing to me then, and still is. But the Steinwedels did come too punctually, five minutes before the appointed time.
>
> [pps from Mischka] She is still young and inexperienced and felt bad about this mishap.
>
> [ppps from Helga] And Mischka just has a thick skin.

They didn't take long to get their act together as hosts: it was something Mischka was naturally good at and probably Helga too. A few months later, when Jensen's wife was hospitalised with typhus, leaving Jensen and his daughter to fend for themselves, the young Danoses had them round several times for lunch without any sign of anxiety even from Helga. There was some less formal social interaction as well. Dailonis Stauvers, now working as an engineer for Siemens in Nuremburg, came to stay several times. Indeed, a photograph survives of the three of them in bed together, Helga in the middle, but Stauvers assured me this was a staged event: rising early one morning, and finding Mischka and Helga still asleep in their big bed, he fetched his camera, got into bed with them and took the photograph.

Thanks to Helga's presence in Heidelberg, the American occupation of the city became more visible to Mischka. He had noticed it at the start, writing to Olga shortly after his arrival about his 'contradictory' impressions of the city: its historic beauty, on the one hand, and the conspicuous American presence, on the other: 'At the moment the traffic here is enormous, since so many American families [*Amifamilien*] live here and the Ami wives drive around in their huge cars. The city isn't as peaceful as you would expect Heidelberg to be.' While Mischka was busy at the institute, Helga had time on her hands. She had been a student at Hanover, and tried to get into a similar program at the University of Heidelberg, but with no success: returned soldiers had first priority. This was a disappointment to her and to her family, who expected her to get a degree, like her elder sister Mechthild. She had the idea of becoming a typist for the Americans, a topic she and Mischka researched thoroughly, as witness Mischka's report to Olga that 'the Yanks pay better than the Germans' and had lots of jobs available and few takers who knew English, but their working week was eccentric in German terms in that they didn't work on Saturday and Wednesday afternoon. The young Danoses had borrowed a typewriter (for which I personally am very grateful—the letters get much easier to read) so that Helga could practise.

Whether she ever got the typing job is unclear, but as of July 1951 she was working four and a half hours every morning for the 'Ami wives', assisting them to find domestic help. 'They are very demanding,' she wrote to Olga:

> They require some knowledge of English, American-style cooking, looking after children and cleaning. You can imagine that there are not very many girls who will do all that for DM 135 a month, working 10 hours a day with one free day a week. Most of the girls are not used to the cheekiness of the children [and] prefer to work for less money in a German household.

Both Helga and Mischka had to spend a considerable time in their last year in Heidelberg trying to sort out Olga's financial affairs, which seem to have been a major mess.

Olga at first left power of attorney with Mischka, but then, at his request, added Helga. Judging by Helga's letters on the topic, she worked hard and uncomplainingly on Olga's behalf. Mischka, however, sounded increasingly uneasy, particularly about an unsettled debt of DM 300, which may have been the money lent to Olga by Martha Heimers. At one point he sent Olga a long, formal letter—his impatience and irritation barely disguised—seeking detailed clarification on a number of issues involving rent on the Fulda house. (If Olga ever provided such detailed clarification, it is not in the surviving papers.) This, incidentally, is an early indication that Mischka could, if he put his mind to it, be quite businesslike, more so than Olga. But he regarded it as time wasted. 'This was again an unphilosophical letter,' was his vexed conclusion to one communication with Olga, as if philosophy were what one normally expected in family correspondence.

It is true that Mischka was writing less about philosophy in his letters to Olga than he had done in the Hanover years. No doubt this was partly because there was always so much urgent financial, domestic and departure business to deal with, but I also get the feeling that Mischka was changing, making the transition from being a student to being a professional scientist. This came as something of a surprise, since when I knew him he was allergic to many aspects of science professionalism, at least in its American guise, particularly the emphasis on making a career. In his conversations with me, Heidelberg ('the Tea Colloquium') was shorthand for pure physics, done for the love of it. At the time, however, Heidelberg had other aspects and new experiences to offer. These included being a promising young scientist starting to make a career.

Mischka had gone to Heidelberg as Jensen's assistant, but early in 1951 Jensen arranged for him to become assistant to

Professor Otto Haxel, Heidelberg's newly appointed Professor of Experimental Physics. This seems to have carried more responsibilities, including setting up a new practicum. Mischka had started to go to conferences, notably one at Bad Neuheim in the autumn of 1950. Among the great men of physics he encountered there was the 82-year-old Arnold Sommerfeld from Munich, Heisenberg's teacher, then in the last year of his life. Despite his age, Mischka reported admiringly, he was 'not in the least spiritually tired ... took part in all the discussions and never said anything trivial or stupid'. In August of the next year, a bunch of *Prominenzen* (big names) from Germany and abroad converged on Heidelberg to celebrate Bothe's sixtieth birthday. On Misha's lips, the word *Prominenzen* was generally pronounced with a certain reserve, but on this occasion he may have been using it without irony.

Mischka was at the university to do a PhD, and its writing and submission were milestones of the Heidelberg period. In January 1951, Helga assured Olga that 'the doctoral work is expected to be soon finished—at least the written part', and said she was regularly going up to the institute with Mischka to help proofread his tables and text. But actually it went right up to the wire—a lifelong habit of Misha's, who usually met deadlines but found it pedestrian to do so without a bit of drama. In this case, however, my impression from his later account was that he had genuinely misjudged the time needed to finish and almost panicked at the end. But he described it to Olga with a certain flourish. 'We went to bed at 5.30 [obviously Helga was still at her proofreading duties] and had to submit it at 11.30. It was thus not just ready at 11 [the cut-off time] but already at 5.' Olga responded with the proper appreciation that 'it is a matter of wonder, my dear Mi, that you were ready with the [doctoral] work in such a timely manner; a whole six hours before the submission time'. Prudently, however, she withheld her congratulations 'until I get the news that you have the diploma in hand'.

The doctoral defence was held in the Dean's office at the University of Heidelberg at the end of February 1951. Mischka described it as 'more a comedy than an exam', evidently meaning that the examiners—Jensen, Bothe and another—treated it as a formality and wandered in and out, Jensen enlivening the occasion with witty sallies at Bothe's expense. The result was a magna cum laude ('very good'), a big step up from Mischka's Hanover performance.

Of course such an event had to be properly celebrated. At Jensen's urging, they gave a party at 31 Rohrbacher Street. Helga wanted to ask only seven or eight people, since the room was small, but 'suddenly there were eleven of us. Mischka didn't count properly as he was issuing the invitations.' Schnapps and liqueur were served, and the party got 'quite cheerful and boisterous'. Around 2 am, a tipsy Jensen wanted to dance. But there was no room and no music, so they trooped over to Jensen's place in the institute and the revelry continued.

Mischka was very relieved at the PhD result, writing to Olga that 'the doctoral exam was the first (and also the only) final exam in which I ever got a "very good" … Now there can't be any more exams. If one goes further [i.e. to the German second doctorate, the Habilitation], that doesn't have an exam.' Although he didn't tell Olga this, he had, at least in retrospect, a feeling that he had blown it 'floundering around in the orals', and that he would have got a summa cum laude, the top grade, if he had performed up to standard. He and Jensen had evidently been having some tussles about some of Mischka's bold theoretical forays. Telling Helga at a party a few weeks later about the high regard in which he held Mischka, both as a person and a scientist, Jensen added that 'in his opinion Mischka could achieve more in the experimental field than the theoretical and he thinks that Michael's very lively imagination doesn't help him in theory and even hinders'. This Helga passed on to Olga, perhaps innocently, since she wasn't very interested in the ins and outs of Mischka's attitudes to physics. But to Mischka, it can't have been welcome news. He was deeply committed to becoming a theorist, not an experimentalist, and that 'lively imagination' was exactly what he thought of as his great strength. (Jensen came round to the same view later, or perhaps simply accepted a fait accompli. In any case, Mischka stayed with theoretical physics, and Jensen continued to support him.)

'My dear Doctor Michael!' Olga wrote joyfully from New York with congratulations. She was enormously pleased, and practical woman that she was, her mind had already turned to publication. This was no doubt connected to her earlier urging that Mischka do 'everything that I don't know but you do' to make himself a good job candidate if and when he followed her to America. Even before the finishing of the dissertation, publication reports became a major feature of his letters to her.

His first scientific publication, co-authored with Helmut Steinwedel, appeared in the American *Physical Review* in September 1950. The subject was related to a letter authored by Steinwedel and Jensen and published in the same *Physical Review* issue, and clearly Mischka and the rest of Jensen's team were all working in broadly the same area (oscillations within the atomic nucleus and the nuclear shell model), for which Jensen later received a Nobel Prize. But that's as far as my lay understanding goes, and Olga's too, most likely. Still, she was very keen to get a copy of an offprint, and Mischka— after expressing some doubts about what use it could be to her—finally sent her one. Other publications quickly followed, both co-authored and single-authored. Mischka had got so professional in his approach that he even knew the relative prestige of various journals, noting that some people considered it 'almost improper' to publish in one journal, aimed at American physics teachers, 'but it's not that dangerous'.

Olga's growing interest in Mischka's publications was directly related to his emigration plans and their hopes that he would find employment suitable to his qualifications. After all, 'it's not some ordinary mortal that's coming, but a gentleman who is a doctor of physics, theoretical physics no less', as she wrote proudly (in idiomatic Russian, to encourage Helga's study of the language). Mischka's departure for New York in November 1951 was a long time in gestation. Not long after the marriage, Mischka filled in an IRO enquiry affirming his interest in emigration and adding Helga's details to his file, but this was not yet a commitment. In March 1950, Simon Mirkin offered to sponsor him for immigration, and around the same time a letter from Olga confirms that he had definitely decided to go. But it was clear in Mischka's mind that he had to finish his PhD in Heidelberg before leaving, and it was not until the end of the PhD was in sight—in the autumn of 1950, shortly before Olga's departure—that he started taking concrete steps towards emigration.

One factor in his decision to depart, though probably not a major one, was that 'one has to anticipate the Russians', meaning presumably Soviet incursion into Western Europe. The timing of this anxiety, which neither Mischka nor Olga had expressed before, is odd, since the key developments raising international Cold War tensions—the Marshall Plan, the creation of two separate Germanies and the consolidation of Communist regimes in Eastern Europe—had all occurred a year or more earlier. Presumably it was the outbreak of the Korean War in June 1950 that had increased their anxiety about Soviet aggression and the chances of a Third World War.

Olga reported shortly after her arrival in New York that people there were very worried about the danger of war.

Mischka took up the theme a few months later, in connection with a conversation with Olga's protégé Daniel Kolz, who had received an invitation to go to the States as a music student in mid 1950 but had not yet departed. Apparently Kolz was having second thoughts, as alternative career possibilities presented themselves in Paris. Rather surprisingly, as there had been no previous hint he had any interest in politics, he turned out to be resistant to the growing anti-Communism and anti-Sovietism around him. According to Mischka's report of the conversation to Olga, Kolz

> has been thinking about being able to stay in Paris, that means also Europe, [reasoning] that it can't be so dangerous under the Russians as everyone says, and that probably it can't be prevented that the Russians come and also stay. He is against the Yanks and the rest rearming; that will just cause conflict that is unnecessary; the Russians will be the victors anyway.

Frustratingly, Mischka does not say what he thinks of this point of view, and no reaction from Olga is recorded. It is hard to imagine that either would have agreed with Kolz. The family's experience in Latvia had led them to see Soviet presence in a country as an unalloyed evil.

But the family, or at least one member of it, was also experiencing unpleasantness from the other side of the Cold War, namely American anti-Communism. Mary Sakss had survived the arrest by the Soviets of her two daughters and her own imprisonment by the Germans in the Ravensbrück concentration camp. Outdoing even Olga, she then proceeded to drop more than ten years from her age for the purpose of

DP documentation. She was in a DP camp in Geestacht near Hamburg for a while, and then at some point went to the Black Forest in the French zone, perhaps in connection with her singing career. Then she applied for resettlement by the IRO in the United States. On 1 February 1949, she left the Black Forest and came to Fulda, where Olga was living, 'in order to emigrate to America'.

But this emigration never took place, the reason apparently being that the Americans blacklisted her for contacts with Communists. According to Misha, Mary

> had gone to the Soviet repatriation office, in the British zone, to enquire about her two deported daughters; of course without any success. This was reported by a fellow DP to the Americans (actually Mary had a well-founded suspicion, a clear opinion about the author of that denunciation: an ex-aizsargs—a paramilitary Latvian organisation—who made it known that he doubted that Mary would be given a visum to the States).

In the 1990s, Misha told this as a story of rank injustice, and it certainly seems likely to have upset the whole family. But apart from some passing mentions of Mary not being in a good state, there is no mention of it in Olga's and Mischka's correspondence, which suggests that they thought it a topic best avoided in postal communication for political reasons. Mary died on a concert tour in Denmark in December 1953, never having succeeded in obtaining a US visa or contacting her daughters.

For Mischka, the big political issue of these years was a practical one arising out of Helga's youthful membership of the League of German Girls (BDM, the female equivalent of the Hitler Youth). US immigration rules banned entry into the United States of persons who had belonged to a 'total-itarian' party, a concept encompassing both the Nazi Party in Germany and the Communist Party in the Soviet Union, and for several years this ban was also understood to cover members of the BDM. Membership of the organisation had actually been compulsory for Helga's age cohort, but she might well have joined it anyway. The Heimer family were evidently patriotic Germans (Helga's older brother had been killed in action at Normandy in 1944) who were not actively, if at all, anti-Nazi. Helga's older sister Mechthild had joined the BDM voluntarily and enjoyed its hikes and camps. By the time Helga came of age for it, membership was mandatory, but she also enjoyed the artistic and sporting side, while being bored by the political lectures.

Mischka became aware of the problem late in 1950. Visiting the American consulate in Frankfurt, he had learnt that a 'new security law' in the States—in fact, the notorious Internal Security Act of 23 September 1950 introduced by Senator Pat McCarran—banned the entry of BDM members, among others. His reaction was both indignant and legalistic:

The paradox is that none of those who belong to the 1920–1935 cohort can go to the States, since membership in the Hitler Youth was mandatory under the terms of the Youth Education Act of 1936 or 1935. Acting contrary to the reg-ulations was punishable by a prison sentence. It is quite probable that this law will not last for very long, but it exists for the moment and creates an obstacle for us. In about ten days they expect to get more exact specifications on the reg-ulations, and then we will see whether there the clause that affects us has been removed. If these expectations are not fulfilled, one must do all one can to show 'public opinion' that at least some points of this law are simply stupid and overall many points are out of touch with reality. Social categorisation of people according to party membership is in general relatively problematic; in the final analysis, an individual's behaviour cannot be predicted ...

The 'hateful law', as Helga called it, and the possibility of its amendment or revocation, became a staple of the Danoses' transatlantic correspondence from the winter of 1950–51. Late in the old year, Olga wrote to say that the immigration specialist on the American Committee for Émigré Scholars, Writers and Artists, with which she had contact in New York, had said that 'the amendment to the law on Hitler Youth is currently being worked on and one hopes for positive results in two or three months'. Early in the new year, Mischka and Helga went to the pastor in her home parish in Hanover to make a formal declaration that membership in the BDM was compulsory and that Helga did not take a leadership role within the organisation. Mischka and Olga both anxiously followed the American debate and the practice of the US authorities in Frankfurt. Mischka assured Olga early in 1951 that 'so far as we can find out unofficially, it seems that the Yanks are going in the direction of normalisation, that they now make trouble for those who were particularly active and slide the others through'. In March, Olga's informants were still saying that a change in the law was expected in the next three months, and Mischka, in response, reported that the story was in the German newspapers every day and there must be a positive resolution soon, since 'public opinion is quite intensively engaged in the States too'. On 4 April 1951, Olga was finally able to report that 'the law on relaxation of entry has gone through. People aged 16 and under who belonged to an unfortunate organisation are not affected [that is, are no longer subject to the ban]. So Helgalein is in the clear ...'

In fact, the Danoses had quite a skewed understanding of the American debate, or at least one very different from contemporary historians. They assumed that the concern in the United States was about admitting Nazis into the country. Actually this seems to have been only a minor and peripheral issue. With the United States now in the grip of the almost hysterical anti-Communism associated with the Cold War and McCarthyism, the real concern was about letting in Communists. The man behind the Internal Security Act of September 1950, Senator McCarran, was a crusading anti-Communist. Olga and Mischka were right in thinking that it was only a matter of time before the exclusions of members of Nazi affiliates were revoked, since McCarran and his allies in Congress had no investment in banning them. What held things up for months, however, was unwillingness to make the same revocation with regard to Soviet Communism, plus a degree of racially based distaste for admitting the Jews and Slavs, especially ex-Soviet Russians, who were commonly suspected of Communist sympathies.

But none of this was important to Mischka at the time: his aim was to get to the United States, and this was an obstacle in the way that had to be overcome. Indeed, it was certainly time to get moving if he was going to leave. By mid 1951, when Mischka was still waiting for embarkation news, almost one million DPs had already departed for resettlement. The 1949 DP Act was about to expire in the United States, the IRO was soon to close down, and the DPs still left in Europe were panicking: 'The final rush ... saw long lines winding through the camps. Some DPs were carried on stretchers. All clung to precious documents as they desperately tried to get papers approved before the end of 1951 ...' Mischka had left it to the last minute. At the time of his PhD defence, they had still heard nothing definite from the IRO, and

Helga—though not Mischka—was ready to give up the whole idea of emigrating.

The crucial resettlement letter from the IRO arrived in March 1951, instructing them on the steps they must take 'before you leave for your new home in the USA'. They had to register with the Resettlement Office in Mannheim, submit all documents within fourteen days, go through medical inspection and then 'wait to be assigned transport'. That made departure seem very close. Helga and Mischka began to worry about packing and whether they could take their 'beautiful big down quilt' with them, despite prohibitions on import of anything containing feathers (with typical disdain for formal rules, Olga assured them that there would be no problem—'Mirkin will be meeting you, so the controller will not be strict').

Then things started to go into slow motion. In mid May, with all their papers in, including an attestation from the Heidelberg police that they had no criminal records, they had still not been called for medical inspection. Mischka's job with Haxel ran out at the end of June, but in mid July they were still waiting, finally being informed that what was delaying their case was a bureaucratic complication: they were departing from the American zone, but Mischka's DP registration had been in the British. Still, they had now at least been assigned a number for their departure. A last screening (political checking) took place in late August.

Finally, in mid October, they were cleared for departure and told to return to Ludwigsburg with luggage for embarkation on the next transport to the United States. (The US processing officer who signed this document was Ruth Adams: I like to think, though with no proof, that this was the Ruth Adams I knew later in Chicago, longtime activist editor of the anti-nuclear *Bulletin of the Atomic Scientists*, to which Misha in his later incarnation was a subscriber.) They sailed out of Bremerhaven on the *General Ballou* on 3 November. Their cohort of departing DPs—those who left in the second half of 1951—was both the smallest since mass resettlement had begun in mid 1947 and the last that the IRO would ever record. The DP resettlement process was essentially over, and the IRO itself was on the point of disbanding. Left behind in Central Europe were around a hundred thousand DPs who, because of age or illness, couldn't be resettled, plus a somewhat smaller number who, like Mischka and Olga, had found employment in the German economy but, unlike them, had decided to remain.

The *General Ballou*, a former troop ship like the one Olga had sailed on the previous year, was carrying 1126 DPs to New York, along with twenty-eight ethnic Germans, sixteen individual migrants and two repatriating Americans. It came direct from Korea, adding to the sense of a world on the brink of war. The voyage, according to Helga, was nightmarish. Women and men slept on different decks (women on the fourth of five), some in three-tiered bunks and others swinging around in four-tiered hammocks, with hundreds together in the same hall. Helga at first got a hammock but later managed to move to a bunk. Although she and Mischka were not seasick, practically everyone else was, with the predictable messy consequences. Helga was not only revolted but disapproving. It was mainly a psychological effect, she thought: one person would start throwing up over the railing and then everyone else would follow suit. Meals were the worst. In the first place, there was the strange American food served—almost no sauerkraut, pickled cucumber or herring. But then there was the problem of one's neighbours at table:

They are almost without exception very primitive and dirty people, and Germany can be happy to have been able to get rid of many thousands of these sorts to America. The people are often so impertinent and undisciplined that you can sometimes scarcely bear it. When for example during the meal someone sitting opposite you throws up, it takes a lot of energy and self-control to take the plate and move to the next nearest table to sit and keep on eating …

Encountering DPs en masse was a shock to the gently brought up Helga. Some of them (Ukrainians and Russians) were illiterate, and as for the rest, particularly the Poles, 'it is unimaginable how low the level of these people is'. It provoked Helga—for the first time, she said—to feel real prejudice against certain ethnic groups. The Jews on board were irritating because of their aggressive sense of superiority and entitlement. The Poles treated their children badly and 'are frightfully primitive; neither they nor their children undress at night, and 70% of the people on this ship have still not bathed a single time during our trip. You can probably imagine how badly these people stink. Moreover, there are enough showers with running hot water available.' It was altogether a great relief to arrive in New York on 14 November 1951 and be met by the dutiful Mirkin.

Mischka wrote a postscript to Helga's fourteen-page letter to her family—the longest she ever wrote—but his concerns were completely different. To be sure, it was nice to encounter clean lavatories in America, with liquid soap and paper towels provided free, but Mischka mentioned them only in passing in the context of praising Americans for being very well dressed, 'even the toilet lady'. His main point, however, was such typical Misha that I had to laugh, remembering how on our walks together I would notice people and he only technology. He wanted his in-laws to appreciate the oddness of New York traffic engineering, with freeways running over ordinary streets and houses:

> Outside and above the window runs a street [freeway]. One truck after the other goes by on the snow. Under that, which is at a height of one storey, is the real street. When one wants to get off [the freeway], one must take an exit. Then one finds oneself on the actual street.

So this was New York. They had taken the exit onto a new life.

Afterword

Olga on her land in Florida, mid 1950s.

'*We made it!*' That was what Misha would always say, with a note of gleeful satisfaction and even triumph, after we had run for a bus or landed safely in a plane, or sometimes just as we sat down to dinner together after coping with the vicissitudes of the day. I loved this phrase. It made our life together a series of little successes, not to mention the big, astonishing success of the marriage itself.

So that's how I imagine him feeling when he arrived in New York to start a new life, liberated from the miseries and uncertainties of the old one. Indeed, that is exactly how he described it to me, except that he didn't say, 'when I arrived in

New York' but 'when I went to Columbia' (meaning Columbia University in New York). In his story, 'going to Columbia' was a wonderful moment of liberation and relief, with physics and eating ice-cream in the sun beside the Hudson River fused in his memory. Columbia was the proper place for him to be in, the one that his life's trajectory required. (In talking to me, Misha would use the Russian word *zakonomerno*, meaning 'fitting the pattern established by underlying laws'; the Germans have a word for this too, but English doesn't.) Columbia University in New York was the next stage in that natural progression that had brought him from the Radio Club in Riga to Dresden, Hanover, Heidelberg and finally to New York. Columbia, with Isidor Rabi and Charles Townes as its current eminences, was one of the leading New World centres of nuclear physics.

Columbia appeared so immediately in Misha's arrival tale that he might have gone there straight from the boat. The arrival story he told me contained no other information except an affectionate mention of the Danoses' apartment, a fifth-floor walk-up under the El in the Bronx, and a rather horrifying account of piloting a small seaplane, rented by a friend, underneath the George Washington Bridge on the Hudson River, for a lark, despite not having learnt to fly. The point of this anecdote, which Misha related with pleasure, was that technical processes like flying a plane can be easily grasped by watching for a while. I gather from it that part of the new life was recovering a feeling of invulnerability.

It was a surprise, therefore, to hear a very different story of the arrival in New York from Helga. She said that at first Misha (now Mike to much of the world) had no job or affiliation in New York, wandering aimlessly around the city streets for almost a year, while Helga slaved away at uncongenial office jobs to support them. It was only when Jensen, arriving on an American visit, read Misha the riot act for exploiting Helga and fixed him up with a postdoc with Townes that Columbia came into the picture. That is partially but not fully confirmed by Misha's own CVs, which date his employment at Columbia from March 1952—in other words, four months after his arrival.

There was supposed to be a job for Misha when he arrived, but it fell through. The American Committee for Émigré Scholars, Writers and Artists, prompted by Olga, had arranged it, and on the basis of her letters to Misha, it always looked dicey to me. Of course, Misha had signed up with the IRO for university positions, and Olga, in her enthusiasm, even imagined that a professorial position might come through for such a distinguished immigrant. But that was a very long shot and never came to anything. In fact, what the committee thought it had on offer was a job as an engineer in New Jersey, based on Misha's Hanover degree. In any case, no job eventuated. After an interlude of however long it actually was, four months or fourteen, Misha got a postdoc at Columbia, which he held until 1954. In that year, he took a position as a researcher in theoretical nuclear physics at the US government's National Bureau of Standards (later, National Institute of Standards and Technology) in Gaithersburg, Virginia, a suburb of Washington, where he remained based for more than forty years.

So, give or take a few months of unemployment and demoralisation, *we made it!* still applies as far as Misha was concerned. He was back on dry land, with a road and a destination before him.

For Olga, it wasn't so straightforward. She was in her mid fifties, as against Misha's twenty-nine. She hadn't wanted to come to the United States, and for her there was no Columbia to serve as a mecca. Her American diary—kept in a different notebook from the 'book of my marriage', which ended in 1948—reveals a lot of misery and carries a note of bitterness and cynicism absent in the earlier volume. You have to be a commodity in America, was her assumption, and the question starkly posed was: 'To whom shall I sell myself?' To a man with money was the first answer that came to mind, and there is an entertaining discussion in the diary of how one might go about the process: 'If you sell yourself as a servant, you ask the bosses for a recommendation. From earlier positions where you have served. Do you perhaps need recommendations from former lovers for this other kind of service?'

None of Olga's current admirers fitted the bill. One of them had money and professed devotion but was married and was never going to leave his wife. Another admirer, back in Europe, had astonished her by sending 'a desperate and quite open-hearted love letter' after she left, but she was pretty sure she wouldn't have married him even if he had had money. Where, if anywhere, the 'good Nazi' Seeliger fitted in was unclear. In an affectionate letter to Olga from 'Your little bear' in April 1952, he talked about his dream of going to America so that 'one day I'll be waiting at your door in a Cadillac, as it was once in Riga when I came from the front'. If this was a suggestion that she should sponsor his immigration, Olga seems not to have obliged.

My sense of these diary entries is that Olga may have been semi-serious about finding a man with money to marry, but she was also expressing both her sense of what life in America demanded and a degree of instinctive revulsion from it. When she did actually marry, it was not for money or worldly advantage. Her choice was a Japanese butler in the Florida household of the Maytags, the washing-machine millionaires. Tadasu Okada, perhaps an artist in another life, is remembered by Helga as a kind and gentle man; his letters to Misha, whom he called Michika, are affectionate and seemingly naive, but this may be an artefact of his English. Olga came to know him because she herself was working for the Maytags as their housekeeper. This choice of employment was part of Olga's semi-defiant reaction to immigration: on arrival, she only half-heartedly tried to get the kind of culture-oriented, white-collar jobs like translation that someone of her background would be expected to go for, but instead went into domestic service. Her first jobs were as a cleaner, so the job with the Maytags (whom she seems to have liked) was a step up.

After leaving the Maytags, Olga made several efforts to set herself up in business as a maker of garden furniture (using her experience as a sculptor), and on the basis of the published record—an interview-based article in the *Miami Herald*—would appear to have made a success of it. But I am a bit doubtful of this article, probably written as a PR exercise by one of Olga's American admirers. According to the diary, the first business collapsed, and she was only tentatively embarking on a new one in the months before her death in 1956. The main efforts were put into acquiring a plot of land in Homestead, Florida, and with Tadu's perhaps unwilling help—'he has never worked so hard or so much in his life'—clearing and planting it. (Who knew that she had agricultural skills, miller's daughter though she was? But perhaps she was just making it up as she went along.) She saw the property as something for her sons, particularly the two left behind, writing that 'I connect this property with the remnants of the hope that still sometime things will come good for my suffering children in Riga'.

After Misha and Helga's arrival, the three of them lived together for about a year. At close quarters, Olga's lifestyle was a bit much for Helga—she was untidy and unpredictable, likely to go off for a weekend without explanation, Helga remembered. The crisis came when Olga's Fulda protégé, Daniel Kolz, finally arrived in New York, evidently having abandoned his Parisian plans, and Olga thought he should live with them, at least at first. But it turned out that Helga felt differently. From her point of view, the Bronx place was her and Misha's home, and she was strongly opposed to Kolz moving in. So Olga moved out, abruptly and after a big blow-up, and never came back. Her diary conveys a strikingly clear-sighted understanding of Helga's problems with her: 'I am too different from her mother, from her sense of what a 60-year-old woman ought to be. She cannot respect me, indeed from time to time she despises me. On top of that, she thinks I influence Mi and that offends her.' Olga understood how 'hard for both of them' (Helga and Misha) the night of the quarrel had been. Still, after that night, 'I wanted at all costs not to be in the house, which suddenly was not my "home".'

The parting of ways with Misha was painful. In her diary, remembering the 'black-haired lad' she had given birth to thirty-one years before, she wrote sadly that 'a wall has been going up between us, slowly but surely', and now 'I have run away from the black-haired lad, the only one left to me'. This was her first diary entry after her move to Florida, where she remained until her death from liver cancer three years later. They corresponded, but Misha wrote rarely, and Olga started to feel that her own letters were a burden to him. She imagined the scene in the Bronx, where 'Helga will say to him in her nice little-child voice, "Misha, you really must write to your mother," and Mi will look guilty and make his boyish grimace and rather unhappily wonder what he can write to me about.'

When he did write, she was upset by the absence of any-thing personal—'there is all sorts of stuff in the letter about Stauvers ... a sailing boat, the weather and the subway but nothing about himself, his work or Helga'—and decided to tear up the cheque for $30 he had sent. Helga's pregnancy with their first child was noted with an aphorism in Olga's diary ('Helga was Misha's wife. Now Misha is Helga's husband'), and Johanna's arrival in 1954 created a new bond, the subject of correspondence with Helga, and a reason for visits between Florida and Washington after Misha and Helga moved there in the spring of 1954. Occasionally, Olga tried to re-establish closer emotional contact with Misha—'Please, Mishutka, don't be so distant'—but judging by the correspondence between them, the old, easy, intimate relationship was never recaptured.

Olga never went back to Europe. She didn't have the money, and Helga says she didn't have the desire either: there was nothing for her to go back for. But Europe returned to her, in a way, in the last year of her life, when Soviet controls were relaxed and communication was resumed with her sons Jan and Arpad. The first contact was a telegram from Arpad on 15 September 1955, which, Olga recorded, changed everything: she no longer always felt tired; 'the foundation mood is no longer sad'. Long letters followed from both Arpad and Jan, the former unmarried, the latter with three children and about to embark upon his third marriage. There was even a letter from Olga's niece Ariadna, returned to Riga after long years of exile in the Soviet Union to find her father gone and her mother dead. The photograph Ariadna enclosed showed her as beautiful as ever, but a different character from before— almost ethereal, all the spunk knocked out of her. She had spinal problems that made it difficult for her to look after her children and died not long after her return, aged barely forty.

Olga could exchange letters with and send parcels to her relatives in Riga. But the Soviet Union hadn't opened up to the extent that they could visit Olga in America or vice versa, even if they could have afforded it. Olga's idea that each of them would have an acre of land in Florida to fall back on had always been impractical and turned out to be a mirage. Tadasu inherited the plot and continued to live there, according to Helga's memory, and that was more or less the last they heard of it. So the family that war had divided remained divided—perhaps even more so, from Olga's point of view, than it had been in the years in Germany, when at least she had had Mischka.

As for Misha's American life, I could just say, 'Reader, I married him', like Charlotte Bronte, but a lot of water flowed under the bridge before our first midair meeting in 1989. His marriage to Helga lasted twenty years, produced two children (Johanna, born in New York in 1954, and Tamara, born in Washington in 1956) and ended against Helga's will. In 1969, Misha married Victoria Nieroda, an American of Polish origin who became a writer and painter. That marriage, which also lasted twenty years, produced a son, named Arpad like the uncle and grandfather he never knew. Olga was gone when Vicky came on the scene, but she would surely have approved of the fact that Vicky believed in Misha's genius, as Olga had said his wives must do.

Throughout all three marriages, Misha worked at the National Bureau of Standards (later the National Institute of Standards and Technology) and lived in Washington DC in the area of MacArthur Boulevard, his first house there having been acquired from the physicist Hans Suess, whom he had got to know back in Heidelberg. Misha was a reverse commuter, living in DC and driving out to Gaithersburg every day in his big old American Cadillac, of which he was very proud, pronouncing the word 'Cadillac' as if it were French. His loyalty to the bureau, as he called it, was unshakeable and, to my mind, excessive, at least in the downsizing years I observed, but the great advantage of staying there was that he had a place to do his 'gadgeteering'—that is, develop inventions using his photonuclear expertise—with some congenial old colleagues, as well as continue his theoretical work. I thought he would have been much better off moving earlier in his career to a good research university, with graduate students and postdocs. But he pointed out that he would then have had to apply for grants to support his research, and would have been no good at it. Perhaps he was right.

We were married for the last ten years of his life, with him still at the bureau and based in Washington and me working at the University of Chicago, where I was a professor of history. In that period, he learnt a lot about Soviet history (much more than I managed to learn about nuclear physics, hard though I tried), improved his childhood Russian (more successfully than I improved my German) and spent more time than before in the Soviet Union, which satisfied an old prophesy of his by collapsing back into Russia in 1991.

Commuting works if you don't have small children, animals or house plants and money is not too tight. Some weeks, Misha would drive his old Cadillac from Washington to Chicago, which took him ten or eleven hours; on one winter day, the automatic window-closing seized up at the first tollgate, leaving him to drive almost the whole way home with the driver's window open, but he didn't mind. He was never bored by the drive because he thought about physics problems and listened to music. Other weeks, I would commute by plane, and he would pick me up on a Thursday evening at what was then National Airport, just ten minutes from our house. We would go home to our little cottage near the canal, pour a glass of wine, put on some music and make dinner together (Misha was the main cook, recently self-taught and working it out from first principles of chemistry). These are very happy memories, even though the music I thought of as my homecoming theme—Schubert's '*Rosamunde*' quartet—is sad. The sadness was for happiness coming so late.

We spent a lot of time in Europe. Unlike Helga, Misha hadn't fully left Europe behind him. He and Helga spoke German at home, and their children grew up bilingual. More strikingly, in terms of self-identification, he spoke German, not English, to the son of his second marriage, even though Vicky didn't know the language. His spoken English had an accent and a few idiosyncrasies—the extra syllable in 'surrepetitious' was a favourite of mine, and his version of 'very good' dropped the 'y' to rhyme with the German *sehr gut*. A flock of ducks on the Georgetown Reservoir was 'kiloducks' (ducks to the power of three), and he greeted stray dogs on the canal towpath with a gentle '*Nun, Hund*'.

Misha was back in Heidelberg on a Humboldt Fellowship in 1959 and visited regularly thereafter. Much of the work in photonuclear physics for which he was best known was done in collaboration with a Frankfurt-based German physicist, Walter Greiner. But Misha apparently never contemplated moving back to Europe and dissuaded Jensen from putting him up for a job in Heidelberg in the 1960s on grounds of his feeling of 'pressure' in Germany. I could see the effects of that pressure for myself when we spent extended periods together in Frankfurt, Tübingen and Berlin in the 1990s. He seemed like a native in Germany, knew everything and liked to show it to me, and yet there was an inner resistance to the place. I was happier there than he was.

At some point in the past, Misha had evidently seriously tried to become American. That meant, in the first instance, feeling gratitude to, and admiration for, the United States for taking him in. Later, he moved to a more critical position, joining the anti-war movement (in the days of the Vietnam War) and the Union of Concerned Scientists. But that was criticism from within and, moreover, criticism that he felt was itself a demonstration of the strength of American democracy. In the 1960s and '70s, Misha understood his US citizenship (acquired in the mid 1950s) as something that carried an obligation of active political engagement; in this sense he was very different from Mischka back in Germany. He even wrote letters to the President.

By the time I met him, however, that phase was over. I thought of him as alienated from America (though perhaps, as I was alienated myself, there was some degree of projection, as well as influence). He still felt an obligation of citizenship, but now the emphasis was on international citizenship, including but not limited to membership in the international community of physics. Although he never spelled this out, that sense of international citizenship seemed to carry a strong identification with Europe. Not Latvia, not Germany, but a broader civilised Europe that was personified by Paris. When I met Misha, he owned a studio apartment on Rue de la Folie-Méricourt in the XI arrondissement, and was spending three months a year there working with his collaborator, Vincent Gillet, of the Saclay Nuclear Research Centre. Misha was passionately attached to Paris, knew the city and its restaurants and concert halls inside out, and was so committed to improving his French (one of the European languages he *didn't* know from childhood) that he even read Georges Simenon's crime stories, a genre that he otherwise shunned. There were no bad memories in Paris. It was the Europe Misha could live with, as well as the one he couldn't live without.

I know a lot more about Misha as a result of writing this book. But I also feel I understand more about the particular historical moment he found himself in, the gathering and then dispersal of displaced persons in Europe after the Second World War. That's interesting because I work on that historical moment as an academic historian too. Once I even published an article about DPs in a scholarly journal, using Misha, Olga and his friend Bičevskis as case studies, though I'm not sure that I should have done. The journal's referee commented that the picture you get from this kind of material is completely different from what you get from archives. I noticed that myself, in my two capacities as personal biographer and impersonal historian. Most archives are institutional, and that gives them a bureaucratic and rule-oriented perspective favouring the general and the typical rather than the individual and idiosyncratic. But individuals are not statistical averages. Once you have real individual people in your sights, you constantly notice anomalies, divergences from the expected norms.

The question for a historian is whether this is good or bad. In Stalin's time, Soviet historians were suspicious of life stories unless they were exemplary, and dubious about biography because, in focussing on the quirks of individual lives, it obscured broader truths about collective experience. I take the second point, if not the first. But at the same time, 'collective experience' is a generalisation constructed, consciously or not, on a sense of the average; no single actual person ever lived it. Granted that individual experience is a construct, too, in that we have access to it only because somebody told the story, it's one step closer to real (unedited) life.

If I had just read the archives, I would know that young Latvian men of Misha's generation were in danger of being called up into the Waffen-SS during the German occupation, but it would not have occurred to me that one way of beating this would be to go to Germany as an exchange student. I would expect that Mischka and Olga, being DPs, would live in DP camps in Germany (the bureaucracies, hence the archives, knew in principle that some DPs were 'free-livers', but since those DPs were unavailable for direct observation, that's about all they knew). From the archives, I would not be aware of the DP grapevine that in some mysterious way brought occasional information into and out of Riga, and I would know next to nothing about the possibility and process of DPs 'going on to the German economy', including why anyone with a good berth as a ward of UNRRA would consider doing so.

Most of these aspects of the Danoses' experience were not typical of DPs as a whole. But apart from the question of what was typical, there's the question of what was possible (that is, conceivable) within the parameters of DP experience. In that scholarly article I wrote about them, I showed how much agency the Danoses had as DPs ('agency' being the academic shorthand for ability to influence what happened to them) and drew the broader conclusion that DPs in Europe at the end of the Second World War had more agency than they are given credit for and were not just passive victims at the mercy of strange armies and governments. But of course Mischka, Olga and Bičevskis were on the fortunate end of the DP spectrum. They were educated, with transportable skills; they knew German; they even had German acquaintances to leave the odd suitcase with. Their wartime experience was not bad, in comparative terms. They were not prisoners of war, or forced labourers, or concentration camp inmates, or Jews (Mischka may have been half Jewish, but was not perceived as such by others or himself). They survived, and had each other as support in the last stages of the war and the years after.

In terms of comparative refugee experiences, DPs in Europe after the Second World War were relatively fortunate. Life in the European DP camps of the 1940s was strikingly better than what awaits Syrian refugees in Turkey or Afghans and Iraqis trapped in Nauru today. Thanks to the policy of the Allied military governments and the protection of UNRRA, DPs lived better than the surrounding German population and were not subject to violence. Some of them even had the chance of a first-rate free education in German universities. The DPs' situation was also vastly better than that of the Palestinians whose refugee camps in Jordan are now more than half a century old, with no solution in sight. The IRO resettled all but a small fraction of them outside Europe, in quite tolerable conditions, within six years of the end of the war; and the DPs' individual preferences, as well as the host countries' selection, played a role in where they ended up. Australia, with its requirement of two years' assigned manual work for DP immigrants, was one of the harsher resettlement environments. Yet Mischka's friend Bičevskis not only had a job as an engineer within a few years of arrival but had also bought a plot of land in the Sydney suburbs and was building a house for his family.

Even in the best of circumstances, however, uprooting and displacement are no picnic, and wartime displacement with the attendant exposure to violence and death is particularly traumatic. It would be a rare DP without the equivalent of Misha's nightmarish wartime moments (seeing the Jewish graves in Riga, the Dresden bombing, near-death from diphtheria in Flensburg). Virtually all DPs had lost or left behind family members, as was the case with the Danoses. Moreover, survival brings survivor's guilt. Olga was stricken with guilt when her ex-husband died, still in Riga and thus on the other side of the Iron Curtain, and she would privately reproach herself until the end of her life for having failed to get two of her sons out in 1944. Misha still found it painful to talk about the fate of his father and his brother Arpad half a century later. All DPs would have carried similar psychic burdens into their new lives.

But this is a book about the singularity of Mischka and Olga's stories, not their representativeness. The idea of singularity was very important to Misha; he hated to be put in any category, including the category of DP (that's why I am not sure that I should have written that scholarly article). He didn't like to see his life in the 1940s as formed by war, flight and displacement. These were simply contingent circumstances in the 'real' story of his life, which was how he left Riga on his journey to become a theoretical physicist, honed his skills in Heidelberg and ended up achieving his goal in America.

At the same time, Misha saw himself as a witness to historic events and took this role seriously: as his big musings on the Soviet occupation of Riga, VEF, the Jewish graves outside Riga, the Dresden bombing, the Heidelberg Tea Colloquium and other topics demonstrate. He was a first-class witness because of his ability to remember exactly and stick to what he saw with his own eyes, and these musings are remarkable historical documents. The Dresden bombing description, for example, is probably unique among eyewitness accounts that survive. Most survivors were in one place during the bombing, usually hiding in basements from which they could only guess what was happening above. Mischka was outside, going on foot for a night and a day through many parts of the city, including the shattered centre, with bombs falling around him.

I learnt a lot about Mischka through writing this book, and in the process understood more about Misha too. In fact, I often thought about it as a collaborative process—*we* now understood more about him—as if I were taking up where his autobiographical musings left off. Learning more about Mischka didn't change my basic view of Misha, but it added something. That man I met on the aeroplane in 1989 was remarkably free of context from my point of view, almost as if a Martian had landed in the seat next to me. He acquired context, of course, as I got to know him, but something of that feeling remained. He was the man who had miraculously turned up from nowhere and saved my life. Since he had done that, I took it for granted that he was the stronger of the two of us. He didn't agree, but I attributed that to partiality. It was only in retrospect that the picture in my mind started to change, with me, the rescued one in my scenario, looking stronger than I had thought at the time, and he, the rescuer, more vulnerable. Mischka's vulnerabilities helped me see Misha's. And Olga's protective responses made me recognise something similar in myself that I had earlier discounted.

Writing this book brought some bad moments. Some of them involved pain on Misha's behalf, when he was in danger, as in the Dresden bombing. Some of them were when I found Mischka not quite up to the Misha standard—for example, in the stiffness and occasional pomposity of his youthful letter-writing style. His letters, I felt, didn't adequately convey the humour, liveliness and simple niceness of the man I knew (who was recognisable as, though distinct from, the man Helga fell in love with). I was reminded of how, at his wake in Washington in 1999, a woman from the old National Bureau of Standards crowd who remembered Misha and Helga as the centre of a lively social circle in the 1960s burst out almost angrily after a series of solemn tributes, including mine: 'But Mike was fun! Why don't you say what fun he was?' I did try to show that in this book, but the Mischka-of-the-record sometimes got in my way. *Show yourself as you really are*, I would mentally admonish him; *make the readers like you*. I wanted it to be as it was when I introduced Misha to my friends and students in the 1990s and they all immediately loved him.

The worst moments were when something in the documents made me critical of Mischka. For example, I wasn't too keen on the way he wrote about women or treated Nanni; I didn't think much of his national stereotyping; and there were some rather loud silences about the Jewish question and Nazism. If he were alive, I could either have expressed these criticisms and heard his response or kept quiet about them. With him being dead and unable to respond, it's all a lot stickier. I hate the idea of anyone else criticising him. But at the same time, I couldn't help putting it all out there so that they could, if so inclined. The historian's Hippocratic oath, as far as I am concerned, is 'don't leave things out because you don't like them'. I seemed unable to break this, even for Misha. Not that he would have wanted me to. I was an experimentalist in his definition, and experimentalists aren't meant to ignore data.

The big worry was whether writing about his life as I have done was a kind of betrayal. I would wake up in the middle of the night with the anguished thought that, in some particular passage, I should be protecting him more. Along with that went another, contradictory fear, also capable of waking me up in the early hours: that in such and such a paragraph, I *was* protecting him and shouldn't be. I got used to getting up in the morning and removing the offending paragraph that had unduly/insufficiently protected him.

This was originally meant to be a book about Mischka's life as a displaced person, but I soon saw that it was really a story about Olga as well. The two of them went through similar experiences, but I became fascinated by the way similar experiences meant quite different things for a young man with a future and for a middle-aged woman with just the past. Ever since I first read Olga's American diary, the stark contrast between her reactions to the new life and Misha's was on my mind. I became very fond of Olga, about whom at the beginning I knew little. Towards the end, I started to wonder if, with her more spontaneous and exuberant writing style and flamboyant personality, she was hijacking my Mischka book. I decided that even if she was, I would let her.

So the book that was meant to be a celebration of Misha turns out to be a celebration of Olga as well, and of the exceptional closeness and mutual support that existed between them in the years in Germany. The closeness didn't fully survive the move to the States, or at least went into temporary eclipse, which became permanent on her unexpectedly early death. Misha didn't talk about that eclipse, but I think it was part of his sense of loss and pain about the past. There may be things in this book about Mischka that would make Misha wince, as we all tend to do when confronted by our younger selves. But I think he would be glad to see Olga back with him on centre stage. In Misha's original *We made it* mantra, she was the other half. They made it through together.

Notes

Introduction
The Anti-Death League
This is a farcical creation of Kingsley Amis in his 1966 novel of the same name, set in an army camp somewhere in England. All who are against death are invited to join the league, which, however, appears to be non-existent.

Memoir of Australian childhood
This is Sheila Fitzpatrick, *My Father's Daughter: Memories of an Australian Childhood* (Melbourne: Melbourne University Press, 2010).

'Writing not just to record but also to communicate'
Misha wrote several musings about how to read his musings. He copied letters he wrote that he considered particularly important into his diary. And in the longest of all his diary entries, on the Dresden bombing of February 1945, he breaks off the narrative in the middle to talk about the problems of getting one's point across to a listener. Thanks to my German translator, Diana Weekes, for pointing this out, and to Mark McKenna for asking the question.

Chapter 1: Family
My principal sources on the Danos family background are my interviews with Jan Danos and Arpad Danos, Kata Bohus's research, the musing 'Stories from my Grandfather's Times', some fragments in Olga's papers, Arpad's school records, and letters from Arpad Danos and Ivan Danos on the Deutsch/Danos family in Hungary (details in Sources).

End of serfdom
Misha's musing implies that his serf ancestors were emancipated in 1861, which is the date for the Russian Empire in general. But in most of Latvia, serfs were emancipated forty years earlier, following a model of Prussian reform. Misha's dating may be simply a mistake,

but it could be that Julia's forebears came from a part of Latvia where emancipation came late.

Historical background and population statistics on Latvia
These are largely drawn from Daina Bleiere et al., *History of Latvia: The Twentieth Century* (Riga: Jumava, 2006). Quotation on Riga's transformation is on p. 53.

Deutsch/Danos name change
At least one other probably Jewish family in Budapest changed its name from Deutsch to Danos at the turn of the century (email correspondence with Jonathan Danos circa 2007), and several Hungarian Danoses are Jewish and have left Holocaust memoirs. According to Kata Bohus, it was more common for Jews than for Germans in Hungary to obey the edict on name change.

Disappearance of Olga's father
Misha's version says he was never heard from again. In an undated autobiographical fragment written in English (3/29), Olga writes in the context of the First World War that 'my father was killed', but given the fallibility of her English, she may just have meant he was dead. In any case, it suggests that the family had some news of his fate.

Olga's first marriage
Olga appears to have told the children when they were young that it was an engagement, not a marriage. But Jan says that when he and Arpad Jr left Riga for Kurland in 1944, hoping to escape from the imminent Soviet reoccupation, Olga told them, in case they never met again, that it was a marriage. (Misha, being already outside Latvia, evidently missed this correction.)

Arpad's singing voice
His sons identified him as a tenor, although a review in Riga's Russian newspaper *Segodnia* (16 May 1920) describes him as 'a lyrical voice of soft timbre, even one might say of baritone colouration'. Thanks to Līvija Baumane-Andrejevska of Riga for sending me this review.

Chapter 2: Childhood
Principal sources for this chapter are Olga's and Misha's diaries, interviews with Jan and Arpad Danos, and (on Olga's fashion atelelier) Līvija Baumane's essay.

Separation of parents
Jan Danos dates this to the mid 1930s, which is also what Misha told me and Helga remembers him telling her. However, Olga's diary for 2 March 1944 unambiguously states that 'On 13 June 1943 I left my husband. I live alone in my workshop.'

Lovers
The mention of the lover is in her diary entry of 2 April 1948, on her husband's death. There are also references in 1940s entries to her husband's jealousy, and a postwar letter from Paul Seeliger, a German official in wartime Riga well known to the Danoses, suggests that an intimate relationship had existed between them at some point.

'Home to the Reich'
About fifty-one thousand Germans left in the first wave in 1939, leaving about ten thousand Germans in Latvia, most of whom left early in 1940 after the country's annexation by the Soviet Union. *History of Latvia*, p. 218.

'Cannon fodder for Adolf'
This is Jan Danos's quotation of his father, in an interview with me on 8 September 2006.

Chapter 3: Riga under the Soviets
Principal sources for this chapter are the musings 'Plebiscite to Join the Union', 'VEF' and 'Mass Deportations in '41', as well as those on socialism and the Soviet Union; Misha's diaries; interviews with Helen Machen; and Līvija Baumane's essay.

June 1941 deportations
See Björn M. Felder, *Lettland im Zweiten Weltkrieg* (Paderborn: Ferdinand Schöningh, 2009), pp. 153–61. The report dated 17 May 1941 that apparently anticipates the event is published in Russian as 'Spetssoobshchenie V.N. Merkulov I. V. Stalinu ob itogakh operatsii po arestu i vyseleniiu "antisovetskikh elementov" iz pribaltiiskikh respublik 17 maia 1941 g.', in *Lubianka: Stalin i NKVD-NKGB-GUKR 'Smersh' 1939-mart 1946* (Moscow: Mezhdunarodnyi fond 'Demokratiia', 2006), pp. 279–81.

Russia replaces Germany as Latvia's 'primary enemy'
The quotation is from *History of Latvia*, p. 260.

Ariadna's deportation
Misha remembered Ufa as the destination, but an article on Ariadna's father, Professor Paul Sakss, says it was Vorkuta (Valdemārs Kārkliņš, 'Brīnišķīgs ceļojums', *Latviu mūsika/Latvian Music*, no. 18, 1988, p. 1905). Thanks to Dailonis Stauvers for supplying me with a copy.

Soviet everyday
The book referred to is Sheila Fitzpatrick, *Everyday Stalinism: Ordinary Life in Extraordinary Times: Soviet Russia in the 1930s* (New York: Oxford University Press, 1999).

Chapter 4: Riga under the Germans
The chapter draws on my interview with Bičevskis'; the musings on 'Nazi Latvia', 'Saving Jews', 'Mass Graves' and 'Koelln and Seeliger'; and Mischka's 'Rittergut' document. On Olga's and Mary's saving of Jews, additional sources are emails from Barry Mirkin and Margers Vestermanis; the *Spokane Daily Chronicle* report on Mirkin and Olga (1 November 1950); and Olga's interview with the *Miami Herald* (27 June 1954).

German attack on Riga, 1941
A four-pronged assault on Latvia, including one direction towards Riga, was part of the initial German assault on the Soviet Union of 22 June 1941. By 8 July, the German Army had occupied the entire territory of Latvia. *History of Latvia*, pp. 263–4.

Ice hockey
According to Latvian sports historian Andris Zeļenkovs, Misha played in the LSB-2 and US-2 teams in 1939–40, the latter being the university's second team.

German policy towards Latvia
From July 1941, Latvia was ruled by the Reich through Alfred Rosenberg's Ministry for the Occupied Eastern Territories (*Reichsministerium die besetzten Ostgebiete*), but its administration, based in Riga, was Latvian under German supervision. There was even talk about future extension of Latvian autonomy, especially in cultural matters. *History of Latvia*, pp. 267–8, 272–3.

Riga ghetto
The move of Riga's Jews to the Riga ghetto was completed on 25 October 1941. Jews were being exterminated in Latvia's smaller

towns throughout the autumn, but it was late in November that the mass killing of Jews from the Riga ghetto began. By mid December, about twenty-five thousand Riga Jews had been killed and buried in pits in the Rumbula Forest, leaving about six thousand Jews alive in Latvia. Trainloads of Jews from Germany and Austria were then brought in and accommodated in the Riga ghetto, most of them to be killed in their turn. *History of Latvia*, pp. 278, 282–4. For a more detailed account, see Andrew Ezergailis, *The Holocaust in Latvia 1941–1944* (Washington, DC: US Holocaust Memorial Museum, 1996).

Saving Jews
Latvian historian Margers Vestermanis has compiled a list of 420 Latvians who saved Jews: Vestermanis, *Juden in Riga* (1995) and email of 16 August 2015. This is an ongoing project, and we have been in communication about adding Mary Sakss and Olga Danos to the list. The date of Mary's arrest—21 October 2015—was kindly supplied by Dr Vestermanis.

For accounts of how individual Jews from the ghetto were saved by being assigned to work for Latvian businesses in the city (usually tailoring shops, like Olga's) and staying overnight on the premises when execution round-ups were imminent, as well as 'vanishing' from the convoy taking them from the ghetto to work in the city and back, see Bernard Press, *The Murder of the Jews in Latvia* (Evanston: Northwestern University Press, 2000), and the testimony of David Silberman and Lev Aronov in Gertrude Schneider (ed.), *Muted Voices: Jewish Survivors of Latvia Remember* (New York: Philosophical Library, 1987).

Olga's relations with Seeliger
See 'Lovers' in the notes to chapter 2, above.

Baltic–German wartime university exchange
Detailed information is in Margot Blank, *Nationalsozialistische Hochschulpolitik in Riga (1941 bis 1944): Konzeption und Realität eines Bereiches deutscher Besatzungspolitik* (Lüneberg: Verlag Nordostdeutsches Kulturwerk, 1991), pp. 64–73.

Chapter 5: Wartime Germany
The principal sources for this chapter are correspondence between Misha in Germany and Olga in Riga; Olga's diary; the letter to Olga from 'Der Alte'; the musings 'Medical Experimentations' and 'Cleansing

of Concepts: Informers vs denouncers in Nazi, Soviet, DDR'; interviews with Jan Danos, Arpad Danos, Helen Machen and Mrs Wally Ayers; and letters to Mischka from Waldtraut Herrnberger, including her 'Verpflichtung'.

Dick Whittington

Misha's oral account of his travels had a folkloric ring. I don't remember if he knew or invoked the English Dick Whittington story, but a possible German parallel is the youth sent off into the wide world by his miller father in Joseph von Eichendroff's early nineteenth-century *Aus der Leben eines Taugenichts*. Thanks to Reinhard Meyer-Kalkus for alerting me to this source.

Dr Hans Boening

A card in Olga's papers identifies him, as of late 1944, as President Dr Boening, Reich Inspector of Labour Draft Plenipotentiaries (Reichsinspecteur des Generalvollmächtigen für den Arbeitseinsatz) with a Reichenburg address. A note on the back, dated 1 December 1944, reads 'A request to Hr Dir. Wesseloky, AEG-Godenbach, to be willing to receive and advise Frau O. Danos'. After the war, Boening kept in contact with Olga—her papers contain a card from him with an Oldenburg address (Federal Republic of Germany) sent to her in New York in 1953.

Dresden Technical University

It is remarkable that Mischka's studies at the TH were so comparatively normal, given that the university was only semi-functional, with some departments completely closed in connection with manpower call-ups. See Victor Klemperer, *I Will Bear Witness: A Diary of the Nazi Years, 1942–1945*, trans. Martin Chalmers (New York: Modern Library, 2001), pp. 355–6 (entry for 10 September 1944). Klemperer, a former professor of the Dresden TH, had been dismissed as a Jew.

Mauserl

The reference is to a German fairy story, 'Hauserl und Mauserl', that Olga must have read her children. It is set in Vienna.

Divorce

The visit to the lawyer is described in her diary for 2 May 1944. She does not return to the topic in later entries.

Letter from 'Der Alte'
Thanks to Jan Danos for identifying the handwriting and the enclosed photograph as those of his father, and for deciphering and interpreting the text.

Chapter 6: The Bombing of Dresden

This chapter is based on the 1996 Musing 'Dresden' and Mischka's diary entries for 12–22 April 1945, written two months after the bombing. The translation of the diary is a joint effort by me and a professional translator, Diana Weekes, for whose help I am very grateful.

On Nanni and the aftermath of the bombing, I draw on the musing 'Shell Shock: Dresden, 1944, 1945' and Mischka's diary.

'Christmas trees'
This is what Germans called the flairs dropped by bombing units to light up their targets.

Vonnegut
The reference is to the American novelist Kurt Vonnegut, whose *Slaughterhouse Five* (1969) describes the bombing of Dresden, which Vonnegut himself, as an American POW, experienced. I never asked Misha what he thought of Vonnegut's novel, but Matthew Lenoe, one of my Chicago students from the 1990s, did. He says Misha replied 'that the reality was so surreal that he didn't think you could top it with a surreal novel about the event' (email to author, 22 October 2016).

Chapter 7: Displaced Persons in Flensburg

Principal sources are Mischka's diary and letters to Olga; the musing 'Occupation Forces in 1945' (quotation on British arrogance); letters to Mischka from Nanni; interviews with Bičevskis and his 'Bičevskis Family History' email.

Pferdewasser school
In a pencilled latter to Olga dated 25 March 1945, Mischka referred to having 'gone to Pferdewasser [in Flensburg, where the Timm Kroeger School was located], but it was overcrowded', in a sentence wedged in between remarks about his suitcase and his hospital committal. But since he was taken semi-conscious from the station straight to the hospital, he couldn't have done this, so it sounds like delirium. Probably the original plan was for Olga and Mischka to meet at the school.

Flensburg 1945

Information from *Flensburg, 700 Jahre Stadt: Eine Festschrift* (Flensburg: 1984) and *Lange Schatten: Ende der NS-Diktatur and frühe Nachkriegsjahre* (Flensburg: 2000). The latter includes concert programmes and excerpts from the *Flensburger Stadt-Chronik/Flensburg News*, from which I have quoted.

Eisenhower edict

General Dwight D. Eisenhower (later US president) was Supreme Commander of the Allied Forces in Europe.

DPs

In providing historical context on DPs, I have drawn to a large extent on my own scholarly research. The quotations on allied attitudes to DPs are from the UNRRA archives, New York, S-0425-0010-17 ('Report on General Situation and Living Conditions of Displaced Persons and UNRRA, 1946') and ibid., S-0402-0003-0001 (June 1945 report on 'UNRRA and Displaced Persons' by Harold Ingham). Good general works on the topic are Mark Wyman, *DPs: Europe's Displaced Persons, 1945–1951* (Ithaca, NY: Cornell University Press, 1989) and Ben Shephard, *The Long Road Home: The Aftermath of the Second World War* (London: Vintage Books, 2011).

Mischka's apologia

This is the undated (1946) 'Rittergut' statement [see Sources].

Reopening of German universities

Information from David Phillips, 'The Re-opening of Universities in the British Zone: The Problem of Nationalism and Student Admissions', in David Phillips (ed.), *German Universities after the Surrender: British Occupation Policy and the Control of Higher Education* (Oxford: University of Oxford Department of Educational Studies, 1983).

Zeilsheim and Frankfurt Jewish listing

The certification of Michael Danos's residence at Zeilsheim DP camp is signed Sidney Flatow, UNRRA Team 503. The listing of Michael Danos in the Jewish community document is in his ITS (International Tracing Service) file [see Sources]. Simon Mirkin's ITS file contains a document headed 'Central Committee of Liberated Jews in the American Occupied Zone', dated December 1946, which gives Zeilsheim as his current address.

HIAS
This is the US-based Hebrew Immigrant Aid Society, in operation since the late nineteenth century and active after the war in helping care for and resettle Jewish DPs in Europe.

Chapter 8: Olga, from Flensburg to Fulda

Principal sources are Olga and Mischka's letters; Olga's diary; Simon Mirkin's 1946 letter to Olga; and interviews with Jan Danos and Arpad Danos.

Mary Sakss
Mary listed her profession as 'singer' on the DP documents in her ITS file. There are a number of photographs of her performing, sometimes in Latvian national dress, in the Danos papers (which include some of Mary's papers, sent to Olga after her death).

British zone work requirement for DPs
The British zonal authorities announced at the end of April 1946 that work would become mandatory for DPs, and this new policy became operative in October. UNRRA, however, was unhappy about it, and its implementation seems to have been patchy at best. As of 20 June 1946, only about 30 per cent of employable DPs were in fact employed, and of those, 80 per cent were working for UNRRA; see Wolfgang Jacobmayer, *Vom Zwangsarbeiter zum heimatlosen Ausländer* (Göttingen: Vandenhoeck & Ruprecht, 1985), pp. 159–61, and UNRRA's monthly labour reports, in the UNRRA archives, S-0425-0010-13. On the difficulties of setting up small businesses without German credentials (*Meisterbriefe*), see Tillmann Tegeler, 'Esten, Letten und Litauer in Nachkriegsdeutschland', in Christian and Marianne Pletzing (eds), *Displaced Persons: Flüchtlinge aus den baltischen Staaten in Deutschland* (Munich: Martin Meindenbauer, 2007), p. 24.

Simon and Boris Mirkin
Information on their wartime experiences comes from Simon's 1946 letter to Olga and their ITS files.

Princess Volkonsky's story
The memoir, well known in its time and translated into various languages, is Princess Peter Wolkonsky [Sophia A. Volkonsky/Volkonskaia], *The Way of Bitterness: Soviet Russia, 1920* (London: Methuen, 1931).

An excerpt appears in Sheila Fitzpatrick and Yuri Slezkine (eds), *In the Shadow of Revolution: Life Stories of Russian Women* (Princeton, NJ: Princeton University Press, 2000).

Repatriant's visit
Voluntary repatriation of 'displaced persons' to the Soviet Union was possible, free of cost, and strongly encouraged by the Soviets, but few took advantage of it because of dislike of the Soviet regime or fear of being arrested on return. Letters from relatives, such as Olga received from Arpad Jr, were let through by the Soviets in order to encourage repatriation.

Chapter 9: Student in Hanover
The principal sources for this chapter are my interviews with Bičevskis and Stauvers; Mischka's diary; and correspondence between Mischka and Olga, and between Mischka and Nanni.

Hanover after the war
I have drawn on Frederick Taylor, *Exorcising Hitler: The Occupation and Denazification of Germany* (London: Bloomsbury, 2011); Perry Biddiscombe, *The Denazification of Germany: A History 1945–1950* (Stroud, Gloucestershire: Tempus, 2007); and Douglas Botting, *In the Ruins of the Reich* (London: George Allen & Unwin, 1985). The quotations are from British war correspondent Leonard Mosley, in Botting, p. 22, and from Botting, p. 164.

DP student life
Bella Brodzki and Jeremy Varon, 'The Munich Years: The Students of Post-war Germany', in Johannes-Dieter Steinert and Inge Weber-Newth (eds), *Beyond Camps and Forced Labour: Current International Research on Survivors of Nazi Persecution: Proceedings of the International Conference, London, 29–31 January 2003* (Osnabrück: Secolo-Verlag, 2005), p. 156.

Latvians in German universities
Information, statistics and student names are from the 'Latvian students in universities in British Zone' section in the 'Report on German Universities, March 1946', UNRRA archives, S-0408-0033-06; the Stauvers interview; and Juris Andrejs Zusevics (ed.), *Zelta Lapas Gaisma: Latviesu Student Eiropas augstskolas pec otra pasaules kara* (Holland, MI: Amerikas Latviesu Apvienibas Latviesu Instituts, 1990).

Theoretical positions at Hanover TH filled by experimentalists
Alan D. Beyerchen, *Scientists under Hitler: Politics and the Physics Community in the Third Reich* (New Haven, CT: Yale University Press, 1977), p. 172.

Michael Danos as physicist
See the recollections of Walter Greiner, Jan Rafelski, Max Huber, Vincent Gillet and Evans Hayward in Walter Greiner (ed.), *Proceedings of the Symposium on Fundamental Issues in Elementary Matter, 25–29 September 2000, Bad Honnef, Germany: In Honor and Memory of Michael Danos* (Debrecen: EP Systema, 2001), pp. 415–30.

Soviet zone of Germany
On the situation in universities, see Taylor, *Exorcising Hitler*, p. 329 and Biddiscombe, *Denazification*, p. 137; on travel in and out of the zone, see J.P. Nettl, *The Eastern Zone and Soviet Policy in Germany 1945–1950* (Oxford: Oxford University Press, 1951), pp. 260–3.

Mischka as pole vaulter
Mischka vaulted a personal best of 3.7 metres at the British zonal championships in 1946. He was aiming at 4 metres, if he could only get a decent pole, at a time when 4.5 metres was the world record. (Now, with fibreglass poles, it is over 6 metres.)

Job with Jensen
Mischka was working as Jensen's assistant since at least June 1948. His original title was *Leiter*, with a salary of DM 80 a month. When Steinwedel, Jensen's former assistant, left for Heidelberg, Mischka took over as Jensen's official *Wissenschaftlicher Assistent*.

Chapter 10: Physics and Marriage in Heidelberg
Principal sources are correspondence between Mischka and Olga; the musing 'Quasi-kruzhki Elsewhere' on the Heidelberg Tea Colloquium; Berthold Stech's memoir 'J.H.D. Jensen: Personal Recollection'; interviews with Helga Danos; and letters to Mischka from Nanni Schuster.

Jensen
J.H.D. (Hans) Jensen (1907–1973) received his doctorate at the University of Hamburg in 1932 and then worked there as a lecturer (Privatdocent). An older colleague at Hamburg, the chemist Paul Harteck, brought him into the wartime Uranium Club, and they wrote

some important papers together on separation of uranium isotopes. In 1933, he joined the National Socialist German University Lecturers' League, which at Hamburg was more or less obligatory if you wanted to be *habilitiert* (that is, receive the second doctorate), and became a candidate member of the Nazi Party in 1936, the year of his Habilitation, and a full member in 1937. His postwar *Persilschein* from Heisenberg argued that he had joined these organisations only in order to avoid unnecessary difficulties in his academic career. After the war, he was professor of theoretical physics at Hanover TH, and then became an *ordinarius* professor (at the top of the academic ladder) at the University of Heidelberg in 1949, which remained his base for the rest of his career. In the 1950s and 1960s, he held visiting professorships at a number of universities in the United States. In 1963, he won the Nobel Prize for physics (with Maria Goeppert-Meyer) for their work on the nuclear shell model.

Development of physics in Germany
I have drawn particularly on Klaus Hentschel (ed.), *Physics and National Socialism: An Anthology of Primary Sources* (Basel: Birkhäuser Verlag, 1996), including biographies of Jensen, Bothe et al.; Mark Walker, *German National Socialism and the Quest for Nuclear Power* (Cambridge: Cambridge University Press, 1989); Alan D. Beyerchen, *Scientists under Hitler: Politics and the Physics Community in the Third Reich* (New Haven, CT: Yale University Press, 1977); and Robert Jungk, *Brighter than a Thousand Suns* (Harmondsworth, Middlesex: Penguin, 1960). On physics at the University of Heidelberg, my main source was Charlotte Schönbeck, 'Physik', in Wolfgang U. Eckart, Volker Sellin and Eike Wolgast (eds), *Die Universität Heidelberg im Nationalsozialismus* (Berlin and Heidelberg: Springer Medizin Verlag, 2006), pp. 1087–149.

Nobel laureates
Listed at en.wikipedia.org/wiki/List_of_Nobel_laureates_by_country #Germany, accessed 27 August 2016. Rudolf Mössbauer was a student of the Heidelberg experimentalist and Tea Colloquium participant Heinz Maier-Leibniz, who Misha thought should have shared Mössbauer's 1961 Nobel Prize ('Quasi-Kruzhki' musing).

Chapter 11: Olga's Departure
This chapter draws largely on the correspondence between Mischka and Olga.

Olga's changing birthdate

Misha gave Olga's birth date as 1897 in 'Stories from my Grandfather's Time'. According to her AEF DP registration, dated 15 January 1946, she was born on 2 November 1899. Another record in the same ITS file, dated 26 July 1948, gives the date as 2 October 1905.

Authoritarian personality theory

On its application by US agencies in Germany, see David Monod, *Settling Scores: German Music, Denazification and the Americans, 1945–1953* (Chapel Hill: University of North Carolina Press, 2005), pp. 65–6. Misha's version is in his musing 'Psycho-sociology in Germany'.

DP departures

See notes for chapter 12, below.

Daniel Kolz

In addition to Helga Danos's testimony, there is also a fragment in German in Olga's papers (3/23) suggesting a romantic dimension to the relationship.

Music in postwar Germany

I have drawn on Toby Thacker, *Music after Hitler, 1945–1955* (Aldershot, Hampshire: Ashgate, 2007); Monod, *Settling Scores* ('beasts of war' quotation, p. 39); and Alex Ross, *The Rest is Noise: Listening to the Twentieth Century* (London and New York: Harper, 2009), pp. 373–85.

Chapter 12: Mischka's Departure

The principal sources for this chapter are the correspondence between Mischka and Helga in Heidelberg and Olga in New York; interviews with Helga Danos; and Helga's long letter to her parents about their trip.

Haxel

Otto Haxel (1909–1998) came to Heidelberg from Göttingen, where he had worked under Heisenberg and collaborated with Fritz Houtermans (which perhaps explains why Mischka had so many Houtermans stories). At the time of his move to Heidelberg, he and Jensen were collaborating on work on the nuclear shell model ('magic numbers'), which in turn was related to Mischka's dissertation topic and first publication.

Michael Danos: work and publications in Heidelberg

In an application for federal employment in the mid 1950s, Misha described his work for Jensen as 'theoretical research in nuclear physics, particularly interaction of electromagnetic radiation with atomic nuclei. Includes: quantum theory, electrodynamics, hydrodynamics'. In his subsequent position with Haxel, he did 'experimental work on the physics of surfaces, particularly metal surfaces. Includes: work with Geiger counters, electronics, ultra violet radiation, x-rays'.

His publications in these years were:

Helmut Steinwedel and Michael Danos, 'Proton Density Variation in Nuclei', *Physical Review, vol.* 79, no. 6, 1951, pp. 1019–20. This letter was published immediately after a letter by Helmut Steinwedel, J. Hans D. Jensen and Peter Jensen, entitled 'Nuclear Dipole Vibrations', in the same issue.

Michael Danos, 'Has Pressure Direction?', *American Journal of Physics, vol.* 19, no. 4, April 1951, p. 248. This was the journal Mischka identified as low-status; he later left the article out of his CVs.

Michael Danos and Helmut Steinwedel, 'Multiple Oscillations of Protons v. Neutrons in Atomic Nuclei', *Zeitschrift für Naturforschung 6A*, 1951, p. 217.

M. Danos, 'Resonances in (y, n) Processes', in *Zeitschrift für Naturforschung 6A*, 1951, p. 218.

An additional article by Michael Danos and Helmut Steinwedel was reported in their *Physical Review* letter to be forthcoming in *Sitzungsberichten den Heidelberger Akademie, Wiss. Math.natur Klass* but does not appear in any of his CVs.

Mary Sakss

The story of her denunciation and failure to get a US visa is in the musing 'Donosi v. Informers'. Her ITS file confirms her plans to emigrate to the United States but does not indicate an outcome. With regard to age, she was Olga's older sister by several years, but the 1945 DP registration in her ITS file gives her date of birth as 1898. A later German ID in the same file gives it as 1908.

US immigration and anti-Communism

My sources on this debate are Robert A. Divine, *American Immigration Policy, 1924–1952* (New Haven, CT: Yale University Press, 1957); Carl J.

Bon Tempo, *Americans at the Gate: The United States and Refugees during the Cold War* (Princeton, NJ: Princeton University Press, 2008); Gil Loescher and John A. Scanlan, *Calculated Kindness: Refugees and America's Half-Open Door, 1945 to the Present* (New York: Free Press, 1986); and Haim Genizi, *America's Fair Share: The Admission and Resettlement of Displaced Persons, 1945–1952* (Detroit: Wayne State University, 1993).

DP departures
The great majority of DPs had left by the time Mischka and Helga did—almost a million, which is about the number of DPs that were initially on UNRRA's books. More than three hundred thousand of the group had gone to the United States, but both US and overall numbers were dropping sharply in 1950–51. Statistics are from Kim Salomon, *Refugees in the Cold War* (Lund: Lund University Press, 1991), p. 191. The quotation on 'the final rush' is from Wyman, *DPs*, p. 202.

USS *General Ballou*
Information on sailing is from the IRO records in Archives nationales (Paris), AJ/43/271.

Afterword
Misha's New York employment
The Columbia starting date could have been backdated, in which case the period of his unemployment could have lasted until the autumn of 1952, as Helga's account suggests. There is a fuzziness in the documents that suggests something is being glossed over: for example, Misha's application for naturalisation in the mid 1950s appears to conflate his employment history after arrival with Helga's.

Tadasu Okada (also known as James T. Okada)
According to Okada's petition for naturalisation, lodged in New York in 1950, he was born in Numaza, Japan, on 17 November 1884 (www. fold3.com/document/22454494/, accessed 12 August 2016). The US Social Security Death index gives his birthdate as 18 November 1894 and the date of his death in Miami, Florida, as June 1987 (www. myheritage.com, accessed 12 August 2016).

Olga's marriage to Tadasu Okada
A diary entry for 9 March 1955 says she has been Olga Okada for seven months. A letter from Okada to Misha ('Michika'), 1 October 1954, states that he is now a 'legal husband'.

***Miami Herald* article**
Although there is no byline, the author was probably Jack Bell, nick-named 'the *Miami Herald* towncrier' in one of Olga's several diary entries about him ('towncrier' is in English).

Olga's land
Tadasu Okada continued to live on the property after Olga's death, according to Helga's recollection. There is no will in her papers, and it appears that no attempt was made to distribute it to her sons. Arpad did write to Tadasu after her death enquiring about her estate (*Nachlass*—not specifically land), but Tadasu's answer is unknown.

Misha's German and French collaborations in the US years
Walter Greiner, 'Michael Danos as I Remember Him'; Max G. Huber, 'Trespassing Frontiers—the Legacy of Michael Danos'; and Vincent Gillet, 'In Memory of Michael Danos', in Greiner (ed.), *Proceedings of the Symposium on Fundamental Issues in Elementary Matter*, pp. 415–16, 420–3 and 423–4.

'Case studies' article
The article using the experiences of Mischka, Olga and Bičevskis is Sheila Fitzpatrick, '"Determined to Get on": Some Displaced Persons on the Way to a Future', *History Australia*, vol. 12, no. 2, 2015, pp. 102–23.

Eyewitness accounts of the Dresden bombing
Victor Klemperer gives one in his memoir *I Will Bear Witness*. Many more have been collected in Walter Kempowski, *Der Rote Hahn: Dresden im February 1945* (Munich: Knaus, 2001), one of the volumes in his monumental 'collective diary' of German experience in the Second World War, *Das Echolot* ('Echo Soundings').

Sources

Danos papers

I have roughly catalogued the papers of Michael and Olga Danos into ten folders, numbering the separate files within them, which usually contain one document or letter. Many of the letters are undated, but I have generally been able to establish an approximate dating on the basis of content. They are mainly in German, as are the diaries, though Latvian, Russian, English and (in Olga's diaries) Italian also make their appearance. Misha's diaries also contain some copies of letters to various addressees. These papers are currently in my possession, but will be deposited with other papers of Michael Danos in the University of Chicago's Special Collections, which already contains a complete printout and electronic copy of the collected musings.

I have anglicised the spelling of some family names (as was sometimes done within the family): Misha's grandmother Julija Viksne becomes Julia, and his aunt Meri (Mērija) Sakss becomes Mary. I retain the 'Sakss' spelling, though it is grammatically wrong for a woman in Latvian, because this was the name on Mary's identification documents in Germany.

Michael Danos: Musings

'Musing' was Misha's term for the short writings on particular subjects, ranging from physics to current affairs, and from history to autobiography, that often originated as emails to me when he was at home in Washington and I was at work in Chicago in the 1990s. In a note on 'How to Read Musings' (24 March 1993), he wrote that they 'are to be understood to be only hints, sketches, of the material, the essence of the subjects, incomplete. They are not fragments of chapters or of essays. They are more like the wire skeletons sculptors use to support the clay which will be the sculpture.' Some of them, however, were reworked and expanded over a period of time and became small essays. The musings on the Dresden bombing, the Soviet and Nazi occupations of Riga, and the Heidelberg physics Tea Colloquium constitute valuable eyewitness testimony, and I have tried to quote them almost in full.

Interviews
Riga
Balva Berke (nee Eglitis), Jan's first wife (Smarde, Riga, 7 September 2006).
Arpad Danos (Riga, 11 September 2006).
Jan Danos (Riga, 7, 8, 9, 10, 11 and 12 September 2006).
Georgs Jankowskis (Jurmala, Riga, 8 September 2006).

United States
Mrs Wally Ayers (telephone, 23 February 2008).
Helga Danos (Ellicott City, MD, 22 and 23 November 2007).
Victoria Danos (telephone conversation, 15 October 2006).
Helen Machen (Downers Grove, IL, 2 February 2007 and 23 February 2008).
Dailonis Stauvers (telephone, 10, 14 and 21 April 2007).

Australia
Andrejs Bičevskis (Brisbane, 30 July and 1 August 2007).
All the above interviews were done by me. In addition, I have used a taped interview with Helga and Mechthild Heimers by Tamara Danos (Helga's younger daughter) (Carmel, CA, 21 December 1993), which is particularly useful on the question of BDM membership. Thanks to Johanna Danos for giving me access to this.

Miscellaneous documents
Emails
Līvija Baumane-Andrejevska, author of essay on Olga Danos (May, June and July 2015, and January and April 2016).
Kata Bohus, researcher in Hungarian archives (28 October and 19 December 2008, and 20 April 2009).
Barry Mirkin, son of Simon Mirkin (22 and 26 April 2009).
Margers Vestermanis, director of Jewish Museum, Riga (16 August, 29 September and 21 October 2015).
Andris Zeļenkovs, Latvian sports researcher (31 August 2015).

From Jan Danos's collection
Arpad Danos's school records, 1894 and 1897.

Letter from Arpad Danos to his brother Jan about the Deutsch/Danos family in Hungary, undated.
Letter from Ivan Danos, Budapest, to his nephew Jan, 13 March 1961.

From ITS (International Tracing Service) files
Files accessed online at Holocaust Museum, Washington DC, 2009 for:
*   Michael Danos (includes listing in Liste B zur Ausländerzählung, Judische Gemeinde, Frankfurt on Main)
*   Olga Danos
*   Boris Mirkin
*   Simon Mirkin
*   Mary Sakss.

From Hungarian archives
Name change of Arpad Danos (formerly Deutsch) and his brothers, 1898, from Magyar Orszagoseveltar Repertoriuma K150/6162. csomag/1898.ev (supplied by Kata Bohus).

From UNRRA archives, United Nations archive, New York
Documents cited separately in the Notes.

Unpublished memoirs
Andrejs Bičevskis, 'Bičevskis Family History' (email, 1 May 2008).
Berthold Stech, 'J.H.D. Jensen: Personal Recollection' (www.thphys. uni-heidelberg.de/home/info/historie_dir/jensen_stech.html, accessed 17 May 2016).

Letters
Helga Danos to parents, 9 November 1951, long letter with Mischka's postscript. Thanks to Helga for giving me a copy of this letter.
Paul Sakss to Tadasu Okada, 12 February 1957, asking for Mary's effects (in Olga's possession) to be sent to Ariadna in Riga.
Arpad Danos Jr to Tadasu Okada, undated [after 1956], enquiring about disposition of her estate.

Other documents
German ID [1945?] of Merija Sakks, born 1908.
Waldtraut Herrnberger, 'Verpflichtung', Berlin, 13 May 1944.

Photographs
From Johanna Danos, Jan Danos and my personal collection.

Published writing on Michael and Olga Danos

Līvija Baumane, 'A Local "Fashion Empire" and Its Collapse: The Fashion Designer Olga Danoss', in Līvija Baumane (ed.), *Kādas sievetes portrets: no jūgenda laikmeta līdz Latvijas brīvvalsts gadiem/ A Portrait of a Woman: From the Jugendstil Era to Latvia's Independence* (Riga: Jūgendstila paviljons, 2015), pp. 79–101.

Sheila Fitzpatrick, '"Determined to Get On": Some Displaced Persons on the Way to a Future', *History Australia*, vol. 12, no. 2, 2015, pp. 102–23. This is in a special issue on Second World War DPs, mainly with reference to resettlement in Australia, edited by me and Mark Edele.

Sheila Fitzpatrick, 'A World War II Odyssey: Michael Danos, En Route from Riga to New York', in Desley Deacon, Penny Russell and Angela Woollacott (eds), *Transnational Lives: Biographies of Global Modernity, 1700–Present*, (Basingstoke: Palgrave Macmillan, 2010), pp. 252–62.

Walter Greiner (ed.), *Proceedings of the Symposium on Fundamental Issues in Elementary Matter, 25–29 September 2000, Bad Honnef, Germany: In Honor and Memory of Michael Danos* (Debrecen: EP Systema, 2001). Includes recollections of Michael Danos by Walter Greiner, Jan Rafelski, Max Huber, Vincent Gillet, Evans Hayward, Jan Danos and Sheila Fitzpatrick.

Miami Herald, 'Miami Sculptor Operated Underground in Latvia', 27 June 1954, p. 12F.

Spokane Daily Chronicle, 1 November 1950. Report of Mirkin's meeting of Olga on her arrival in New York.

Documents of Michael and Olga Danos used in the text

Cited by date and catalogue number (folder/file), followed in brackets by topics (italics) and the chapters in which they are used.

Michael Danos: diaries

Five small notebooks with entries from various years, 1939–48 (1a, 1/2, 1/6, 1/7, 1/9).

24 October 1939, 1/7 (*Olga quoted on Arpad Sr's talents*—ch. 2).

Undated (after 13 November 1939), pp. 12–16, 1/7 (*German school, expulsion*—ch. 2).

10 and 11 July [1940], 1/9 (*farm work, 1940*—ch. 3).

14 March 1945, 1a (*travels*—ch. 5; *'life is still beautiful'*—ch. 7).

27 March 1945 (*Hamburg*—ch. 7).

28, 29 March 1945, 1a (*hospital in Flensburg*—ch. 7).

30 March 1945, 1a (*missing Easter*—ch. 7).

2 April 1945, 1/2 (*his father*—ch. 5; philosophy—ch. 7).

13 April 1945, 1/2 (*Dresden bombing*—ch. 6).

15 April 1945, 1/2 (*Dresden bombing*—ch. 6).

18 April 1945, 1/2 (*Dresden bombing*—ch. 6).

20 April 1945, 1/2 (*Dresden bombing*—ch. 6).

22 April 1945, 1/2 (*Dresden bombing*—ch. 6).

1 May 1945, 1a (*physics*—ch. 7).

2 May 1945, 1/2 (*philosophy*—ch. 7).

5 May 1945, 1/2 (*girlfriends*—ch. 7).

9 May 1945, 1/2 (*physics*—ch. 7).

2 July 1945, 1/2 (*physics*—ch. 7).

25 July 1945, 1/2 (*piano listener; girlfriends*—ch. 7).

10 August 1945, 1/2 (*lack of stamina; Estonian nurse*—ch. 7).

2 November 1945, 1a (*Munich 1945*—ch. 7).

3 November 1945, 1a (*meeting with girl on train*—ch. 7).

23 April 1946, 1/6 (*mother love*—ch. 8).

14 July 1946, 1/2 (*sex and marriage*—ch. 9).

23 July 1946, 1/2 (*sex and marriage*—ch. 9).

13 October 1946, 1/6 (*Nanni*—ch. 9).

2 February 1947, 1/2 (*dreams of family in Riga*—ch. 8).

24 July 1947, 1/2 (*physics epiphany*—ch. 9).

9 August 1947, 1/2 (*worry about concentration*—ch. 9).

18 November 1947, 1/2 (*improved memory and concentration*—ch. 9).

4 January 1948, 1/2 (*improved memory and concentration; 'geschlossen'*—
ch. 9).

5 June 1948, 1/2 (*father's death*—ch. 8).

6 June 1948, 1/2 (*father's death*—ch. 8).

Michael Danos: documents

Birth certificate, 2/17 (ch. 1).

DP index card, undated, Mikelis Danos, 2/4.

DP index card from Allied Expeditionary Forces, undated, Michael
Danos, 2/9.

Undated CV, 2/37 (*drafted to work as radio technician 1943*—ch. 4).

Gymnasium grades, 4th class, Riga, 3 September 1937, 2/16.

Letter from VEF, 18 February 1942, attesting that Michael Danos
worked there from 14 December 1940 to 18 December 1941, 2/7.

University of Riga, student record 1943–44, 2/51.

University of Riga grades, 11 March 1944, 2/27.

German-Foreign Student's Club, Vienna, card for Michael Danos, 4 May 1944, 2/15 (ch. 5).

Studienbuch, 10 June 1944, Dresden TH, 2/3.

Enrolment as student at Dresden TH, 12 June 1944, signed by Rector, 2/6.

Heinrich Barkhausen, recommendations for Michael Danos, 17 August 1944, 2/12 and 2/43.

'On the Invention of Student Mischka Danos', letter from head of development group, Ministry of Armaments and War Production, to Dr H. Boening, president of regional labour department, Reichenberg, 16 October 1944, 2/13.

Permission to study in Dresden extended until end of summer semester 1945, from Reichsminister für Wissenschaft, Erziehung und Volksbildung, Berlin, 11 December 1944, 2/5.

DP index card from Allied Expeditionary Forces, 1 August 1945 (renewed 5 September 1945, 17 November 1945, 3 February 1946), 2/25.

Baltic Sports Society of Flensburg, diplomas for wins in athletics, 15 September 1945, 2/67.

Certification of residence at Zeilsheim Assembly Center/Sidney Flatow, UNRRA Team 503, endorsed 15 October 1945 and 31 December 1946, 2/10.

Studienbuch, [1946], Hannover TH, 2/2 (ch. 9).

Student ID card, Hanover TH, 12 January 1946, 2/20.

Hanover TH grades, 12 November 1946, 2/22 (ch. 9).

Hanover TH, engineering degree, 12 May 1948, 2/33.

Hanover TH, final exam result ('ziemlich gut'), 12 May 1948, 2/34.

Hanover TH, appointment as Leiter in theoretical physics on 10 September 1948, 2/41.

Statement from Hans Jensen, 21 December 1948, that Michael Danos is doing doctorate under his supervision; requests permission to take him to University of Heidelberg when he moves, 2/54.

Lebenslauf (CV), 5 January 1949, 2/46 (ch. 2).

Discharge on German economy of Mikelis Danoss, Hanover, 2 May 1949, 2/31.

Marriage certificate of Michael Danos and Helga Heimers, 4 August 1949, 2/4.

Undated CV [1950s], 4/1 (*VEF dates*—ch. 4).

Lebenslauf, 1 February 1951, 2/37 (ch. 2).

University of Heidelberg, PhD ('magna cum laude'), 28 February 1951, 2/35.

IRO resettlement letter in United States for Michael and Helga Danos, 27 March 1951, 2/18.

Certification that Michael Danos has been issued a visa and is ready to go on next transport, signed Ruth Adams, US Processing Officer, 12 October 1951, 2/47.

INS certificate of admittance to the United States as a displaced person, 13 November 1951, 4/9.

Application for federal employment, undated draft [1954?], 4/4 (Afterword).

Application to file petition for naturalisation, Michael and Helga Danos [draft, dated in hand 11 June 1957], 4/11.

Letters from Michael Danos to Olga Danos

13 May 1944, 8/83 (*arrival in Germany; sport*—ch. 5).

16 June 1944, 8/65 (*philosophy; sport*—ch. 5).

21 July 1944, 8/76 (*Barkhausen; philosophy*—ch. 5).

28 July 1944 (but from content actually 28 August), 9/54 (ch. 5).

3 September 1944, 8/93 (*Barkhausen; Kriegseinsatz; Jan and Latvian Legion; Olga's departure plans*—ch. 5).

Undated [December 1944], 8/59 (*studies at Dresden; father*—ch. 5).

3 January 1945, 8/68 (*trip to Munich*—ch. 5).

15 February 1945, 8/66 (*leaving Dresden*—ch. 5).

26 February 1945, 8/81 (*telegram on bombing*—ch. 5).

25 March 1945, 8/73 (*letter in pencil from hospital*—ch. 7).

6 April 1945, 8/67 (*two postcards from hospital*—ch. 7).

26 October 1945, 8/80 (*university tour*—ch. 7).

14 November 1945, 8/92 (*enrolment at Brunswick TH*—ch. 7).

14 November 1945, 8/74 (*Brunswick*—ch. 7).

1 December 1945, 3/24 (*Brunswick*—ch. 7).

15 January 1946, 8/84 (*admitted to Hanover TH*—ch. 7).

23 January 1946, 8/84 (*working hard in Hanover*—ch. 7).

24 January 1946, 8/70 (*more information on Hanover*—ch. 7).

9 May 1946. 8/85 (*Hanover TH; attitude to study*—ch. 9).

27 May 1946, 8/47 (*Heisenberg; sports*—ch. 9).

26 June 1946, 8/53 (*physicists; concentration problems*—ch. 9).

26 July 1946, 8/86 (*'experienced woman'*—ch. 9).

26 October 1946, 8/88 (*cold*—ch. 8; *German types*—ch. 9).

4 November 1946, 8/78 (*Bogdanovs's exploits*—ch. 9).

Undated [1946], 8/75 (*Nanni*—ch. 9).

19 January 1947, 8/44 (*business advice on Olga's sculpture*—ch. 8).

28 February 1947, 8/71 (*his progress in physics*—ch. 9).

19 March 1947, 8/43 (*relationship with Olga*—ch. 8; *his progress in physics (including quotation)*—ch. 9).

9 May 1947, 8/50 (*concentration problems, exams*—ch. 9).

22 May 1947 (postmark), 8/52 (*Mirkin*—ch. 8; *grades conflict*—ch. 9; *'German physics'*—ch. 10).

17 October 1947, 8/56 (*exams; Sennheiser; Germans*—ch. 9).

25 October 1947, 8/57 (*exams; colloquium paper; progress in physics; improvement in memory*—ch. 9).

15 November 1949 (postmark), 9/34 (*mothers and married sons; married life; departure plans*—ch. 12).

Undated [after 4 February 1948], 8/98 (*Arpad's letter*—ch. 8; *Marjorie Broadhurst's letter*—ch. 9).

Undated [spring 1948], 8/92 (*departure of friend Pablo to Canada*—ch. 11).

Undated [before 20 June 1948], 8/100 (*work as* Assistent*; Helga*—ch. 9).

Undated [mid-1948], 8/42 (*Arpad's letter*—ch. 8).

13 July 1948, 8/99 (*Sennheiser; Jensen*—ch. 9).

Undated [before 2 August 1948), 8/106a (*German types*—ch. 9).

2 August 1948, 8/103 (*against Hamburg radio job; sports; progress in physics*—ch. 9; *job for Mischka in New York*—Afterword).

Undated [autumn 1948?], 8/39 (*Helga*—ch. 10).

Undated [August–September 1948?], 8/106p (*Nanni*—ch. 10; *friends' departures*—ch. 11).

14 January 1949, 8/106g (*Helga*—ch. 10).

Undated [September 1948], 8/106j (*his progress in physics*—ch. 9).

Undated [early 1949], 8/95 (*Helga*—ch. 10; *destinations discussion*—ch. 11).

Undated [April–May 1949], 8/106 (*Helga*—ch. 10).

Undated [before 1 May 1949], 8/39 (*move to Heidelberg*—ch. 9; *Olga's DP status; life in Heidelberg; Jensen and Nazis*—ch. 10).

Undated [May 1949], 8/54 (*Heidelberg move; '1.5 Frauen'; Helga; Jensen*—ch. 10; *Ami families*—ch. 12).

Undated [May 1949], 8/30 (*Jensen*—ch. 10).

Undated [May-June 1949], 8/32 (*Heidelberg salary, conditions; Jensen*—ch. 10).

27August 1951, 8/4 (*Bothe celebration*—ch. 10).

Undated [June 1949], 8/31 (*panic attack*—ch. 10).

Undated [mid-1949], 8/33 (*nerves*—ch. 10).

Undated [autumn 1949], 8/34 (*Gieseking*—ch. 11).

Undated [late 1949?], 8/36 (*Nanni*—ch. 10; *married life*—ch. 12).

27 February 1950, 8/2 (*Gieseking*—ch. 11; *married life*—ch. 12).

Undated [February 1950?], 8/106 (*married life*—ch. 12).

Undated [mid-1950], 8/37 ('*Germanen*'—ch. 11).

Undated [June–July 1950], 8/104 (*politics*—ch. 12).

Undated [August 1950], 8/104 (*departure plans*—ch. 12).

Undated 8/101 [September 1950] (*Gieseking; Bach-Hindemith*—ch. 11).

Undated [late 1950], 8/106l (*friend Mārtiņ Kregŝde in New York*—ch. 11).

Undated [late 1950], 8/24 (*Sommerfeld; Helga and BDM [quotation]*—ch. 12).

Undated [late 1950], 8/101 (*Helga and BDM*—ch. 12).

Undated [January 1951], 8/5a (*Kolz on Russians; politics*—ch. 12).

Undated [January 1951?], 8/5s (*politics; Helga and BDM*—ch. 12).

Undated [December 1950], 8/106 (America—ch. 12).

Undated [early 1951], 8/5g (*friend Ilo Kurlis in Boston*—ch. 11).

Undated [early 1951], 8/5d (*finishing the dissertation*—ch. 12).

Undated [early 1951], 8/5g ('*Germanium*'—ch. 11; *Olga's financial affairs; departure*—ch. 12).

1 February 1951, 8/5e (*job in New Jersey*—Afterword).

7 March 1951, 8/5a (*finishing the dissertation; departure plans*—ch. 12).

Undated [March 1951], 8/5c (*PhD defence*—ch. 12).

15 March 1951, 9/58 (*Helga and BDM*—ch. 12).

4 April 1951, 8/58 (*departure plans*—ch. 12).

25 April 1951, 8/4a (*departure*—ch. 12).

16 May 1951, 8/4d (*politics*—ch. 12).

16 July 1951, 8/4e (*Helga's work in Heidelberg*—ch. 12).

18 July 1951, 8/4b (*Olga's financial affairs; departure*—ch. 12).

27 August 1951 (postmark), 8/4c (*Bothe's 65th birthday celebration [it was actually his 60th]; departure*—ch. 12).

Undated [mid-1953], 8/14 (*non-intimacy of letter offends Olga*—Afterword).

Undated [mid-1953], 8/18 (Afterword).

Letters from Olga Danos to Michael Danos

20 May 1944, 9/40 (*preparations for departure*—ch. 5).

9 July 1944, 9/45 (*plans for Arpad; Mauserl; her illness*—ch. 5).

15 July 1944, 9/45 (*departure plans*—ch. 5).

28 August 1944, 9/54a (*departure plans*—ch. 5).

14 October 1944, 9/44 (*Jan and Arpad's attempt to leave Riga, 1944; Olga's trip to Germany*—ch. 5).

2 October 1944, 9/42 (*news from Sudetenland*—ch. 5).

8 November 1944, 5/79 (*news from Sudetenland*—ch. 5).

18 November 1944. 9/43 (*workshop problems*—ch. 5).

11 December 1944, 9/44 (ch. 5).

5 January 1946, 9/57 (*Mischka's antisocial behaviour*—ch. 7; *plan to go to Riga*—ch. 8).

1 March 1946, 9/57m (*business*—ch. 8).

12 March 1946, 9/57 (*'money no obstacle'; English admirer*—ch. 8).

22 March 1946, 9/57 (*her six languages*—ch. 8).

24 March 1946, 9/57n (*'lazybones'; plan to go to Riga*—ch. 8).

29 May 1946, 9/57a (*business*—ch. 8).

14 July 1946, 9/57 (*Seeliger*—ch. 8).

24 July 1946, 9/56a (*business*—ch. 8; *friends' departures*—ch. 11).

Undated [after 26 July 1946]. 9/56a (*business*—ch. 8).

Undated [August 1946], 9/56a (*proposed move to US zone*—ch. 8).

Undated [August 1946], 9/56b (*proposed move to US zone; sculpture*—ch. 8).

7 January 1947, 9/59 (*sculpture*—ch. 8).

15 January 1947, 9/57a (*sculpture*—ch. 8).

Undated [after 15 January 1947], 9/57 (*sculpture*—ch. 8).

21 March 1947, 9/54b (*Misha's attitude to her; her upbringing of sons*—chs 2, 8).

22 May 1947 (postmark), 8/52 (ch. 8).

26 September 1947, 9/2 (*friends' departures*—ch. 11).

27 July 1948, 9/48 (*DP status renewed; Arpad's death*—ch. 8; *Fulda*—ch. 11).

10 September 1948, 9/41 (*destinations discussion; Fulda*—ch. 11).

21 September 1948, 9/47 (*Koellner*—chs 4 and 8; *news of Jan*—ch. 8; *letter from Arpad*—ch. 8).

11 January 1949 (postmark), 9/3 (*Fulda*—ch. 11).

Undated [early 1949], 9/4 (*her DP status; Heidelberg; 'Helgalein' and prospective marriage*—ch. 10).

27 February 1949 (unsent), 9/50 (*mentions letters to son Arpad*—ch. 8; *separation from Mischka*—ch. 11).

2 April 1949, 9/55 (*Gieseking*—ch. 11).

23 June 1949, 9/5 (*reassurance on nerves*—ch. 10).

Undated [after 12 November 1949], 9/28 (*comment on Nanni's letter*—ch. 10).

29 [November or December] 1949, 9/25, (*Gieseking*—ch. 11; *relationship with Mischka after marriage*—ch. 12).

Undated [1949], 9/30 (*departure plans*—ch. 11).

11 June 1949, 9/8 (ch. 10; *Gieseking*—ch. 11).

23 June 1949, 9/5, (*Olga's business card*—ch. 8; *Mischka's nervous problems*—ch. 10).

28 September 1949, 9/24 (*Daniel Kolz*—ch. 11; *Mischka's wedding*—ch. 12).

Undated [soon after 12 November 1949], 9/28 (*panic attack*—ch. 10; *destinations discussion; Mary Sakss*—ch. 11).

27 February 1950, 8/2 (*Olga's illness*—ch. 11).

Undated [March 1950], 9/31(*departure plans; illness*—ch. 11).

27 March 1950, 9/23 (*Mischka's departure plans*—ch. 12).

28 April 1950, 9/22 (*Daniel Kolz; illness*—ch. 11).

31 July 1950, 9/20 (*Jan and Arpad's attempt to leave Riga, 1944*—ch. 5; *illness; departure*—ch. 11).

Undated [mid-1950], 9/10 (*illness*—ch. 11).

Undated [mid-1950], 9/21 (*illness; operation*—ch. 11).

Undated [14 August 1950], 9/18 (ch. 11).

Undated [August 1950], 9/18 (*Mischka's departure plans*—ch. 12).

26 January 1951 [misdated 1950], 9/58 (*job for Mischka in New York*—Afterword).

11 September 1950, 9/16 (*Mischka's departure plans*—ch. 12).

13 September 1950, 9/17 (*departure, 'so much fear!'*—ch. 11).

16 September 1950, 9/12 (*sculpture*—ch. 11).

16 September 1950, 9/13 (*sculpture*—ch. 11).

21 September 1950, 9/14 (*sculpture*—ch. 11).

27 September [must be October] 1950, 9/34 (*voyage*—ch. 11).

21 October 1950, 9/15 (*departure*—ch. 11).

2 November 1950, 9/35 (*voyage*—ch. 11).

26 [November] 1950, 9/58 (*Helga and BDM*—ch. 12).

28 November 1950, 9/37 (*job in New York*—Afterword).

12 December 1950, 9/39 (*politics*—ch. 12).

17 February 1951 [misdated 1950]. 9/36 (*America*—ch. 12).

11 March 1951, 9/58 (*congratulations on PhD*—ch. 12).

18 September 1953, 9/66 (*'don't be so distant'*—Afterword).

Other letters to and from Michael Danos
From 'Mutti' Loefer, Vienna, 25 May 1944, 5/228 (ch. 5).

From Waldtraut Herrnberger, 7 June 1944, 5/123 (*comment on Misha as 'theorist' in Riga*—ch. 9); 22 June 1944, 5/113; 18 July 1944, 5/116; 31 July 1944, 5/47; 17 November 1944, 5/98 (ch. 3).

From Arpad Danos (brother), 13 August 1944, 6/8 (*departure plans*—ch. 5).

From Marianne (Nanni) Schuster, 8 October 1944, 5/58 (*trip to Chemnitz*—ch. 5); 24 November 1945, 5/168 (*life in Soviet zone*—ch. 7); 22 February 1946, 5/164; 4 February 1947, 5/163 (*'diplomatic problems' between Saxony and Hanover*—ch. 9); 9 February 1946, 5/166; 24 April 1947, 5/158; 23 June 1947, 5/177 (*visit, return trip, argument on man–woman relations, including typed copy of Mischka's letter*—ch. 9); 20 July 1947, 5/176; 17 September 1947, 5/5 (*'faithless tomato'*—ch. 9); 8 January 1949, 5/4 (*waiting to leave*—ch. 10); 2 April 1949, 5/43 (*in Goettingen*—ch. 10); 14 April 1949, 5/178 (*signed Marianne Schuster*—ch. 10); 9 May 1949, 5/16 (*in Reutlingen*—ch. 10); 27 May 1949, 5/17 (*in Tübingen*—ch. 10; 16 June 1949, 5/20 (*in Tübingen*—ch. 10).

To Nanni Schuster, 26 July 1946 [in diary], 1/6; to M.S. [Nanni Schuster], 12 October 1946 [in diary], 1/1 (*suspicion of academicism*—ch. 9).

To unnamed girl ('Mädel', probably Nanni), 14 December 1945, 1/1 [in diary] (*university tour*—ch. 7).

To F.B., 27 July 1946 [in diary], 1/1 (*suspicion of academicism; doubts suitability for marriage; Sennheiser*—ch. 9).

To Ch.K., 19 January 1948 [in diary], 1/1 (*doubts suitability for marriage; Nanni*—ch. 9).

From Marjorie Broadhurst to MD and Andrejs Bičevskis, 4 February 1948, 5/19 (ch. 9).

To Helga Heimers, 15 May 1949, 10/13 (*Jensen and Nazis*—ch. 10); 22 May 1949, 10/12 (*Jensen and Nazis*—ch. 10); 27 June 1949, 10/8 (*nervous problems*—ch. 10).

To Dr Malkus, 23 June [1949], 10/8. Thanks to Helga for giving me a copy of this letter.

To Willy and Martha Heimers, 21 July 1949, 10/48 (*early interest in radio*—ch. 2; *Heidelberg salary; decision to marry Helga*—ch. 10). Thanks to Helga Danos for giving me a copy of this letter.

Telegram to Martha Heimers, 11 December 1953, 3/75 (*Mary's funeral*—ch. 12).

From Tadasu Okada, 1 October 1954, 9/76 (*'now legal husband'*—Afterword); 11 December 1956, 9/74 (*news of Olga's incurable liver cancer*—Afterword).

Michael Danos: occasional writings

'Eine Erwiderung', undated essay, 2/46 (*response to Manfred Büttner's essay on nihilism*—ch. 9).

Fragment, undated [1949], 10/8 (*too old for Nobel prize*—ch. 10).

'Rittergut', undated [1946] autobiographical statement, 2/46 (*on leaving Riga*—ch. 4).

Michael Danos: musings

'Stories from my Grandfather's Times', 20 June 1998 (ch. 1).

'Early Training for Arrogance', 28 July 1995 (*servants upstairs*—chs 1 and 2).

'Buying of Apples', 25 February 1997 (chs 1 and 2).

'Feynman and I', 7 March 1992 (*reaction to brother's illness*—ch. 2; *Barkhausen*—ch. 5; *self-doubt*—ch. 9; *'floundering in orals'*—ch. 12).

'Levels of Society', 22 September 1994 (*books and lived experience*—ch. 3).

'VEF, Valsts Electrotechniska Fabrika', 13 July 1994 and 4 June 1998 (ch. 3).

'Plebiscite to Join the Union', 11 October 1995 (*Soviet arrival in Riga, occupation*—ch. 3).

'Mass Deportations in '41', 8 February 1995 (*deportations of cousins*—ch. 3; ch. 4).

'Everyday in the Soviet Union', 9 October 1994 (ch. 3).

'Dubna 1967', 21 February 1998 (ch. 3).

'What is Special about the Soviet Case?', 30 March 1996 (ch. 3).

'Civilising the Russians', 4 September 1994 (ch. 3).

'Socialism-Communism', 29 June 1992 (ch. 3).

'Assassinators', 6 August 1993 (*Sovietology*—ch. 3).

'Nazi Latvia', 16 November 1994 (ch. 4).

'Saving Jews: Why?', 4 January 1995 (ch. 4).

'Mass Graves', 22 July 1996 (ch. 4).

'Koelln and Seeliger', 23 April 1996 (chs 4 and 8).

'Beria: Individual vs Soviet System', 6 March 1994 (*Koelln and Seeliger*—ch. 4).

'Medical Experimentations', 24 January 1997 (*German nurse*—ch. 5).

'Dresden', 20 and 21 January 1996 (*departure*—ch. 5; *bombing*—ch. 6).

'Cleansing of Concepts: Informers vs Denouncers in Nazi, Soviet, DDR', 21 March 1995 (ch. 5; *Flensburg hospital encounters*—ch. 7).

'Shell Shock: Dresden, 1944, 1945', 25 April 1997 (*Teschen-Bodenbach bombing story*—ch. 5; *making rucksack*—ch. 7).

'Occupation Forces in 1945', 26 July 1994 (*arrogance of British*—ch. 7).

'Quasi-kruzhki Elsewhere: Memories [Heidelberg Tee-Colloquium; Philippe Lenard; Houtermanns]', 14 September 1994 (*Tea Colloquium*—ch. 10; *attitude to Germany*—ch. 11).

'Währungsreform', 23 February 1997 (ch. 11).

'Donosi [Denunciations] v. Informers', 2 May 1994 (*Mary Sakss*—ch. 12).
'Psycho-sociology in Germany', 11 March 1995 (ch. 11).
'Flying a Little Plane in New York', 23 May 1997 (Afterword).

Olga Danos: diaries
'Book of my marriage', 1922–48, 3/1a.
1 April 1927 (*husband lacks occupation*—ch. 2).
April, Easter [1927] (*husband has voice problems*—ch. 2).
18 October 1928 (*Russia 1918*—ch. 1).
2 March 1944 (*separation from husband*—ch. 5).
2 May 1944 (*visit to lawyer about divorce*—ch. 5).
30 October 1945 (*only entry for year*—ch. 7).
9 March 1946 (*thoughts of Riga family; repatriant's visit*—ch. 8).
31 March 1946 (*thoughts of Riga family; letters to them*—ch. 8).
10 March 1947 (*Arpad Sr's jealousy*, ch. 2).
24 June 1947 (*child-raising practices; thoughts of Riga family*—chs 2 and 8).
2 April 1948 (*reference to unnamed lover*—ch. 2; *Arpad's death*—ch. 8).
19 May 1948 (*meeting Arpad*—ch. 1; *Arpad's death*—ch. 8).

American diary, 1950–56, 3/1
1 January 1951 (*new life in United States*—Afterword).
16 January 1951 (*new life in United States*—Afterword).
10 January 1953 (*recalling Misha's birth*—chs 1 and 2; *quarrel with Misha and Helga*—Afterword).
6 July 1953 (*Jack Bell*, 'Miami Herald *towncrier'; sculpture business*—Afterword).
14 July 1953 (*Jack Bell; sculpture*—Afterword).
28 July 1953 (*quarrel*—Afterword).
12 August 1953 (*thinks of tearing up cheque from Misha*—Afterword).
24 August 1953 (*news of Helga's pregnancy*—Afterword).
8 July 1954 (*fears for sons in Soviet Union*—ch. 3).
8 March 1955 (*fears for sons*—ch. 3).
9 March 1955 (*land as inheritance for sons; seven months as Olga Okada*—Afterword).
26 June 1956 (last entry) (*land for sons*—Afterword).

Olga Danos: documents
Certification from IRO, that Olga Danos has been screened and 'found eligible for work and emigration'; preferred destination, Argentina, 26 October 1948, 2/26 and 3/56.

Bescheinigung (declaration) signed by Simon and Ilse Mirkin, authorising the return to Olga of rent paid for Florengasse 53, 7 June 1951, 9a/51d.

Other letters to and from Olga Danos
From Arpad Sr ('Der Alte'), 1 October 1944, 3/53 (*last letter to Olga*—ch. 5; ch. 7).

From Simon Mirkin, 15 September 1946, 3/21 (ch. 7); 5 October 1950, 3/17 (*Olga's departure*—ch. 11).

From Helga Danos, undated [June 1950], 8/37 (*Helga's work in Heidelberg*—ch. 12); (with postscript from Mischka), 28 November 1950, 8/106m (*Helga and BDM; Mischka's publications*—ch. 12); 11 January 1951, 8/5f (*Mischka's job*—ch. 12).

To Martha Heimers, 23 July 1950, 9/9 (ch. 12).

To Helga Danos, 2 December 1950, 9/58 (*what Mischka needs in a wife*—ch. 12); 15 March 1951, 9/58 (*paskha*—ch. 12); 16 July 1951, 8/4e (*departure*—ch. 12).

From Paul Seeliger, 20 April 1952, 3/6 (chs 2 and 4, Afterword).

From Jan Danos, 21 November 1955, 6/20 (*contact with Riga*—Afterword).

From Arpad Danos, postcard, undated [after 11 January 1956], 6/21 (*contact with Riga*—Afterword); telegram, 19 September 1956, 6/29 (*contact with Riga*—Afterword).

From Ariadna Sakss, 29 July 1956, 3/37 (ch. 3; Afterword).

From Press Advisor (name illegible), friend from Flensburg, 2 November 1956, 3/34 (ch. 7).

Olga Danos: occasional writings, fragments
Undated autobiographical fragment, 3/29 (*her mother's illness*—ch. 1).

Undated autobiographical fragment, 3/31 (*her time in Russia; houses owned by Viksnes*—ch. 1).

Autobiographical fragment, 19 May 1952 (date crossed out), 3/13 (*her wedding*—ch. 1).

Autobiographical fragment, 12 April 1919, in Russian, 3/43 (*jealousy, quotation*—ch. 2).

Undated autobiographical fragment, [early 1920s], in Russian, 3/46 (*jealousy*—ch. 2).

Autobiographical fragment, 14 April 1945, 3/51 (*Glücksburg*—ch. 7).

Fragment, in form of letter without addressee, mainly in German, 14 July 1947, 3/71 (*'buffoon' quotation*—ch. 8).

Undated [1950], untitled fragment in English on yellow lined paper, 3/28 (*friend's persuasion to go to America; unfavourable picture of United States ['heartless robots']*—ch. 11).

'The Voyage', undated fragment, 9/15 (*voyage to United States*—ch. 11).

Undated fragment in German, 3/33 (*Daniel [Kolz?]*—ch. 12).

Handwritten essay in German, Ponte Vedre Beach, 25 September 1955, 3/31 (*telegram from Riga*—Afterword).

Fragment in German, 29 August 1956, 9/83 (*contact with Riga*—Afterword).

Acknowledgements

I have accumulated many debts in the writing of this book. Janis (Jan) Danos and the late Andrejs Bičevskis provided indispensable information through interviews and the sharing of documents. Helga Danos, the late Arpad Danos (Misha's brother), Dailonis Stauvers and Helen Machen were generous with time and information. Other family members and friends who shared memories of Misha were his son Arpad Michael Danos, his daughter Johanna Danos, his second wife Victoria Danos, and his longtime friend and office mate Evans Hayward, as well as friends of Misha's youth, Balva Berke and Georgs Jankowskis, to whom Jan introduced me in Riga.

Barry Mirkin contributed invaluable information on his father, Simon Mirkin, as well as photographs and press cuttings of Olga's arrival in New York in 1950. Jan Danos and Johanna Danos also provided photographs from their family collections.

Kata Bohus carried out research on the Deutsch/Danos family in the Hungarian archives on my behalf. Livija Baumane provided wonderful data on Olga's fashion atelier in Riga, and Andris Zeļenkovs shared information on the Latvian sporting scene before the war. Scholars who answered questions on various issues that came up in the course of the research include Holly Case, Bjorn Felder, Norman Naimark and Atina Grossmann. I am particularly grateful to Dr Margers Vestermanis of the Jewish Museum in Riga for his help.

For translation assistance, I thank Diana Weekes (who translated the Dresden diary) and Eva von Kügelschen; Johanna Danos and Barbara Helwing for German, Rita Lesnik and Arpad Michael Danos for Latvian, and Marco Duranti for Italian.

The institutions that supported me as I worked on this book are the University of Chicago, the Research School of Humanities at the Australian National University (2008 Fellowship), the Wissenschaftskolleg zu Berlin (2008–9 Fellowship), and the University of Sydney, which has been my academic home since 2012.

Because this was an unusual project for me, I leaned more heavily than usual on my friends for advice and encouragement: among them Jörg Baberowski, Phyllis Booth, Lorraine Daston, Desley Deacon, Orlando Figes, Marsha Siefert, Alfred Rieber, Yuri Slezkine, and Bernard Wasserstein. Donald Berger, Katerina Clark, Ann Curthoys, and Anne Nesbett all read chapters, as did Jan Danos and Helga Danos. I am particularly grateful to the long list of friends who read and commented on the entire manuscript: Ruth Balint, Lynn Dalgarno, Kay Dreyfus, Barbara Gillam, Kitty Hauser, Mark McKenna and Ross McKibbin. Their reactions, questions and criticisms were enormously valuable.

Index